OFFICIAL BLUE BOOK OF UNITED STATES COINS™

The Official BLUE BOOK®

HANDBOOK OF
UNITED STATES COINS

R.S. YEOMAN

E

KENNET

65th Edition
2008

Illustrated Catalog and Prices Dealers Pay for Coins—1616 to Date

Containing mint records and wholesale prices for U.S. coins from 1616 to the present time, including colonials, regular issues, commemoratives, territorials, gold, Proof sets, and mint sets. Information on collecting coins—how coins are produced—mints and mintmarks—grading of coins—location of mintmarks—preserving coins—starting a collection—history of mints—and interesting descriptions of all U.S. copper, nickel, silver, and gold coins. Illustrated.

The Handbook of United States Coins™
THE OFFICIAL BLUE BOOK OF UNITED STATES COINS™

THE OFFICIAL BLUE BOOK and THE OFFICIAL BLUE BOOK OF UNITED STATES COINS are trademarks of Whitman Publishing, LLC.

WCG™ • OCG™

www.whitmanbooks.com

Printed in the United States of America.

The WCG™ pricing grid used throughout this publication is patent pending.

3101 Clairmont Road • Suite C • Atlanta GA 30329

OCG™ Collecting Guide

Whitman Publishing, LLC, does not deal in coins; the values shown here are not offers to sell or buy but are included only as general information. Descriptions of coins are based on the most accurate data available, but could contain beliefs that may change with further research or discoveries. Correspondence regarding this book may be sent to the publisher at the address above.

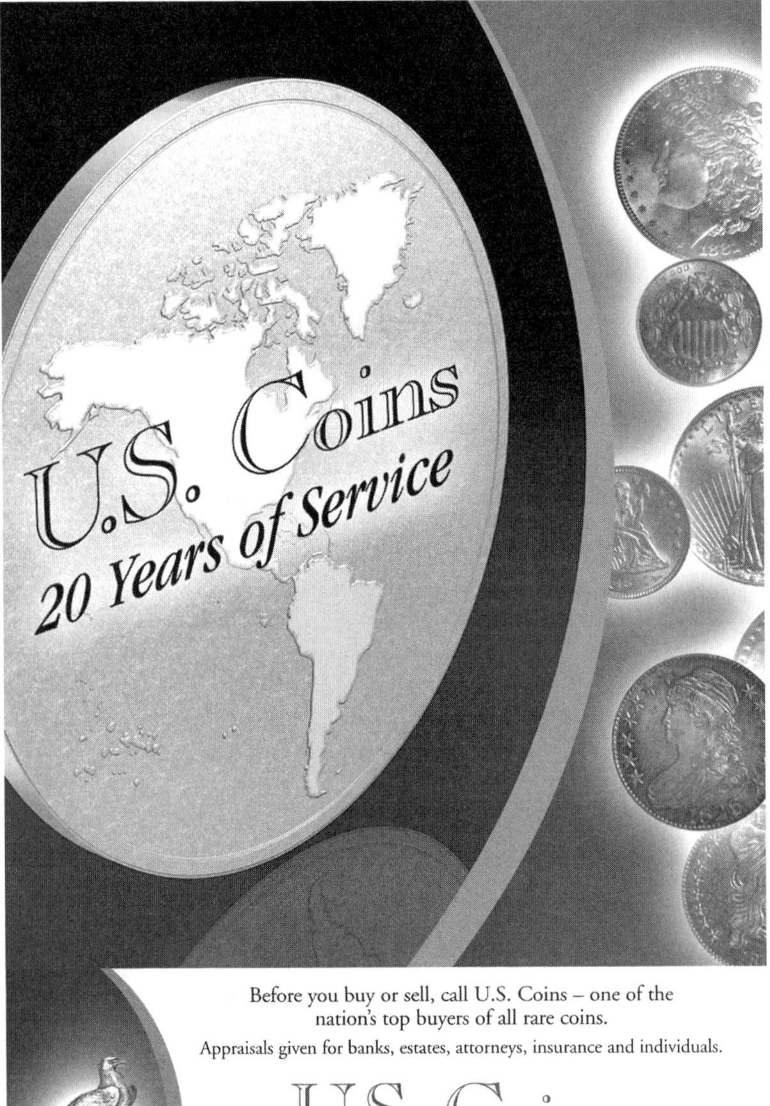

U.S. Coins
20 Years of Service
Before you buy or sell, call U.S. Coins – one of the nation's top buyers of all rare coins.
Appraisals given for banks, estates, attorneys, insurance and individuals.
U.S. Coins
AUTHORIZED DEALER : PCGS, NGC, ANACS
8435 Katy Freeway, Houston, Texas 77024
713-464-6868 713-464-7548 fax www.buyuscoins.com
TOLL FREE: 888-502-7755 LOUISIANA OFFICE: 337-291-1191

TABLE OF CONTENTS

CONTRIBUTORS TO THE SIXTY-FIFTH EDITION

Special Consultants: Philip Bressett, Tom Hallenbeck

Whitman Publishing extends its thanks to these members of the coin buying community who have contributed pricing for this year's *Handbook of United States Coins*. Their data were compiled and then reviewed by editor Kenneth Bressett and the special consultants listed above. This process ensures input from a broad range of dealers and auctioneers from across the country—experts who buy, sell, and trade coins every day and know the market inside and out.

Mark Albarian
Jeff Ambio
H. Robert Campbell
Elizabeth W. Coggan
Gary Cohen
Steve Contursi
Sheridan Downey
Mike Fuljenz
Chuck Furjanic
Kenneth Goldman
J.R. Grellman Jr.
James Halperin
Gene Henry
John W. Highfill
Karl D. Hirtzinger
Jesse Iskowitz
Steve Ivy
Brad Karoleff
Richard A. Lecce
Julian M. Leidman
Stuart Levine
Denis W. Loring
Dwight N. Manley
Robert T. McIntire
Lee S. Minshull
Scott P. Mitchell
Michael C. Moline
Paul Montgomery
Richard Nachbar
Robert M. Paul
William P. Paul
Joel Rettew Jr.
Joel Rettew Sr.
Greg Rohan
Maurice Rosen
Gerald Scherer Jr.
Richard J. Schwary
Frank E. Van Valen
David Wnuck

Special credit is due to the following for service in past editions of the *Handbook*:

Gary Adkins
David Akers
John Albanese
Buddy Alleva
Richard S. Appel
Michael Aron
Richard M. August
Richard A. Bagg
Mitchell A. Battino
Lee J. Bellisario
Jack Beymer
Mark R. Borckardt
Q. David Bowers
Fonda Chase
Alan R. Cohen
Marc Crane
John Dannreuther
Tom DeLorey
Silvano DiGenova
Kenneth Duncan
Steven Ellsworth
John Feigenbaum
Dennis Gillio
Ronald Gillio
Lawrence S. Goldberg
Ron Guth
John Hamrick
James J. Jelinski
A.M. Kagin
Mike Kliman
John J. Kraljevich Jr.
David Leventhal
Kevin Lipton
Andy Lustig
Chris McCawley
Harry Miller
Robert Mish
Charles Moore
Chris Napolitano
Paul Nugget
Mike Orlando
John M. Pack
William S. Panitch
Robert J. Rhue
Tom Rinaldo
Leonard R. Saunders
Mary Sauvain
Cherie Schoeps
James A. Simek
William J. Spencer
Lawrence Stack
Anthony J. Swiatek
Anthony Terranova
Jerry Treglia
Fred Weinberg
Douglas Winter
Mark S. Yaffe

Special photo credits are due to the following:

American Numismatic Rarities, Douglas F. Bird, Steve Contursi, Bill Fivaz, Ira & Larry Goldberg Coins & Collectibles, heritagecoins.com, Tom Mulvaney, the Museum of the American Numismatic Association, Noyes–Lusk DVD Photo Project, Numismatic Guaranty Corporation of America (NGC), Brent Pogue, Sarasota Rare Coin Gallery, the Smithsonian Institution, Rick Snow, Spectrum, Stack's Rare Coins of New York, Superior Galleries, Anthony Swiatek, and the United States Mint.

Since 1942, annually revised editions of the Official Blue Book™ of United States Coins have aided thousands of people who have coins to sell or are actively engaged in collecting United States coins. The popular coin-folder method of collecting by date has created ever-changing premium values, based on the supply and demand of each date and mint. Through its panel of contributors, the Blue Book has, over the years, reported these changing values. It also serves as a source of general numismatic information to all levels of interest in the hobby.

The values shown are representative prices paid by dealers for various United States coins. These are averages of prices assembled from many widely separated sources. On some issues slight differences in price among dealers may result from proximity to the various mints or heavily populated centers. Other factors, such as local supply and demand or dealers' stock conditions, may also cause deviations from the prices listed. While many coins bring no premium in circulated grades, they usually bring premium prices in Mint State and Proof. Extremely rare and valuable coins are usually sold at public auction, and prices vary according to current demand.

THIS BOOK LISTS PRICES MANY COIN DEALERS WILL PAY.

Premium prices are the average amount dealers will pay for coins (according to condition) if required for their stock. This book is not a retail price list.

IF YOU HAVE COINS TO SELL

Whitman Publishing, LLC, is not in the rare coin business; however, chances are that the dealer from whom you purchased this book is engaged in the buying and selling of rare coins—contact him first. In the event that you purchased this book from a source other than a numismatic establishment, consult your local telephone directory for the names of coin dealers (they will be found sometimes under the heading of "Stamp and Coin Dealers"). If you live in a city or town that does not have any coin dealers, obtain a copy of one of the trade publications (such as *Coin World* or *Numismatic News*) or check the Internet in order to obtain the names and addresses of many of the country's leading dealers. Information or sample copies may be obtained by writing to the individual publisher.

Current average *retail* valuations of all U.S. coins are listed in Whitman's *A Guide Book of United States Coins*™ by R.S. Yeoman, edited by Kenneth Bressett, Whitman Publishing, LLC, Atlanta, GA ($16.95 hardcover; $14.95 coilbound).

HOW TO READ THE CHARTS

A dash in a price column indicates that coins in that grade exist even though there are no current sales or auction records from them. (The dash does *not* necessarily mean that such coins are excessively rare.) Italicized prices indicate unsettled or speculative values. A number of listings of rare coins do not have prices or dashes in certain grades. This indicates that they are not available or not believed to exist in those grades.

Mintages of Proof coins are listed in parentheses.

Italicized mintages are estimates.

Numismatics or coin collecting is one of the world's oldest hobbies, dating back several centuries. Coin collecting in America did not develop to any extent until about 1840, as our pioneer forefathers were too busy carving a country out of wilderness to afford the luxury of a hobby. The discontinuance of the large-sized cent in 1857 caused many people to attempt to accumulate a complete set of the pieces while they were still in circulation. One of the first groups of collectors to band together for the study of numismatics was the American Numismatic Society, founded in 1858 and still a dynamic part of the hobby. Lack of an economical method to house a collection held the number of devotees of coin collecting to a few thousand until Whitman Publishing and other manufacturers placed low-priced coin boards and folders on the market in the 1930s. Since that time, the number of Americans collecting coins has increased many-fold.

THE PRODUCTION OF COINS

To collect coins intelligently it is necessary to have some knowledge of the manner in which they are produced. Coins are made in factories called "mints." The Mint of the United States was established at Philadelphia by a resolution of Congress dated April 2, 1792. The act also provided for the coinage of gold eagles ($10), half eagles, and quarter eagles; silver dollars, half dollars, quarter dollars, dimes (originally spelled "disme"), and half dismes or half dimes; and copper cents and half cents. The first coins struck were one-cent and half-cent pieces, in March of 1793 on a hand-operated press. Most numismatic authorities consider the half disme of 1792 the first United States coinage, quoting the words of George Washington as their authority. Washington, in his annual address, November 6, 1792, said, "There has been a small beginning in the coining of the half dimes, the want of small coins in circulation calling the first attention to them." Though the half disme is considered America's first coinage, it was not the first coinage produced by the Mint; these coins were produced off premises in July of 1792 before the mint was completed. In the new Philadelphia Mint are a number of implements from the original mint, and some coins discovered when the old building was wrecked. These coins included half dismes, and the placard identifying them states that Washington furnished the silver and gave the coined pieces to his friends as souvenirs.

Prior to the adoption of the Constitution, the Continental Congress arranged for the issuance of copper coins under private contract. These are known as the *Fugio cents* from their design, which shows a sundial and the Latin word "fugio"—"I Fly" or, in connection with the sundial, "Time Flies." The ever-appropriate motto "Mind Your Business" is also on the coin.

In the manufacture of a given coin, the first step is the cutting of the die. Prior to the latter part of the 19th century, dies for United States coins were "cut by hand." Briefly, this method is as follows: the design having been determined, a drawing the exact size of the coin is made. A tracing is made from this drawing. A piece of steel is smoothed and coated with transfer wax, and the tracing impressed into the wax. The engraver then tools out the steel where the relief or raised effect is required. If the design is such that it can all be produced by cutting away steel, the die is hardened and ready for use. Some dies are not brought to a finished state, as some part of the design can perhaps be done better in relief. In that case, when all that can be accomplished to advantage in the die is completed, it is hardened, a soft-steel impression is taken from it, and the unfinished parts are then completed. This piece of steel is in turn hardened and, by a press, driven into another piece of soft steel, thus making a die which, when hardened, is ready for the making of coins.

This hand method of cutting dies accounts for the many die varieties of early United States coins. Where the amount of coinage of a given year was large enough to wear out many dies, each new die placed in the coining press created another die variety of that year. The dies being cut by hand, no two were exactly alike in every detail, even though some of the major elements such as the head or wreath, were sunk into the die by individual master punches. Of the cents dated 1794, more than sixty different die varieties have been discovered.

Thousands of dies are now used by the mints of the United States each year, but they are all made from one master die, which is produced in the following manner:

After the design is settled upon, the plaster of paris or wax model is prepared several times the actual size of the coin. When this model is finished an electrotype (an exact duplicate in metal) is made and prepared for the reducing lathe. The reducing lathe is a machine that works on the principle of the pantograph, only in this case the one point traces or follows the form of the model while another much smaller point in the form of a drill cuts away the steel and produces a reduced-size die of the model. The die is finished and details are sharpened or worked over by an engraver with chisel and graver. The master die is used to make duplicates in soft steel which are then hardened and ready for the coining press. To harden dies, they are placed in cast-iron boxes packed with carbon to exclude the air, and when heated to a bright red are cooled suddenly with water.

In the coinage operations the first step is to prepare the metal. Among the alloys that have been used are the following: silver coins, 90% silver and 10% copper; five-cent pieces, 75% copper and 25% nickel; one-cent pieces, 95% copper and 5% zinc. (The 1943 cent consists of steel coated with zinc; and the five-cent piece of 1942–1945 contains 35% silver, 56% copper, and 9% manganese.) Under the Coinage Act of 1965, the composition of dimes, quarters, and half dollars was changed to eliminate or reduce the silver content of these coins. The copper-nickel "clad" dimes, quarters, half dollars, and dollars are composed of an outer layer of copper-nickel (75% copper and 25% nickel) bonded to an inner core of pure copper. The silver clad half dollar and dollar have an outer layer of 80% silver bonded to an inner core of 21% silver, with a total content of 40% silver. Current cents are made from a core of 99.2% zinc, 0.8% copper, with a plating of pure copper. Dollars are composed of a pure copper core with outer layers of manganese-brass.

Alloys are melted in crucibles and poured into molds to form ingots. The ingots are in the form of thin bars and vary in size according to the denomination of the coin. The width is sufficient to allow three or more coins to be cut from the strips.

The ingots are next put through rolling mills to reduce the thickness to required limits. The strips are then fed into cutting presses which cut circular blanks of the approximate size of the finished coin. The blanks are run through annealing furnaces to soften them; next they move through tumbling barrels, rotating cylinders containing cleaning solutions which clean and burnish the metal; and finally into centrifugal drying machines.

The blanks are next fed into a milling machine which produces the raised or upset rim. The blank, now called a *planchet*, is now ready for the coining press.

The planchet is held firmly by a collar, as it is struck under heavy pressure varying from 40 tons for the one-cent pieces and dimes to 170 tons for silver dollars. Upper and lower dies impress the design on both sides of the coin. The pressure is sufficient to produce a raised surface level with that of the milled rim. The collar holding the blank for silver or clad coins is grooved. The pressure forces the metal into the grooves of the collar, producing the "reeding" on the edge of the finished coin.

HOW A PROOF COIN IS MADE

Selected dies are inspected for perfection and are highly polished and cleaned. They are again wiped clean or polished after every 15 to 25 impressions and are replaced frequently to avoid imperfections from wear. Coinage blanks are polished and cleaned to assure high quality in striking. They are then hand fed into the coinage press one at a time, each blank receiving two blows from the dies to bring up sharp, high-relief details. The coinage operation is done at slow speed. Finished Proofs are individually inspected and are handled by gloves or tongs. They also receive a final inspection by packers before being sonically sealed in special plastic cases.

Certain coins, including Lincoln cents, Buffalo nickels, quarter eagles, half eagles, eagles, and double eagles, between the years 1908 and 1916, were made with Matte Proof (nickel and silver) and Sand Blast and Satin Proof (gold) finishes. These later Proofs have a dull frosted surface which was either applied to the dies, or produced by special treatment after striking.

MINTS AND MINTMARKS

In addition to the Philadelphia Mint, the U.S. government has from time to time established branch mints in various parts of the country. At present a branch mint operates in Denver and another in San Francisco. Starting in 1968, Proof sets and some of the regular coins were produced at the San Francisco Mint and Assay Office. The Denver Mint has operated since 1906. A mint was operated at New Orleans from 1838 to 1861 and again from 1879 to 1909. Mints were also in service at Carson City, Nevada, from 1870 to 1893; at Charlotte, North Carolina, from 1838 to 1861; at Dahlonega, Georgia, from 1838 to 1861; and at San Francisco since 1854. The U.S. government also operated a mint in the Philippines in the early 1900s.

Coins struck at Philadelphia before 1979 (except 1942 to 1945 five-cent pieces) do not bear a mintmark. Historically the mintmark was used only for branch mints. Recent exceptions include the Lincoln cent and the Kennedy half dollar, which both use the P for Philadelphia. All coins struck after 1967 have the mintmark on the obverse. The letters signifying the various mints are as follows:

C—Charlotte, North Carolina (gold coins only; 1838–1861)
CC—Carson City, Nevada (1870–1893)
D—Dahlonega, Georgia (gold coins only; 1838–1861)
D—Denver, Colorado (1906 to date)
O—New Orleans, Louisiana (1838–1861; 1879–1909)
P—Philadelphia, Pennsylvania (1793 to date; P not used in early years)
S—San Francisco, California (1854 to date)
W—West Point, New York (1984 to date)

The mintmark is of utmost importance to collectors because, historically, coinage of the branch mints has often been much smaller than quantities struck at Philadelphia. Many early coins of the branch mints are very scarce.

DISTINGUISHING MARKS

The illustrations and explanations in this section will help the collector identify certain well-known varieties.

Half Cents of 1795–1796 Showing Location of Pole to Cap

The end of the pole lies parallel with the lines of the bust, which is pointed. On some coins, the pole is missing due either to engraver error (while cutting the die) or to an error in "relapping" (when the die is ground to remove wear, clash marks, etc.).

Pole to Cap

No Pole to Cap

Stemless Wreath Variety of Half Cents and Large Cents

For this variety, the difference is on the reverse side. Illustrations below show both Stemless and Stems to Wreath types for comparison—stemless wreath found on the 1804, 1805, and 1806 half cents; and on the 1797, 1802, and 1803 large cents.

Stemless Wreath

Stems to Wreath

1864 Bronze Indian Head Cent With "L" on Ribbon

A small "L," the initial of the designer James B. Longacre, was added to the Indian design late in 1864 and was continued through 1909. For coins in less than Fine condition, this small letter will often be worn away. The point of the bust is rounded on the 1864 variety without "L"; the bust is pointed on the variety with "L." The initial must be visible, however, for the 1864 variety to bring the higher premium. If the coin is turned slightly so that the portrait faces the observer, the highlighted details will usually appear to better advantage.

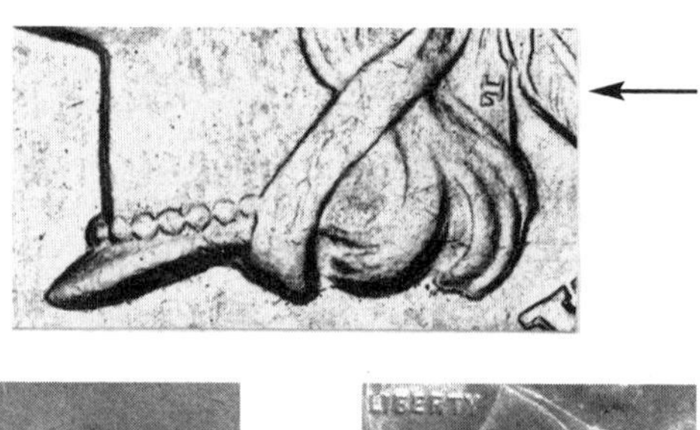

During 1909, initials appeared on the reverse. Starting in 1918, they appear below the shoulder.

1918-S, 8 Over 7
A variety of the kind on this quarter dollar is rarely found in coinage of the 20th century.

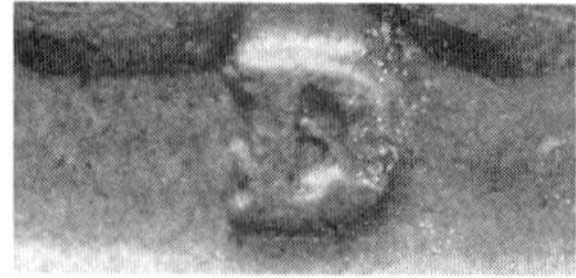

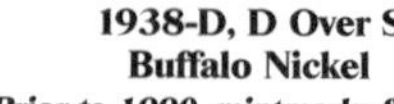

1938-D, D Over S
Buffalo Nickel
Prior to 1990, mintmarks for all mints were usually applied directly to working dies at Philadelphia in a hand-punching operation. Occasionally, a die was accidentally marked with one letter on top of another.

1942, 2 Over 1
Mercury Dime
Dies are produced by impressing the raised coin design of a hub into the end of a cylinder of steel. In early years the Mint made use of old dies by repunching the dates on their dies with new numbers. That practice was stopped prior to 1909. Since that time, all overdated coins have been the result of errors that occur when two different-dated hubs have been used in die preparation, and one is impressed over the other by accident.

1955, Doubled-Die Obverse
Lincoln Cent

Large Date Cent
(1960)

Small Date Cent
(1960)

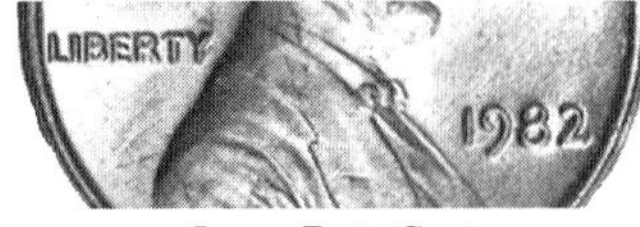
Large Date Cent
(1982)

Small Date Cent
(1982)

CONDITIONS OF COINS

Essential Elements of the Official ANA Grading System

PROOF—A specially made coin distinguished by sharpness of detail and usually with a brilliant, mirrorlike surface. *Proof* refers to the method of manufacture and is not a condition, but normally the term implies perfect condition unless otherwise noted.

GEM PROOF (PF-65)—Brilliant surfaces with no noticeable blemishes or flaws. A few scattered, barely noticeable marks or hairlines.

CHOICE PROOF (PF-63)—Reflective surfaces with only a few blemishes in secondary focal places. No major flaws.

PROOF (PF-60)—Surface may have several contact marks, hairlines, or light rubs. Luster may be dull and eye appeal lacking.

MINT STATE—The terms *Mint State (MS)* and *Uncirculated (Unc.)* are used interchangeably to describe coins showing no trace of wear. Such coins may vary to some degree because of blemishes, toning, or slight imperfections, as described in the following subdivisions:

PERFECT UNCIRCULATED (MS-70)—Perfect new condition, showing no trace of wear. The finest quality possible, with no evidence of scratches, handling, or contact with other coins. Very few regular-issue coins are ever found in this condition.

GEM UNCIRCULATED (MS-65)—An above average Uncirculated coin that may be brilliant or lightly toned and that has very few contact marks on the surface or rim. MS-67 through MS-62 indicate slightly higher or lower grades of preservation.

CHOICE UNCIRCULATED (MS-63)—Has some distracting contact marks or blemishes in prime focal areas. Luster may be impaired.

UNCIRCULATED (MS-60)—Has no trace of wear but may show a number of contact marks, and surface may be spotted or lack some luster.

CHOICE ABOUT UNCIRCULATED (AU-55)—Evidence of friction on high points of design. Most of the mint luster remains.

ABOUT UNCIRCULATED (AU-50)—Traces of light wear on many of the high points. At least half of the mint luster is still present.

CHOICE EXTREMELY FINE (EF-45)—Light overall wear on highest points. All design details are very sharp. Some of the mint luster is evident.

EXTREMELY FINE (EF-40)—Light wear on design throughout, but all features sharp and well defined. Traces of luster may show.

CHOICE VERY FINE (VF-30)—Light, even wear on the surface and highest parts of the design. All lettering and major features are sharp.

VERY FINE (VF-20)—Moderate wear on high points of design. All major details are clear.

FINE (F-12)—Moderate to considerable even wear. Entire design is bold with overall pleasing appearance.

VERY GOOD (VG-8)—Well worn with main features clear and bold, although rather flat.
GOOD (G-4)—Heavily worn, with design visible but faint in areas. Many details are flat.
ABOUT GOOD (AG-3)—Very heavily worn with portions of lettering, date, and legend worn smooth. The date may be barely readable.

Important: Damaged coins, such as those that are bent, corroded, scratched, holed, nicked, stained, or mutilated, are worth less than those without defects. Flawless Uncirculated coins are generally worth more than values quoted in this book. Slightly worn coins ("sliders") that have been cleaned and conditioned ("whizzed") to simulate Uncirculated luster are worth considerably less than perfect pieces.

Unlike damage inflicted after striking, manufacturing defects do not always lessen values. Examples include colonial coins with planchet flaws and weakly struck designs; early silver and gold with weight-adjustment "file marks" (parallel cuts made prior to striking); and coins with "lint marks" (surface marks due to the presence of dust or other foreign matter during striking).

Brief guides to grading are placed before each major coin type in this book. For more on grading, consult the *Official ANA Grading Standards for United States Coins*.

PRESERVING AND CLEANING COINS

Most numismatists will tell you to "never clean a coin" and it is good advice! Cleaning coins will almost always reduce their value. Collectors prefer coins in their original condition.

Some effort should be made to protect Uncirculated and Proof coins so they won't need cleaning. Tarnish on a coin is purely a chemical process caused by oxygen in the air acting on the metal, or by chemicals with which the coin comes in contact. One of the most common chemicals causing tarnish is sulphur; most paper, with the exception of specially manufactured "sulphur-free" kinds, contains sulphur due to the sulphuric acid that is used in paper manufacture; therefore do not wrap coins in ordinary paper. Also keep Uncirculated and Proof coins away from rubber bands (a rubber band placed on a silver coin for a few days will produce a black stripe on the coin where the band touched). The utmost in protection is obtained by storing the coin in an airtight box, away from moisture and humidity, and by using holders made of inert materials.

Many coins become marred by careless handling. Always hold the coin by the edge. The accompanying illustration shows the right and wrong way to handle numismatic specimens. It is a breach of numismatic etiquette to handle another collector's coin except by the edge, even if it is not an Uncirculated or Proof piece.

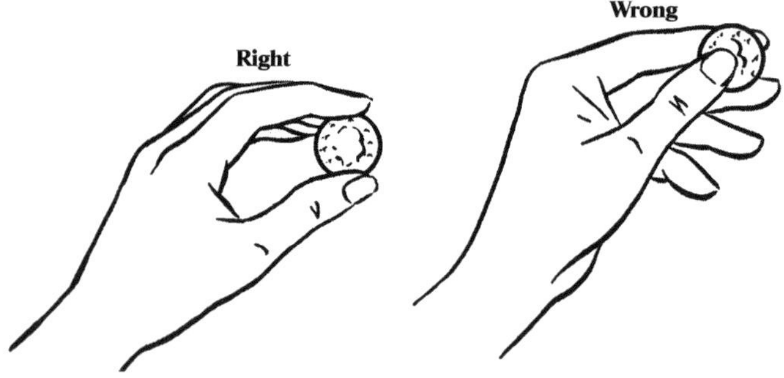

STARTING A COLLECTION

One may start a collection of United States coins with very little expense by systematically assembling the various dates and mintmarks of all the types and denominations that are now in general circulation. Whitman's many different coin folders and albums make this possible.

With the exception of the price paid for the coin folder, collecting coins received in everyday business transactions entails no expense whatsoever; a Jefferson nickel taken out of circulation, for example, can always be spent for five cents if the occasion arises. Filling an album or two out of circulation is probably the best method of determining whether coin collecting appeals to you. Not everyone can be a successful coin collector. It requires patience, intelligence of a high order, and a certain desire to know the meaning behind a lot of things that at first glance appear meaningless. You may not be cut out to be a collector but you'll never know until you look further into the subject, and if by the time an album or two of coins are collected you have no burning desire to acquire many more different coins, you will probably never be a collector. However, chances are that you will be, because if you have read this far in this book, it shows that you are interested in the subject.

Perfection is the goal of every endeavor and coin collecting is no exception. After an album has been filled with circulated specimens, the next step will be to replace them with coins in Uncirculated condition, or perhaps to start collecting an obsolete series; in either case, it will be necessary to purchase some coins from dealers or other collectors. The most logical way to keep abreast of the market, or obtain the addresses of the country's leading dealers, is to subscribe to one or more of the trade publications. These magazines carry advertisements of various dealers listing coins for sale. Moreover, through these sources the beginner may obtain price lists and catalogs from the dealers.

There are several good reference books available at reasonable prices which will be helpful to the collector who wishes to know more about U.S. coins and paper money. R.S. Yeoman's *A Guide Book of United States Coins*™ (the "Red Book") lists retail values of all regular U.S. coins and also lists all coins of the U.S. colonial period and private and territorial gold coins, plus tokens, pattern coins, errors, and other numismatic collectibles.

Most coin, book, and hobby dealers can supply the following titles:

The Official Red Book®: A Guide Book of United States Coins™—R.S. Yeoman, edited by Kenneth Bressett

A Guide Book of Morgan Silver Dollars: A Complete History and Price Guide—Q. David Bowers

The Expert's Guide to Collecting and Investing in Rare Coins—Q. David Bowers

Coin Collecting: A Beginner's Guide to the World of Coins—Kenneth Bressett

History of the United States Mint and Its Coinage—David W. Lange

The Official ANA Grading Standards for United States Coins—Kenneth Bressett, et al.

A Guide Book of United States Type Coins—Q. David Bowers

Join a Coin Club

A beginner should join a "coin club" if he or she is fortunate enough to live in a city which has one. Associating with more experienced collectors will be of great benefit. Practically all the larger cities have one or more clubs and they are being rapidly organized in the smaller towns. Trade publications carry information about coin clubs and special events such as coin shows and conventions.

The American Numismatic Association is a national organization that collectors can join. The ANA web site (www.money.org) has a list of member coin clubs throughout the United States. Contact the ANA by mail at 818 North Cascade Avenue, Colorado Springs, CO 80903, or by phone at 719-632-2646.

Early American coins are rare in conditions better than those listed and are consequently valued much higher.

BRITISH NEW WORLD ISSUES

Sommer Islands (Bermuda)

This coinage, issued around 1616, was the first struck for England's colonies in the New World. The coins were known as "Hogge Money" or "Hoggies."

The pieces were made of copper lightly silvered, in four denominations: shilling, sixpence, threepence, and twopence, indicated by Roman numerals. The hog is the main device and appears on the obverse side of each. SOMMER ISLANDS is inscribed within beaded circles. The reverse shows a full-rigged galleon with the flag of St. George on each of four masts.

Shilling

	G	VG	F	VF	EF
Twopence	$2,600	$4,000	$6,500	$11,000	$21,000
Threepence *(very rare)*			60,000		
Sixpence	2,500	3,800	6,000	12,000	23,000
Shilling	3,000	4,500	12,000	18,000	40,000

Massachusetts

"New England" Coinage (1652)

In 1652 the General Court of Massachusetts ordered the first metallic currency to be struck in the British Americas, the New England silver threepence, sixpence, and shilling. These coins were made from silver bullion procured principally from the West Indies. Joseph Jenks made the punches for the first coins at his Iron Works in Saugus, Massachusetts, close to Boston where the mint was located. John Hull was appointed mintmaster; his assistant was Robert Sanderson.

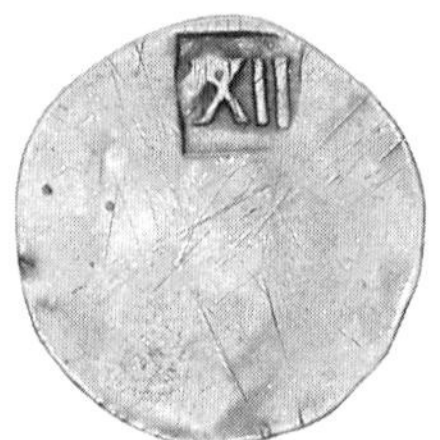

NE Shilling (1652)

	G	VG	F	VF
NE Threepence *(unique)*	—	—	—	—
NE Sixpence *(8 known)*	—	—	—	$110,000
NE Shilling	$22,000	$40,000	$55,000	135,000

Willow Tree Coinage (1653–1660)

The simplicity of the design on the N.E. coins invited counterfeiting and clipping of the edges. Therefore, they were soon replaced by the Willow Tree, Oak Tree, and Pine Tree series. The Willow Tree coins were struck from 1653 to 1660, the Oak Trees 1660 to 1667, and the Pine Trees 1667 to 1682. All of them (with the exception of the Oak Tree twopence) bore the date 1652. Many varieties of all of these coins exist. Values shown are for the most common types.

Sixpence

	Fair	G	VG	F	VF
1652 Willow Tree Threepence *(3 known)*	—	—	—	—	—
1652 Willow Tree Sixpence *(14 known)*	—	$13,000	$20,000	$40,000	$100,000
1652 Willow Tree Shilling	$5,000	11,000	22,000	50,000	115,000

Oak Tree Coinage (1660–1667)

Twopence

Threepence

	G	VG	F	VF	EF	AU
1662 Oak Tree Twopence	$350	$500	$1,000	$2,000	$3,750	$6,500
1652 Oak Tree Threepence	350	550	1,200	2,500	4,500	7,500
1652 Oak Tree Sixpence	350	550	1,600	3,200	5,750	9,000
1652 Oak Tree Shilling	390	600	1,600	2,500	4,800	8,000

Pine Tree Coinage (1667–1682)

The first Pine Tree coins were minted on the same size planchets as the Oak Tree pieces. Subsequent issues of the shilling were narrower and thicker, to conform to the size of English coins.

Shilling, Large Planchet (1667–1674)

Shilling, Small Planchet (1675–1682)

See next page for chart.

	G	VG	F	VF	EF	AU
1652 Pine Tree Threepence	$325	$500	$900	$2,000	$2,750	$4,500
1652 Pine Tree Sixpence	375	550	1,200	3,000	3,400	5,000
1652 Pine Tree Shilling, Large Planchet	400	750	1,500	2,750	4,500	7,200
1652 Pine Tree Shilling, Small Planchet	375	650	1,300	2,300	3,500	5,000

Maryland

Lord Baltimore Coinage

In 1659, Cecil Calvert, Lord Baltimore and Lord Proprietor of Maryland, had coinage struck in England for use in Maryland. There were four denominations: shilling, sixpence, fourpence (groat) in silver, and copper penny (denarium). The silver coins have the bust of Lord Baltimore on the obverse, and the Baltimore family arms with the denomination in Roman numerals on the reverse.

Lord Baltimore Shilling

Fourpence (groat)

	G	VG	F	VF	EF	AU
Penny (copper) *(6 known)*	—	—	—	—	—	—
Fourpence	$800	$1,600	$3,500	$7,000	$10,000	$16,000
Sixpence	700	1,200	2,500	5,000	7,000	10,000
Shilling	1,000	1,700	3,500	7,000	10,000	14,000

New Jersey

St. Patrick or Mark Newby Coinage

Mark Newby, who came to America from Dublin, Ireland, in November 1681, brought copper pieces believed by numismatists to have been struck in England circa 1663 to 1672. These are called St. Patrick coppers. The coin received wide circulation in the New Jersey Province, having been authorized to pass as legal tender by the General Assembly in May 1682. The smaller piece, known as a farthing, was never specifically authorized for circulation in the colonies.

St. Patrick Farthing

	G	VG	F	VF	EF	AU
St. Patrick "Farthing"	$100	$150	$400	$1,200	$2,600	$4,500
St. Patrick "Halfpenny"	160	370	725	1,600	4,000	

COINAGE AUTHORIZED BY BRITISH ROYAL PATENT

American Plantations Tokens

These tokens struck in nearly pure tin were the first royally authorized coinage for the British colonies in America. They were made under a franchise granted in 1688 to Richard Holt. Restrikes were made circa 1828 from original dies.

	G	F	EF	AU	Unc.
(1688) James II Plantation Token Farthing,					
1/24 Part *Real*, tin	$125	$275	$750	$1,000	$2,000
1/24 Part *Real*, Restrike	60	170	375	550	950

Coinage of William Wood

Rosa Americana Coins

William Wood, an Englishman, obtained a patent from King George I to make tokens for Ireland and the American colonies. The Rosa Americana pieces were issued in three denominations—halfpenny, penny, and twopence—and were intended for use in America.

Penny

	VG	F	VF	EF	AU	Unc.
(No date) Twopence, Motto in Ribbon	$90	$170	$375	$700	$1,500	$3,000
1722 Halfpenny, DEI GRATIA REX UTILE DULCI	55	125	210	450	825	1,800
1722 Penny	55	125	210	450	825	1,800
1722 Twopence	80	160	300	550	1,000	2,200

Halfpenny

See next page for chart.

Twopence

	VG	F	VF	EF	AU	Unc.
1723 Halfpenny	$40	$100	$175	$450	$800	$1,750
1723 Penny	40	110	200	400	650	1,500
1723 Twopence *(illustrated)*	90	130	300	500	925	1,900

Wood's Hibernia Coinage

The type intended for Ireland had a seated figure with a harp on the reverse side and the word HIBERNIA. Denominations struck were the halfpenny and the farthing with dates 1722, 1723, and 1724. Although these have no association with the Americas, because of the connection with William Wood many American collectors desire to obtain them.

1722, Hibernia Halfpenny

First Type

Second Type

	VG	F	VF	EF	AU	Unc.
1722 Farthing, second type	$125	$220	$400	$700	$1,000	$2,500
1722 Halfpenny (first or second type)	35	50	100	200	300	500

1723, Hibernia Farthing

1724, Hibernia Halfpenny

	VG	F	VF	EF	AU	Unc.
1723 Farthing	$20	$30	$75	$150	$220	$410
1723 Halfpenny	20	30	75	150	220	410
1724 Farthing	40	85	200	400	600	1,200
1724 Halfpenny	32	75	170	325	500	975

Virginia Halfpennies

In 1773, coinage of a copper halfpenny was authorized for Virginia by the British Crown. The style is similar to the regular English coinage. These pieces did not arrive in Virginia until 1775, but after then they did circulate on a limited basis. Most examples know today are Uncirculated, by virtue of a hoard of several thousand pieces that came to light in the 19th century and was distributed in numismatic channels.

	VG	F	VF	EF	AU	Unc.
1773 Halfpenny	$30	$50	$125	$225	$350	$600

EARLY AMERICAN AND RELATED TOKENS

Elephant Tokens

London Elephant Tokens

The London Elephant tokens were struck circa 1672 to 1694. Although they were undated, two examples are known to have been struck over 1672 British halfpennies. Most are struck in copper, but one is made of brass. The legend on this piece, GOD PRESERVE LONDON, is probably just a general plea for divine aid and not a specific reference to the outbreak of plague in 1665 or the great fire of 1666.

These pieces were not struck for the colonies, and probably did not circulate widely in America, although a few may have been carried there by colonists. They are associated with the 1694 Carolina and New England Elephant tokens, through a shared obverse die.

	VG	F	VF	EF	AU	Unc.
(1694) Halfpenny, GOD PRESERVE LONDON, Thick or Thin Planchet	$150	$270	$500	$875	$1,500	$2,000

Carolina Elephant Tokens

Although no law is known authorizing coinage for Carolina, very interesting piece known as Elephant Tokens were made with the date 1694. These copper tokens were of halfpenny denomination. The reverse reads GOD PRESERVE CAROLINA AND THE LORDS PROPRIETERS. 1694.

The Carolina pieces were probably struck in England and perhaps intended as advertising to heighten interest in the Carolina Plantation.

See next page for chart.

	VG	F	VF	EF
1694 CAROLINA	$2,000	$3,500	$6,000	$10,000

New England Elephant Tokens

Like the Carolina Tokens, the New England Elephant Tokens were believed to have been struck in England as promotional pieces to increase interest in the American colonies.

	VG	F	VF	EF
1694 NEW ENGLAND	$12,000	$17,000	$28,000	$36,000

New Yorke in America Token

Little is known about the origin of this token. The design of a heraldic eagle on a regulated staff with oak leaf finials is identical to the crest found on the arms of William Lovelace, governor of New York, 1663 to 1673. It seems likely that this piece is a token farthing struck by Lovelace for use in New York.

	VG	F
(Undated) Brass	$2,750	$7,000

Gloucester Tokens

This token appears to have been a private coinage by a merchant of Gloucester (county), Virginia. The only specimens known are struck in brass. The exact origin and use of these pieces are unknown.

	F
1714 Shilling, brass *(2 known)*	$50,000

Higley or Granby Coppers

The Higley coppers were private issues. All the tokens were made of pure copper. There were seven obverse and four reverse dies. The first issue, in 1737, bore the legend the VALUE OF THREEPENCE. After a time the quantity exceeded the local demand, and a protest arose against the value of the piece. The inscription was changed to VALUE ME AS YOU PLEASE.

	G	VG	F	VF
1737 THE VALVE OF THREE PENCE, CONNECTICVT, 3 Hammers	$5,000	$8,500	$16,000	$45,000
1737 THE VALVE OF THREE PENCE, I AM GOOD COPPER, 3 Hammers	5,500	9,000	16,000	45,000
1737 VALUE ME AS YOU PLEASE, I AM GOOD COPPER, 3 Hammers	5,500	9,000	16,000	45,000
(1737) VALUE ME AS YOU PLEASE, J CUT MY WAY THROUGH, Broad Axe	5,500	9,000	16,000	45,000
1739 VALUE ME AS YOU PLEASE, J CUT MY WAY THROUGH, Broad Axe	6,000	10,000	18,000	65,000

Hibernia-Voce Populi Coins

These coins, struck in the year 1760, were made in Dublin. Although these have no connection with America, they have been listed in numismatic publications in the United States for a long time and are collected by tradition.

Farthing (1760)

See next page for chart.

Halfpenny (1760)

	G	VG	F	VF	EF	AU	Unc.
1760 Farthing	$130	$180	$300	$900	$1,250	$2,000	$3,750
1760 Halfpenny	40	75	115	200	375	800	1,500

Pitt Tokens

William Pitt is the subject of these pieces, probably intended as commemorative medalets. He was a friend to the interests of America. The halfpenny served as currency during a shortage of regular coinage.

	VG	F	VF	EF	AU	Unc.
1766 Farthing		$4,000	$12,000			
1766 Halfpenny	$175	350	700	$1,400	$2,000	$4,000

Rhode Island Ship Medals

Although this medal has a Dutch inscription, the spelling and design indicate an English or Anglo-American origin. It is believed that this token was struck in England circa 1779–1780 as propaganda to persuade the Dutch to sign the Treaty of Armed Neutrality. Specimens are known in brass, copper, tin, and pewter. As with many colonial issues, modern copies exist.

1778–1779, Rhode Island Ship Medal

Values shown are for brass or copper pieces. Those struck in pewter are rare and valued higher.

	VF	EF	AU	Unc.
Rhode Island Ship Medal	$550	$950	$1,300	$2,200

John Chalmers Issues

John Chalmers, a silversmith, struck a series of silver tokens at Annapolis in 1783. Certain of the dies were by Thomas Sparro, who also engraved bank note plates. As most examples show wear today, these pieces seem to have served well in commerce.

	VG	F	VF	EF	AU
1783 Threepence	$800	$1,600	$2,800	$5,000	$7,000
1783 Sixpence	1,300	3,000	5,000	9,500	15,000
1783 Shilling	650	1,300	2,100	4,000	6,500

FRENCH NEW WORLD ISSUES

None of the coins of the French regime is strictly American. They were all general issues for the French colonies of the New World. The copper of 1717 to 1722 was authorized by edicts of 1716 and 1721 for use in New France, Louisiana, and the French West Indies.

Copper Sou or Nine Deniers

	VG	F	VF
1721B (Rouen)	$80	$200	$375
1721H (La Rochelle)	45	100	200
1722H	45	100	200

French Colonies in General

Coined for use in the French colonies, these circulated only unofficially in Louisiana, along with other foreign coins and tokens. Most were counterstamped RF (République Française) for use in the West Indies. The mintmark A signifies the Paris Mint.

	VG	VF	EF	AU
1767 French Colonies, Sou	$45	$200	$400	$800
1767 French Colonies, Sou, Counterstamped RF	40	100	225	400

SPECULATIVE ISSUES, TOKENS, AND PATTERNS

Nova Constellatio Coppers

The Nova Constellatio pieces were struck supposedly by order of Gouverneur Morris. Evidence indicates that they were all struck in Birmingham, England, and imported for American circulation as a private business venture.

1783, CONSTELLATIO, Pointed Rays

1783, CONSTELATIO, Blunt Rays

1785, CONSTELATIO, Blunt Rays

1785, CONSTELLATIO, Pointed Rays

	VG	F	VF	EF	AU	Unc.
1783, CONSTELLATIO, Pointed Rays	$50	$110	$250	$550	$1,000	$2,000
1783, CONSTELATIO, Blunt Rays	55	125	275	650	1,100	2,750
1785, CONSTELATIO, Blunt Rays	60	125	300	700	1,700	3,000
1785, CONSTELLATIO, Pointed Rays	50	120	270	575	1,000	2,000

Immune Columbia Pieces

Nearly all of these are very rare. Many if not most seem to be unofficial, including pieces produced at the private Machin's Mills mint in Newburgh, New York.

1785, Copper, Star Reverse

1785, George III Obverse

1787, IMMUNIS COLUMBIA, Eagle Reverse

	G	VG	F	VF	EF	AU
1785 Copper, Star Reverse			$8,000	$12,000	$15,000	
1785, George III Obverse	$2,500	$3,750	5,000			
1785, VERMON AUCTORI Obverse, IMMUNE COLUMBIA	3,000	5,000	6,000	16,000		
1787, IMMUNIS COLUMBIA, Eagle Reverse . . .	125	375	800	1,900	3,750	$6,000

Confederatio Coppers

Some Confederatio coppers may have been patterns, but others seem to have been made in limited numbers for general circulation. This will explain why the die with the CONFEDERATIO legend was combined with other designs such as a bust of George Washington, Libertas et Justitia of 1785, Immunis Columbia of 1786, the New York "Excelsiors," Inimica Tyrannis Americana, and others. In all there were thirteen dies struck in fourteen combinations. There are two types of the Confederatio reverse. In one instance the stars are contained in a small circle; in the other, larger stars are in a larger circle.

Typical Obverse

Small Circle Reverse

Large Circle Reverse

	VF
1785, Stars in Small Circle, various obverses.	$28,000
1785, Stars in Large Circle, various obverses.	25,000

Speculative Patterns

1786, IMMUNIS COLUMBIA

Eagle Reverse

Shield Reverse

See next page for chart.

	VF
1786, IMMUNIS COLUMBIA, Eagle Reverse	$30,000
1786, IMMUNIS COLUMBIA, Shield Reverse	25,000
(No date) (1786) Washington Obverse, Shield Reverse	—
1786, Eagle Obverse, Shield Reverse	30,000
1786, Washington Obverse, Eagle Reverse *(2 known)*	—

COINAGE OF THE STATES

New Hampshire

New Hampshire was the first of the states to consider the subject of coinage following the Declaration of Independence.

William Moulton was empowered to make a limited quantity of coins of pure copper, authorized by the State House of Representatives in 1776.

	VG
1776 New Hampshire Copper	$16,000

Massachusetts

The coinage of Massachusetts copper cents and half cents in 1787 and 1788 was under the direction of Joshua Witherle. These were the first coins bearing the denomination "cent" as established by Congress. Many varieties exist, the most valuable being that with arrows in the eagle's right talon (on the left side of the coin).

1787 Half Cent

1787 Cent

1788 Half Cent

1788 Cent

	G	F	VF	EF	AU	Unc.
1787 Half Cent	$40	$110	$300	$650	$1,000	$1,800
1787 Cent, Arrows in Right Talon	4,200	10,000	20,000			
1787 Cent, Arrows in Left Talon *(illustrated)*	40	110	325	700	1,700	2,750
1788 Half Cent	50	125	300	675	1,500	2,000
1788 Cent	40	110	275	650	1,500	2,000

Connecticut

Authority for establishing a mint near New Haven was granted by the state to Samuel Bishop, Joseph Hopkins, James Hillhouse, and John Goodrich in 1785. Today, well over 300 different die varieties are known of Connecticut coppers dated from 1785 to 1788. These pieces circulated widely and effectively; most are seen with significant evidence of circulation.

1785, Bust Facing Right

1785, Bust Facing Left

1786–1787, Mailed Bust Facing Right

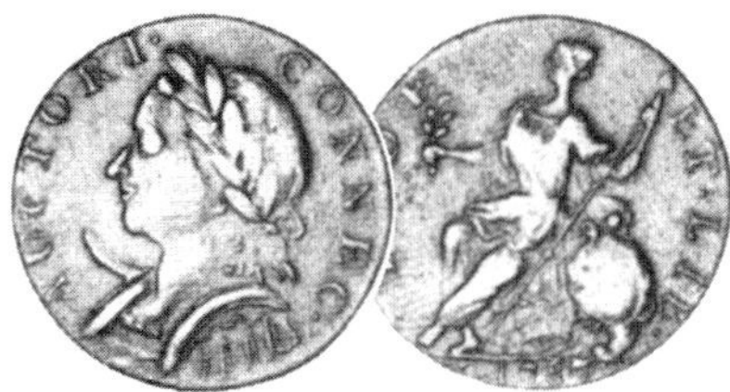

1786–1787, Mailed Bust Facing Left

1787, Draped Bust Facing Left

1788, Mailed Bust Facing Right

See next page for chart.

1788, Mailed Bust Facing Left

1788, Draped Bust Facing Left

	G	VG	F	VF	EF
1785, Bust Facing Right	$35	$45	$95	$300	$725
1785, Bust Facing Left	100	175	300	850	1,100
1786, Mailed Bust Facing Right	40	50	100	275	950
1786, Mailed Bust Facing Left	35	45	100	200	475
1787, Mailed Bust Facing Right	42	65	175	475	800
1787, Mailed Bust Facing Left	25	35	75	200	450
1787, Draped Bust Facing Left	25	35	75	225	500
1788, Mailed Bust Facing Right	25	50	100	300	700
1788, Mailed Bust Facing Left	25	32	80	210	550
1788, Draped Bust Facing Left	25	35	100	250	600

New York and Related Issues

Brasher Doubloons

Perhaps the most famous pieces coined before the establishment of the U.S. Mint at Philadelphia were those produced by a well-known goldsmith and jeweler, Ephraim Brasher of New York.

Brasher produced a gold piece weighing about 408 grains, approximately equal in value to a Spanish doubloon (about $15.00).

The punch-mark EB appears in either of two positions as illustrated. This mark is found on some foreign gold coins as well, and probably was so used by Brasher as evidence of his testing of their value. Many modern forgeries exist.

	EF
1787 New York gold doubloon, EB on Breast	—
1787 New York gold doubloon, EB on Wing	—

Copper Coinage

No coinage was authorized for New York following the Revolutionary War, although several propositions were considered. The only coinage laws passed were those regulating coins already in use.

	G	VG	F	VF
1786, NON VI VIRTUTE VICI	$2,750	$4,250	$7,500	$16,000

	G	VG	F	VF	EF
1787 EXCELSIOR Copper, Eagle on Globe Facing Right	$1,000	$2,000	$4,000	$10,000	$18,000
1787 EXCELSIOR Copper, Eagle on Globe Facing Left	1,000	2,000	3,500	9,000	17,000

1787, George Clinton and New York Arms

1787, Indian and New York Arms

1787, Indian and Eagle on Globe

	G	VG	F	VF	EF
1787, George Clinton and New York Arms	$4,500	$8,000	$13,000	$25,000	—
1787, Indian and New York Arms	3,500	5,000	9,000	18,000	$37,000
1787, Indian and Eagle on Globe	6,000	9,000	16,000	30,000	70,000

Nova Eborac Coinage for New York

**1787, NOVA EBORAC Reverse,
Seated Figure Facing Right**

**1787, NOVA EBORAC Reverse,
Seated Figure Facing Left**

	Fair	G	F	VF	EF	AU
1787, NOVA EBORAC, Seated Figure Facing Right.	$30	$60	$175	$600	$1,500	$2,500
1787, NOVA EBORAC, Seated Figure Facing Left	30	50	150	500	900	1,700

New Jersey

On June 1, 1786, the New Jersey Colonial legislature granted to Thomas Goadsby, Albion Cox, and Walter Mould authority to coin some three million coppers no later than June 1788, on condition that they delivered to the Treasurer of the State "one-tenth part of the full sum they shall strike and coin," in quarterly installments. These coppers were to pass current at 15 to the shilling. Produced in significant quantities, these coins are often seen in the market today and are widely collectible, although certain varieties can be rare and especially valuable.

Narrow Shield

Wide Shield

	G	F	VF	EF	AU
1786 Narrow Shield	$25	$100	$300	$650	$1,100
1786, Wide Shield	30	125	350	800	1,300

Small Planchet

	G	F	VF	EF	AU
1787, Small Planchet, Plain Shield	$30	$100	$300	$650	$1,100
1787, Large Planchet, Plain Shield	35	110	375	700	1,200

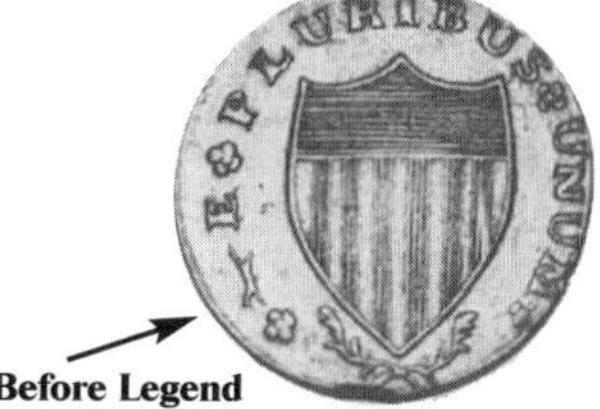

Fox Before Legend

	G	F	VF	EF	AU
1788, Horse's Head Facing Right	$30	$100	$300	$700	$1,200
1788, Similar, Fox in Legend	75	275	600	1,000	3,000
1788, Horse's Head Facing Left	175	500	1,750	4,500	—

Vermont

Reuben Harmon Jr. was granted permission to coin copper pieces beginning July 1, 1785. The franchise was extended for eight years in 1786. However, in 1787 production was shifted to Machin's Mills, Newburgh, New York, in which Harmon had a proprietary interest. Although the Vermont coins were legally issued there, most other products of Machin's Mills were counterfeits, some dies for which were combined with Vermont pieces, creating several illogical pieces below, including the 1785 Immune Columbia and the 1788 Georgivs III Rex.

1785, IMMUNE COLUMBIA **1785–1786, Plow Type** **1786, Baby Head**

	G	VG	F	VF	EF
1785, IMMUNE COLUMBIA	$3,000	$5,000	$6,000	$16,000	—
1785, Plow Type, VERMONTS	175	350	600	1,400	$4,000
1786, Plow Type, VERMONTENSIUM	135	260	500	1,000	2,000
1786, Baby Head	175	350	750	2,000	4,000

1786–1787, Bust Left 1787, BRITANNIA 1787, Bust Right

	G	VG	F	VF	EF
1786, Bust Left	$80	$200	$450	$1,250	$2,500
1787, Bust Left	2,500	5,500	15,000	23,000	—
1787, BRITANNIA	50	85	160	350	900
1787, Bust Right *(several varieties)*	70	135	245	500	1,300

1788, Bust Right

1788, GEORGIVS III REX

	G	VG	F	VF	EF
1788, Bust Right	$60	$110	$225	$500	$1,000
1788, GEORGIVS III REX	325	550	1,400	2,600	7,000

Note: This piece should not be confused with the common British halfpence with similar design and reverse legend BRITANNIA.

PRIVATE TOKENS AFTER CONFEDERATION

North American Tokens

This piece was struck in Dublin, Ireland. The obverse shows the seated figure of Hibernia facing left. Although dated 1781, it is believed to have been struck early in the next century.

	VG	F	VF	EF
1781, Copper or brass	$30	$75	$170	$420

Bar Coppers

The Bar "Copper" is undated and of uncertain origin. It has 13 parallel and unconnected bars on one side. On the other side is the large Roman letter USA monogram. The design was supposedly copied from a Continental button.

	VG	F	VF	EF	AU
(Undated) (Circa 1785) Bar Copper	$900	$1,700	$3,000	$4,500	$6,000

Auctori Plebis Tokens

This token is sometimes included with the coins of Connecticut as it greatly resembles issues of that state. It was struck in England by an unknown maker, possibly for use in America.

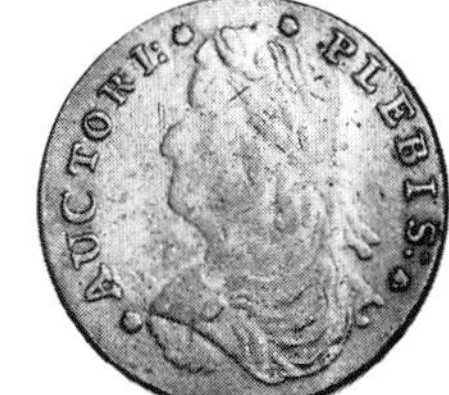

	G	VG	F	VF	EF	AU	Unc.
1787, AUCTORI PLEBIS	$40	$90	$150	$390	$750	$1,500	$3,750

Mott Store Cards

This item has long been considered an early token because of its date (1789). Some scholars believe it was most likely produced circa 1809 as a commemorative of the founding of the Mott Company, and probably served as a business card.

	VG	F	VF	EF	AU	Unc.
1789, Mott Token	$60	$125	$250	$450	$675	$1,250

Standish Barry Threepence

Standish Barry, a Baltimore silversmith, circulated a silver threepence in 1790. The tokens were believed to have been an advertising venture at a time when small change was scarce.

See next page for chart.

	VG	F	VF
1790 Threepence	$4,500	$9,000	$20,000

Kentucky Tokens

These tokens were struck in England about 1792 to 1794. Each star in the triangle represents a state, identified by its initial letter. These pieces are usually called Kentucky Cents because the letter K (for Kentucky) happens to be at the top. In the 19th century these were often called "triangle tokens," from the arrangement of the stars. Values are for the normal issue with plain edge; lettered edge varieties exist and are scarcer.

	VG	VF	EF	AU	Unc.
(1792–1794) Copper, Plain Edge	$50	$120	$225	$375	$650

Franklin Press Tokens

This piece is an English tradesman's token but, being associated with Benjamin Franklin, has accordingly been included in American collections.

	VG	VF	EF	AU	Unc.
1794, Franklin Press Token	$55	$150	$250	$400	$750

Talbot, Allum & Lee Cents

Talbot, Allum & Lee, engaged in the India trade and located in New York, placed a large quantity of English-made coppers in circulation during 1794 and 1795. ONE CENT appears on the 1794 issue.

1794 Cent, With NEW YORK

1795 Cent

	G	VG	VF	EF	AU	Unc.
1794 Cent, With NEW YORK	$25	$40	$150	$270	$400	$800
1794 Cent, Without NEW YORK	200	300	1,200	2,500	3,500	4,500
1795 Cent	25	40	125	240	350	600

WASHINGTON PORTRAIT PIECES

An interesting series of coins and tokens dated from 1783 to 1795 bear the portrait of George Washington. The likenesses in most instances were faithfully reproduced and were designed to honor Washington. Many of these pieces were of English origin and made later than the dates indicate.

	F	VF	EF	AU	Unc.
1783, Large Military Bust	$40	$100	$235	$550	$1,400

	F	VF	EF	AU	Unc.
1783, Draped Bust	$45	$110	$250	$475	$1,300

1783, UNITY STATES

Undated Double-Head Cent

See next page for chart.

	VG	F	VF	EF	AU	Unc.
1783, UNITY STATES	$60	$100	$150	$300	$600	$1,500
(Undated) Double-Head Cent	30	50	150	250	600	1,700

Obverse

Large Eagle Reverse

Small Eagle Reverse

	F	EF	AU	Unc.
1791 Cent, Large Eagle (Date on Obverse)	$225	$450	$750	$1,300
1791 Cent, Small Eagle (Date on Reverse)	250	500	900	1,500

	F	EF	AU
1791 Liverpool Halfpenny, Lettered Edge	$750	$2,200	$3,500

1792, Eagle With Stars, copper	—
1792, Eagle With Stars, silver	—
1792, Eagle With Stars, gold *(unique)*	—

(1792) Undated Cent, WASHINGTON BORN VIRGINIA

1792 Cent, WASHINGTON PRESIDENT

	VG	F	VF
(1792) Undated Cent, WASHINGTON BORN VIRGINIA, copper	$1,200	$2,250	$3,750
1792 Cent, WASHINGTON PRESIDENT, Plain Edge	1,500	3,750	6,000

1792 Getz Pattern

1793 Ship Halfpenny

1795 Halfpenny, Grate Token

	VG	F	VF	EF	AU	Unc.
1792, Getz Pattern, copper	$4,000	$7,000	$14,000	—		
1793 Ship Halfpenny, Lettered Edge	35	110	250	$450	$800	$1,800
1795, Grate Token, Lettered Edge	50	125	250	450	875	1,250
1795, Grate Token, Reeded edge	30	75	110	250	350	600

	F	VF	EF	AU	Unc.
1795, LIBERTY AND SECURITY Halfpenny, Plain Edge	$75	$200	$400	$800	$1,800
1795, LIBERTY AND SECURITY Halfpenny, Lettered Edge	65	160	325	650	1,700
Undated (1795) LIBERTY AND SECURITY Penny	165	300	450	700	1,500

	G	F	VF	EF
1795, NORTH WALES Halfpenny	$60	$150	$385	$800

	F	VF	EF	AU	Unc.
SUCCESS Medal; Large; Plain or Reeded Edge	$135	$275	$500	$900	$1,700
SUCCESS Medal; Small; Plain or Reeded Edge	150	325	600	950	1,800

CONTINENTAL CURRENCY

The Continental Currency pieces probably had some assigned value at their time of issue. The exact nature of their monetary role is uncertain; they might have been patterns, or they might have seen circulation. At any rate, this was the first dollar-sized coin proposed for the United States. They were probably struck in Philadelphia. As with many early pieces, modern replicas exist.

	G	F	VF	EF	AU	Unc.
1776, CURENCY, Pewter *(2 varieties)*	$3,000	$5,000	$10,000	$15,000	$22,000	$40,000
1776, CURENCY, Silver *(2 known)*		150,000				
1776, CURRENCY, Pewter	3,000	5,500	12,000	17,000	26,000	42,000
1776, CURRENCY, EG FECIT, Pewter	3,000	5,500	12,000	16,500	25,000	45,000

FUGIO CENTS

The first coins issued by authority of the United States were the "Fugio" cents. The legends have been credited to Benjamin Franklin by many, and the coins, as a consequence, have been referred to as *Franklin cents*.

1787, With Pointed Rays

1787, With Club Rays

	VG	F	VF	EF	AU	Unc.
Pointed Rays, STATES UNITED at Side of Circle *(illustrated)*	$125	$200	$300	$600	$900	$1,500
Pointed Rays, UNITED STATES at Side of Circle	125	200	300	600	900	1,500
Club Rays, Rounded Ends	250	350	850	1,750	3,000	—

The half cent was authorized to be coined April 2, 1792. Originally the weight was to have been 132 grains, but this was changed to 104 grains by the Act of January 14, 1793, before coinage commenced. The weight was again changed to 84 grains January 26, 1796, by presidential proclamation in conformity with the Act of March 3, 1795. Coinage was discontinued by the Act of February 21, 1857. All were coined at the Philadelphia Mint.

LIBERTY CAP (1793–1797)

AG-3 ABOUT GOOD—Clear enough to identify.
G-4 GOOD—Outline of bust of Liberty clear, no details. Date readable. Reverse lettering incomplete.
VG-8 VERY GOOD—Some hair details. Reverse lettering complete.
F-12 FINE—Most of hair detail visible. Leaves worn, but all visible.
VF-20 VERY FINE—Hair near ear and forehead worn, other areas distinct. Some details in leaves visible.
EF-40 EXTREMELY FINE—Light wear on highest parts of head and wreath.
AU-50 ABOUT UNCIRCULATED—Only a trace of wear on Liberty's face.

Head Facing Left (1793)

	Mintage	AG-3	G-4	VG-8	F-12	VF-20	EF-40	AU-50
1793	35,334	$800	$1,400	$2,500	$3,500	$6,000	$10,000	$15,000

Head Facing Right (1794–1797)

	Mintage	AG-3	G-4	VG-8	F-12	VF-20	EF-40	AU-50
1794	81,600	$110	$250	$350	$600	$1,000	$2,400	$4,250

Pole to Cap

Punctuated Date

No Pole to Cap

	Mintage	AG-3	G-4	VG-8	F-12	VF-20	EF-40	AU-50
1795, All kinds	139,690							
1795, Lettered Edge, With Pole		$75	$180	$300	$500	$1,100	$2,200	$3,250
1795, Lettered Edge, Punctuated Date		75	180	300	500	1,100	2,200	3,250
1795, Plain Edge, Punctuated Date		70	150	250	400	900	2,000	3,000
1795, Plain Edge, No Pole		70	150	250	400	900	2,000	3,000
1796, With Pole	1,390	3,250	6,500	9,000	12,000	20,000	30,000	
1796, No Pole	*	7,000	13,000	19,000	27,500	39,000	60,000	

* Included in number above.

1797, Plain Edge

1797, 1 Above 1, Plain Edge

	Mintage	AG-3	G-4	VG-8	F-12	VF-20	EF-40	AU-50
1797, All kinds	127,840							
1797, Lettered Edge		$200	$600	$950	$2,500	$6,000	$14,000	$30,000
1797, Plain Edge		90	200	300	600	1,000	2,100	3,500
1797, Gripped Edge		4,000	12,000	27,000				
1797, 1 Above 1, Plain Edge		70	210	300	450	850	1,800	2,700

DRAPED BUST (1800–1808)

AG-3 ABOUT GOOD—Clear enough to identify.
G-4 GOOD—Outline of bust of Liberty clear, few details, date readable. Reverse lettering worn and incomplete.
VG-8 VERY GOOD—Some drapery visible. Date and legends complete.
F-12 FINE—Shoulder drapery and hair over brow worn smooth.
VF-20 VERY FINE—Only slight wear in previously mentioned areas. Slight wear on reverse.
EF-40 EXTREMELY FINE—Light wear on highest parts of head and wreath.
AU-50 ABOUT UNCIRCULATED—Wear slight on hair above forehead.

1st Reverse

2nd Reverse

	Mintage	AG-3	G-4	VG-8	F-12	VF-20	EF-40	AU-50
1800	202,908	$16	$30	$40	$60	$125	$275	$400
1802, 2 over 0	20,266	125	320	710	1,750	4,500	13,000	
1803	92,000	16	30	40	60	135	425	650

Plain 4

Crosslet 4

Stemless Wreath

Stems to Wreath

	Mintage	AG-3	G-4	VG-8	F-12	VF-20	EF-40	AU-50
1804, All kinds	1,055,312							
1804, Plain 4, Stems to Wreath		$17	$35	$55	$85	$150	$435	$800
1804, Plain 4, Stemless Wreath		16	30	40	60	85	150	260
1804, Crosslet 4, Stemless Wreath		16	30	40	60	85	150	260
1804, Crosslet 4, Stems to Wreath		16	30	40	60	85	150	260

Chart continued on next page.

1804, "Spiked Chin"

Small 5

Large 5

	Mintage	AG-3	G-4	VG-8	F-12	VF-20	EF-40	AU-50
1804, "Spiked Chin"	*	$17	$35	$45	$65	$100	$175	$300
1805, All kinds	814,464							
1805, Medium 5, Stemless Wreath		16	30	40	60	90	150	260
1805, Small 5, Stems to Wreath		110	310	650	1,250	2,500	4,750	
1805, Large 5, Stems to Wreath		16	30	40	60	90	150	260

* Included in "1804, All kinds" mintage (previous page).

Small 6

Large 6

1808, 8 Over 7

Normal Date

	Mintage	AG-3	G-4	VG-8	F-12	VF-20	EF-40	AU-50
1806, All kinds	356,000							
1806, Small 6, Stems to Wreath		$40	$110	$180	$325	$600	$1,400	$2,750
1806, Small 6, Stemless Wreath		16	30	40	50	70	140	280
1806, Large 6, Stems to Wreath		16	30	40	50	70	140	280
1807	476,000	16	30	40	55	80	220	470
1808, 8 Over 7	*	30	70	120	280	600	1,650	4,000
1808, Normal Date	400,000	16	30	40	55	80	220	470

* Included in number below.

CLASSIC HEAD (1809–1836)

G-4 GOOD—LIBERTY only partly visible on hair band. Lettering, date, stars, worn but visible.
VG-8 VERY GOOD—LIBERTY entirely visible on hair band. Lower curls worn.
F-12 FINE—Only partial wear on LIBERTY, and hair at top worn in spots.
VF-20 VERY FINE—Lettering clear-cut. Hair only slightly worn.
EF-40 EXTREMELY FINE—Light wear on highest points of hair and leaves.
AU-50 ABOUT UNCIRCULATED—Sharp hair detail with only a trace of wear on higher points.
MS-60 UNCIRCULATED—Typical brown to red surface. No trace of wear.
MS-63 CHOICE UNCIRCULATED—Well-defined color, brown to red. No traces of wear.

Brilliant or red Uncirculated coins are worth more than prices shown. Spotted, cleaned, or discolored pieces are worth less.

	Mintage	AG-3	G-4	VG-8	F-12	VF-20	EF-40	MS-60	MS-63
1809,	1,154,572	$14	$25	$30	$35	$55	$90	$300	$400
1810	215,000	14	25	35	60	100	250	900	1,400
1811	63,140	42	75	170	310	700	2,300	3,500	5,200
1825	63,000	14	25	30	35	55	90	450	750
1826	234,000	14	25	30	35	55	85	225	360

13 Stars

12 Stars

	Mintage	AG-3	G-4	VG-8	F-12	VF-20	EF-40	MS-60	MS-63	PF-63
1828, 13 Stars	606,000	$13	$23	$30	$35	$45	$55	$190	$275	
1828, 12 Stars	*	14	24	35	40	50	125	650	900	
1829	487,000	13	23	30	35	45	65	175	325	
1831	2,200									$9,000
1832	51,000	13	23	28	32	40	55	175	250	2,500
1833	103,000	13	23	28	32	40	55	175	250	2,500
1834	141,000	13	23	28	32	40	55	175	250	2,500
1835	398,000	13	23	28	32	40	55	175	250	2,500
1836										8,000

* Included in number above.

BRAIDED HAIR (1840–1857)

VG-8 VERY GOOD—Beads in hair uniformly distinct. Hair lines visible in spots.
F-12 FINE—Hair lines above ear worn. Beads sharp.
VF-20 VERY FINE—Lowest curl worn; hair otherwise distinct.
EF-40 EXTREMELY FINE—Light wear on highest points of hair and on leaves.
AU-50 ABOUT UNCIRCULATED—Very slight trace of wear on hair above Liberty's ear.
MS-60 UNCIRCULATED—No trace of wear. Clear luster.
MS-63 CHOICE UNCIRCULATED—No trace of wear.
PF-63 CHOICE PROOF—Nearly perfect.

Brilliant or red Uncirculated coins are worth more than prices shown. Spotted, cleaned, or discolored pieces are worth less.

	PF-63		PF-63
1840, Original	$2,500	1845, Original	$3,500
1840, Restrike	2,250	1845, Restrike	3,250
1841, Original	2,600	1846, Original	3,250
1841, Restrike	2,500	1846, Restrike	2,600
1842, Original	2,750	1847, Original	2,600
1842, Restrike	2,500	1847, Restrike	2,600
1843, Original	2,500	1848, Original	2,600
1843, Restrike	2,500	1848, Restrike	2,600
1844, Original	3,500	1849, Original, Small Date	2,900
1844, Restrike	2,600	1849, Restrike, Small Date	2,900

Small Date

Large Date

	Mintage	G-4	VG-8	F-12	VF-20	EF-40	AU-50	MS-60	MS-63	PF-63
1849, Large Date	39,864	$17	$23	$30	$40	$75	$100	$225	$275	—
1850	39,812	17	23	30	40	75	100	225	325	$3,000
1851	147,672	15	20	28	35	50	80	135	250	2,700
1852										3,000
1853	129,694	15	20	28	35	50	80	135	250	
1854	55,358	15	20	28	35	50	80	135	250	2,700
1855	56,500	15	20	28	35	50	80	135	250	2,700
1856	40,430	17	22	30	40	60	85	150	300	2,700
1857	35,180	18	25	45	70	80	125	185	320	2,700

Cents and half cents were the first coins struck under the authority of the United States government. Coinage began in 1793 with laws specifying that the cent should weigh exactly twice as much as the half cent. Large cents were coined every year from 1793 to 1857 with the exception of 1815, when a lack of copper prevented production. All were coined at the Philadelphia Mint. Varieties listed are those most significant to collectors. Numerous other die varieties may be found because each of the early dies was individually made.

FLOWING HAIR (1793)

AG-3 ABOUT GOOD—Date and devices clear enough to identify.
G-4 GOOD—Lettering worn but readable. No detail on bust.
VG-8 VERY GOOD—Date and lettering distinct, some details of head visible.
F-12 FINE—About half of hair and other details visible.
VF-20 VERY FINE—Ear visible, most details visible.
EF-40 EXTREMELY FINE—Wear evident on highest points of hair and back of temple.

Chain Reverse (1793)

Obverse

AMERI. Reverse

AMERICA Reverse

	Mintage	AG-3	G-4	VG-8	F-12	VF-20	EF-40
1793, Chain, All kinds	36,103						
1793, AMERI. in Legend		$1,300	$3,800	$7,000	$12,000	$22,000	$37,500
1793, AMERICA		1,200	3,300	6,500	8,750	18,000	32,000

Wreath Reverse (1793)

Obverse

Wreath Reverse

Strawberry Leaf Variety

	Mintage	AG-3	G-4	VG-8	F-12	VF-20	EF-40
1793, Wreath, All kinds	63,353						
1793, Vine/Bars Edge		$300	$1,100	$1,600	$2,500	$3,800	$6,800
1793, Lettered Edge		350	1,250	1,700	2,700	4,000	7,500
1793, Strawberry Leaf	*(4 known)*						

LIBERTY CAP (1793–1796)

1793, Vine and Bars Edge
Chain and Wreath types only.

Lettered Edge (1793–1795)
ONE HUNDRED FOR A DOLLAR

Beaded Border (1793)

Head of 1793 (1793–1794)
Head in high, rounded relief.

Head of 1794 (1794)
Well-defined hair; hook on lowest curl.

Head of 1795 (1794–1796)
Head in low relief; no hook on lowest curl.

	Mintage	AG-3	G-4	VG-8	F-12	VF-20	EF-40
1793, Liberty Cap	11,056	$700	$1,600	$3,500	$6,200	$15,000	$28,000
1794, All kinds	918,521						
1794, "Head of 1793"		225	650	1,300	1,700	4,000	8,500
1794, "Head of 1794"		41	100	175	400	700	1,600
1794, "Head of 1795"		41	100	175	400	600	1,400
1795, Lettered Edge	37,000	41	130	175	400	850	2,000
1795, Plain Edge	501,500	32	110	200	350	700	1,500
1796, Liberty Cap	109,825	60	150	225	500	900	2,300

DRAPED BUST (1796–1807)

AG-3 ABOUT GOOD—Clear enough to identify.
G-4 GOOD—Lettering worn, but clear; date clear. Bust lacking in detail.
VG-8 VERY GOOD—Drapery on Liberty partly visible. Less wear in date and lettering.
F-12 FINE—Hair over brow smooth; some detail showing in other parts of hair.
VF-20 VERY FINE—Hair lines slightly worn. Hair over brow better defined.
EF-40 EXTREMELY FINE—Hair above forehead and left of eye outlined and detailed. Only slight wear on olive leaves.

LIHERTY Error

	Mintage	AG-3	G-4	VG-8	F-12	VF-20	EF-40
1796, Draped Bust	363,375	$37	$62	$140	$300	$650	$1,500
1796, LIHERTY Error	*	75	125	300	500	1,500	3,700

* Included in number above.

Gripped Edge · With Stems · Stemless

	Mintage	AG-3	G-4	VG-8	F-12	VF-20	EF-40
1797, All kinds	897,510						
1797, Gripped Edge, 1796 Reverse		$25	$60	$125	$225	$375	$1,400
1797, Plain Edge, 1796 Reverse		25	60	125	225	375	1,500
1797, 1797 Reverse, With Stems		20	50	100	150	225	650
1797, 1797 Reverse, Stemless		25	60	230	250	600	2,000

1798, 8 Over 7

1799, 9 Over 8

1800 Over 1798

1800, 80 Over 79

	Mintage	AG-3	G-4	VG-8	F-12	VF-20	EF-40
1798, All kinds	1,841,745						
1798, 8 Over 7		$25	$60	$135	$220	$750	$2,200
1798		13	30	45	110	220	800
1799, 9 Over 8	*	700	1,400	2,500	6,000	16,000	
1799, Normal Date		650	1,300	2,200	5,500	14,000	
1800, All kinds	2,822,175						
1800 Over 1798		12	26	50	110	300	1,300
1800, 80 Over 79		12	26	50	100	225	900
1800, Normal Date		12	26	50	100	225	900

* Included in 1798 mintage.

Fraction 1/000

Corrected Fraction

1801 Reverse, 3 Errors

	Mintage	AG-3	G-4	VG-8	F-12	VF-20	EF-40
1801, All kinds	1,362,837						
1801, Normal Reverse		$11	$20	$30	$75	$200	$500
1801, 3 Errors: 1/000, One Stem, and IINITED		25	65	120	325	750	3,000
1801, Fraction 1/000		11	25	40	120	225	750
1801, 1/100 Over 1/000		12	25	42	125	275	850
1802, All kinds	3,435,100						
1802, Normal Reverse		11	22	40	90	175	500
1802, Fraction 1/000		12	28	50	120	250	850
1802, Stemless Wreath		11	22	40	90	175	500

1803, Small Date, Blunt 1

1803, Large Date, Pointed 1

Small Fraction

Large Fraction

	Mintage	AG-3	G-4	VG-8	F-12	VF-20	EF-40
1803, All kinds	3,131,691						
1803, Small Date, Small Fraction		$11	$22	$40	$80	$175	$500
1803, Small Date, Large Fraction		11	22	40	80	175	500
1803, Large Date, Small Fraction		1,000	2,300	4,000	8,000	12,000	
1803, Large Date, Large Fraction		17	32	80	150	360	1,250
1803, 1/100 Over 1/000		11	25	50	100	225	650
1803, Stemless Wreath		11	25	50	100	225	650

Broken Dies

All genuine 1804 cents have crosslet 4 in date and a large fraction. The 0 in date is in line with O in OF on reverse.

	Mintage	AG-3	G-4	VG-8	F-12	VF-20	EF-40
1804 **(a)**	96,500	$300	$600	$1,100	$1,800	$2,750	$6,000
1805	941,116	11	22	40	80	175	500
1806	348,000	11	25	50	95	225	850

a. Values shown are for coins with normal or broken dies.

Small 1807, 7 Over 6 (Blunt 1)

Large 1807, 7 Over 6 (Pointed 1)

	Mintage	AG-3	G-4	VG-8	F-12	VF-20	EF-40
1807, All kinds	829,221						
1807, Small 7 Over 6, Blunt 1		$400	$1,100	$2,000	$4,250	$7,500	$15,000
1807, Large 7 Over 6		11	22	35	70	175	500
1807, Small Fraction		11	22	35	70	225	550
1807, Large Fraction		11	22	35	70	200	500

CLASSIC HEAD (1808–1814)

AG-3 ABOUT GOOD—Details clear enough to identify.
G-4 GOOD—Legends, stars, and date worn, but plain.
VG-8 VERY GOOD—LIBERTY all readable. Liberty's ear visible. Details worn but plain.
F-12 FINE—Hair on forehead and before ear nearly smooth. Ear and hair under ear sharp.
VF-20 VERY FINE—Some detail in all hair lines. Slight wear on leaves on reverse.
EF-40 EXTREMELY FINE—All hair lines sharp. Very slight wear on high points.

See next page for chart.

	Mintage	AG-3	G-4	VG-8	F-12	VF-20	EF-40
1808	1,007,000	$13	$22	$50	$140	$260	$800
1809	222,867	22	50	110	220	600	1,600

1810, 10 Over 09

1810, Normal Date

1811, Last 1 Over 0

1811, Normal Date

	Mintage	AG-3	G-4	VG-8	F-12	VF-20	EF-40
1810, All kinds	1,458,500						
1810, 10 Over 09		$11	$22	$45	$120	$300	$700
1810, Normal Date		11	22	35	120	260	650
1811, All kinds	218,025						
1811, Last 1 Over 0		16	33	60	210	800	2,500
1811, Normal Date		15	35	70	150	400	850
1812	1,075,500	11	20	35	110	250	600
1813	418,000	13	24	50	125	285	650
1814	357,830	11	20	35	110	250	600

LIBERTY HEAD (1816–1857)

G-4 GOOD—Details on Liberty's head partly visible. Even wear in date and legends.
VG-8 VERY GOOD—LIBERTY, date, stars, and legends clear. Part of hair cord visible.
F-12 FINE—All hair lines visible. Hair cords uniformly visible.
VF-20 VERY FINE—Hair cords only slightly worn. Hair lines only partly worn, all well defined.
EF-40 EXTREMELY FINE—Both hair cords stand out sharply. All hair lines sharp.
AU-50 ABOUT UNCIRCULATED—Only traces of wear on hair and highest points on leaves and bow.
MS-60 UNCIRCULATED—Typical brown surface. No trace of wear.
MS-63 CHOICE UNCIRCULATED—Some distracting contact marks or blemishes in prime focal areas. Impaired luster possible.

Matron Head (1816–1836)

13 Stars

15 Stars

Brilliant or red Uncirculated coins are worth more than prices shown. Spotted, cleaned, or discolored pieces are worth less.

	Mintage	G-4	VG-8	F-12	VF-20	EF-40	AU-50	MS-60	MS-63
1816	2,820,982	$8	$11	$16	$32	$70	$125	$250	$375
1817, 13 Stars	3,948,400	8	10	14	27	50	100	200	350
1817, 15 Stars	*	11	13	16	55	225	350	1,000	—
1818	3,167,000	8	10	14	27	50	90	270	350

* Included in number above.

1819, 9 Over 8

1820, 20 Over 19

	Mintage	G-4	VG-8	F-12	VF-20	EF-40	AU-50	MS-60	MS-63
1819	2,671,000	$9	$11	$15	$27	$55	$125	$185	$350
1819, 9 Over 8	*	10	13	18	36	150	175	300	475
1820	4,407,550	8	10	13	30	60	100	200	350
1820, 20 Over 19	*	10	13	18	45	150	200	500	650
1821	389,000	16	27	60	185	500	1,000	3,500	—
1822	2,072,339	9	12	22	50	100	275	450	750

* Included in number above.

1823, 3 Over 2

1824, 4 Over 2

1826, 6 Over 5

	Mintage	G-4	VG-8	F-12	VF-20	EF-40	AU-50	MS-60	MS-63
1823, 3 Over 2	*	$27	$50	$150	$300	$1,000	$1,750	$3,000	—
1823, Normal Date	*	30	55	175	375	1,350	2,200	3,400	—
1824, 4 Over 2	*	10	18	40	150	550	1,100	2,300	—
1824, Normal Date	1,262,000	8	10	16	75	210	350	950	$1,500
1825	1,461,100	8	10	16	45	150	250	800	1,100
1826, 6 Over 5	1,517,425	12	17	37	110	425	600	1,200	2,300
1826, Normal Date	**	8	10	12	45	110	190	400	650
1827	2,357,732	8	10	12	40	80	150	300	600

* Included in number below. ** Included in number above.

Date Size, Through 1828

Date Size, 1828 and Later

	Mintage	G-4	VG-8	F-12	VF-20	EF-40	AU-50	MS-60	MS-63
1828, Large Narrow Date	2,260,624	$8	$10	$14	$40	$70	$150	$400	$650
1828, Small Wide Date	*	8	10	16	50	100	200	500	1,000
1829	1,414,500	8	10	13	40	70	110	250	500
1830	1,711,500	8	10	13	30	60	100	200	400
1831	3,359,260	7	9	11	22	50	100	200	350
1832	2,362,000	7	9	11	22	50	80	175	325
1833	2,739,000	7	9	11	22	50	80	175	325
1834	1,855,100	7	9	11	22	70	100	200	350
1835	3,878,400	7	9	11	22	65	90	200	350
1836	2,111,000	7	9	11	22	55	85	160	300

* Included in number above.

Matron Head Modified (1837–1839)

G-4 GOOD—Considerably worn. LIBERTY readable.
VG-8 VERY GOOD—Hairlines smooth but visible; outline of ear clearly defined.
F-12 FINE—Hairlines at top of head and behind ear worn but visible. Braid over brow plain; ear clear.
VF-20 VERY FINE—All details sharper than for F-12. Only slight wear on hair over brow.
EF-40 EXTREMELY FINE—Hair above ear detailed, but slightly worn.
AU-50 ABOUT UNCIRCULATED—Trace of wear on high points of hair above ear and eye and on highest points on leaves and bow.
MS-60 UNCIRCULATED—Typical brown surface. No trace of wear.
MS-63 CHOICE UNCIRCULATED—Some distracting contact marks or blemishes in prime focal areas. Impaired luster possible.

1839 Over 1836

Brilliant or red Uncirculated coins are worth more than prices shown. Cleaned or discolored pieces are worth less.

	Mintage	G-4	VG-8	F-12	VF-20	EF-40	AU-50	MS-60	MS-63
1837	5,558,300	$7	$9	$11	$22	$65	$90	$160	$240
1838	6,370,200	7	9	11	22	30	85	150	210
1839	3,128,661	7	9	11	22	40	80	150	210
1839, 9 Over 6, Plain Cords	*	110	275	500	1,100	3,000	5,000	—	—
1840	2,462,700	7	9	11	18	40	75	150	275
1841	1,597,367	7	9	11	18	40	75	150	275
1842	2,383,390	7	9	11	18	40	75	150	250

* Included in number above.

"Head of 1840"
Petite Head
(1839–1843)

"Head of 1844"
Mature Head
(1843–1857)

Small Letters

Large Letters

	Mintage	G-4	VG-8	F-12	VF-20	EF-40	AU-50	MS-60	MS-63
1843, Petite, Small Letters	2,425,342	$7	$9	$13	$20	$30	$60	$145	$185
1843, Petite, Large Letters	*	9	11	20	35	70	125	325	575
1843, Mature, Large Letters	*	8	10	16	25	50	90	160	400
1844, Normal Date	2,398,752	7	9	11	20	32	65	120	175
1844, 44 Over 81	*	8	12	18	35	110	225	500	1,000
1845	3,894,804	7	9	13	20	30	70	125	175
1846	4,120,800	7	9	13	20	30	70	125	175
1847	6,183,669	7	9	13	20	30	70	125	175
1847, 7 Over Small 7	*	8	11	17	30	65	150	500	950

* Included in number above.

	Mintage	G-4	VG-8	F-12	VF-20	EF-40	AU-50	MS-60	MS-63
1848	6,415,799	$7	$9	$13	$18	$30	$70	$110	$150
1849	4,178,500	7	9	13	18	30	70	125	190
1850	4,426,844	7	9	13	18	30	70	100	150

1844, 44 Over 81

1851, 51 Over 81

1847, 7 Over "Small" 7

Brilliant or red Uncirculated coins are worth more than prices shown. Spotted, cleaned, or discolored pieces are worth less.

	Mintage	G-4	VG-8	F-12	VF-20	EF-40	AU-50	MS-60	MS-63
1851, Normal Date	9,889,707	$7	$9	$13	$18	$30	$70	$100	$150
1851, 51 Over 81	*	9	11	18	28	70	110	250	425
1852	5,063,094	7	9	13	18	30	70	100	150
1853	6,641,131	7	9	13	18	30	70	100	150
1854	4,236,156	7	9	13	18	30	70	100	150

* Included in number above.

1855, Upright 5's

1855, Slanting 5's

1855, Knob on Ear

	Mintage	G-4	VG-8	F-12	VF-20	EF-40	AU-50	MS-60	MS-63
1855, All kinds	1,574,829								
1855, Upright 5's		$7	$9	$13	$18	$30	$70	$100	$150
1855, Slanting 5's		7	9	13	18	30	70	125	175
1855, Slanting 5's, Knob on Ear		7	10	14	20	35	85	150	250
1856, Upright 5	2,690,463	7	9	13	18	30	70	100	150
1856, Slanting 5	*	7	9	13	18	30	70	100	150

* Included in number above.

1857, Large Date

1857, Small Date

	Mintage	G-4	VG-8	F-12	VF-20	EF-40	AU-50	MS-60	MS-63
1857, Large Date	333,546	$16	$25	$30	$35	$50	$100	$175	$275
1857, Small Date	*	17	27	35	40	55	115	200	300

* Included in number above.

FLYING EAGLE (1856–1858)

The Act of February 21, 1857, provided for the coinage of the small cent. The 1856 Flying Eagle cent was not an authorized Mint issue, as the law governing the new-size coin was enacted after the date of issue. It is believed that nearly 1,000 original strikings and 1,500 or more restrikes were made of the 1856. They are properly referred to as *patterns*.

G-4 GOOD—All details worn, but readable.
VG-8 VERY GOOD—Details in eagle's feathers and eye evident, but worn.
F-12 FINE—Eagle-head details and feather tips sharp.
VF-20 VERY FINE—Considerable detail visible in feathers in right wing and tail.
EF-40 EXTREMELY FINE—Slight wear, all details sharp.
AU-50 ABOUT UNCIRCULATED—Slight wear on eagle's left wing and breast.
MS-60 UNCIRCULATED—No trace of wear. Light blemishes.
MS-63 CHOICE UNCIRCULATED—Some distracting contact marks or blemishes in prime focal areas. Some impairment of luster possible.
PF-63 CHOICE PROOF—Nearly perfect.

1858, 8 Over 7

1856–1858, Large Letters

1858, Small Letters

Brilliant Uncirculated and Proof coins are worth more than prices shown. Spotted, cleaned, or discolored pieces are worth less.

	Mintage	G-4	VG-8	F-12	VF-20	EF-40	AU-50	MS-60	MS-63	PF-63
1856	*2,000*	$4,200	$4,800	$5,200	$6,750	$8,000	$9,000	$11,000	$13,500	$13,500
1857 . . . *(485)*	17,450,000	12	15	19	27	80	100	200	350	4,000
1858, Large Letters *(80)*	24,600,000	12	15	19	27	80	100	200	350	4,000
1858, Small Letters *(200)*	*	12	15	19	27	80	100	200	350	4,000
1858, 8 Over 7	*		50	110	210	420	725	1,900	5,000	

* Included in number above.

INDIAN HEAD (1859–1909)

The small cent was redesigned in 1859, and a representation of Miss Liberty wearing an Indian war bonnet was adopted as the obverse device. The 1859 reverse was also changed to represent a laurel wreath. In 1860 the reverse was modified to display an oak wreath with a small shield at the top. From 1859 to 1863, cents were struck in copper-nickel. In 1864 the composition was changed to bronze, although copper-nickel cents were also struck during that year.

G-4 GOOD—No LIBERTY visible.
VG-8 VERY GOOD—At least some letters of LIBERTY readable on head band.
F-12 FINE—LIBERTY mostly visible.
VF-20 VERY FINE—Slight but even wear on LIBERTY.
EF-40 EXTREMELY FINE—LIBERTY sharp. All other details sharp. Only slight wear on ribbon end.
AU-50 ABOUT UNCIRCULATED—Very slight trace of wear above the ear and the lowest curl of hair.
MS-60 UNCIRCULATED—No trace of wear. Light blemishes.
MS-63 CHOICE UNCIRCULATED—Some distracting contact marks or blemishes in prime focal areas. Impaired luster possible.
PF-63 CHOICE PROOF—Nearly perfect.

Without Shield at Top of Wreath (1859 Only)

With Shield on Reverse (1860–1909)

Variety 1 – Copper-Nickel, Laurel Wreath Reverse (1859)

Brilliant or red Uncirculated coins are worth more than prices shown. Spotted, cleaned, or discolored pieces are worth less.

	Mintage	G-4	VG-8	F-12	VF-20	EF-40	AU-50	MS-60	MS-63	PF-63
1859 . . . . . *(800)*	36,400,000	$7	$8	$10	$28	$55	$100	$135	$265	$850

Variety 2 – Copper-Nickel, Oak Wreath With Shield (1860–1864)

	Mintage	G-4	VG-8	F-12	VF-20	EF-40	AU-50	MS-60	MS-63	PF-63
1860 . . . . *(1,000)*	20,566,000	$6.00	$7	$8	$10	$32	$65	$100	$150	$525
1861 . . . . *(1,000)*	10,100,000	11.00	13	18	32	65	85	140	190	600
1862 . . . . . *(550)*	28,075,000	5.50	6	7	9	22	40	65	100	475
1863 . . . . . *(460)*	49,840,000	5.50	6	7	9	22	40	65	100	475
1864 . . . . . *(370)*	13,740,000	8.00	10	14	25	38	65	100	140	500

Variety 3 – Bronze (1864–1909)

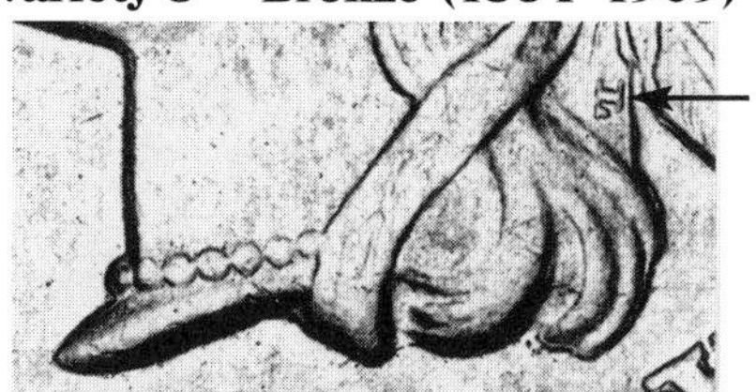

1864, Indian Head Cent With "L"

	Mintage	G-4	VG-8	F-12	VF-20	EF-40	AU-50	MS-60	MS-63	PF-63
1864, All kinds	39,233,714									
1864, No L *(150)*		$4	$6	$9	$22	$32	$42	$55	$85	$500
1864, w/L *(20)*		25	40	60	100	170	190	225	375	—
1865 . . . . . *(500)*	35,429,286	4	5	9	12	20	35	50	85	350
1866 . . . . . *(725)*	9,826,500	22	25	35	65	100	150	175	275	350
1867 . . . . . *(625)*	9,821,000	22	25	35	65	100	150	175	275	350
1868 . . . . . *(600)*	10,266,500	22	25	35	65	100	150	175	275	350
1869 . . . . . *(600)*	6,420,000	35	40	90	150	225	275	300	450	350
1870 . . . *(1,000)*	5,275,000	28	35	85	135	200	275	300	350	350
1871 . . . . . *(960)*	3,929,500	35	45	125	185	225	300	365	500	375
1872 . . . . . *(950)*	4,042,000	40	60	160	225	300	400	450	650	425
1873 . . . *(1,100)*	11,676,500	11	14	24	38	80	100	120	220	275
1874 . . . . . *(700)*	14,187,500	9	11	15	30	55	85	110	165	250
1875 . . . . . *(700)*	13,528,000	10	14	20	35	50	75	110	165	250
1876 . . . *(1,150)*	7,944,000	15	18	20	60	100	145	185	275	250
1877 . . . . . *(900)*	852,500	425	500	700	1,100	1,400	1,800	2,100	2,500	2,500

Brilliant or red Uncirculated coins are worth more than prices shown. Spotted, cleaned, or discolored pieces are worth less.

	Mintage	G-4	VG-8	F-12	VF-20	EF-40	AU-50	MS-60	MS-63	PF-63
1878	(2,350).... 5,797,500	$14.00	$18.00	$25.00	$65.00	$100	$145	$165	$250	$220
1879	(3,200)... 16,228,000	4.00	6.00	8.00	18.00	40	45	50	75	175
1880	(3,955)... 38,961,000	1.75	2.00	3.00	6.00	15	24	30	50	140
1881	(3,575)... 39,208,000	1.75	2.00	3.00	5.00	10	16	26	32	140
1882	(3,100)... 38,578,000	1.75	2.00	3.00	5.00	10	16	26	32	140
1883	(6,609)... 45,591,500	1.75	2.00	3.00	5.00	10	16	26	32	140
1884	(3,942)... 23,257,800	2.25	2.50	3.50	6.00	14	20	30	55	140
1885	(3,790)... 11,761,594	3.00	4.00	6.00	14.00	35	45	60	90	140
1886	(4,290)... 17,650,000	1.75	3.00	8.00	24.00	65	85	100	125	150
1887	(2,960)... 45,223,523	1.25	1.50	1.75	2.25	8	14	25	30	140
1888	(4,582)... 37,489,832	0.80	1.10	1.80	2.75	8	14	25	30	140
1889	(3,336)... 48,866,025	0.80	1.10	1.80	2.75	6	12	22	30	140
1890	(2,740)... 57,180,114	0.80	1.10	1.80	2.75	6	12	22	30	140
1891	(2,350)... 47,070,000	0.80	1.10	1.80	2.75	6	12	22	30	140
1892	(2,745)... 37,647,087	0.80	1.10	1.80	2.75	6	12	22	30	140
1893	(2,195)... 46,640,000	0.80	1.10	1.80	2.75	6	12	22	30	140
1894	(2,632)... 16,749,500	2.00	3.00	4.50	7.00	22	28	30	38	175
1895	(2,062)... 38,341,574	0.85	1.10	1.30	2.00	6	11	22	28	140
1896	(1,862)... 39,055,431	0.85	1.10	1.30	2.00	6	11	22	28	140
1897	(1,938)... 50,464,392	0.85	1.10	1.30	2.00	6	11	22	28	140
1898	(1,795)... 49,821,284	0.85	1.10	1.30	2.00	6	11	22	28	140
1899	(2,031)... 53,598,000	0.85	1.10	1.30	2.00	6	11	22	28	140
1900	(2,262)... 66,831,502	0.80	1.00	1.10	1.50	5	10	18	25	120
1901	(1,985)... 79,609,158	0.80	1.00	1.10	1.50	5	10	18	25	120
1902	(2,018)... 87,374,704	0.80	1.00	1.10	1.50	5	10	18	25	120
1903	(1,790)... 85,092,703	0.80	1.00	1.10	1.50	5	10	18	25	120
1904	(1,817)... 61,326,198	0.80	1.00	1.10	1.50	5	10	18	25	120
1905	(2,152)... 80,717,011	0.80	1.00	1.10	1.50	5	10	18	25	120
1906	(1,725)... 96,020,530	0.80	1.00	1.10	1.50	5	10	18	25	120
1907	(1,475).. 108,137,143	0.80	1.00	1.10	1.50	5	10	18	25	120

Location of Mintmark S on Reverse of Indian Cent (1908 and 1909 Only)

	Mintage	G-4	VG-8	F-12	VF-20	EF-40	AU-50	MS-60	MS-63	PF-63
1908	(1,620)... 32,326,367	$0.80	$1.10	$1.25	$1.50	$4.50	$10	$18	$25	$120
1908S	 1,115,000	32.00	42.00	48.00	55.00	80.00	100	150	250	
1909	(2,175)... 14,368,470	2.00	2.50	2.00	3.00	8.00	14	20	27	120
1909S	 309,000	200.00	230.00	270.00	300.00	350.00	390	485	650	

LINCOLN, WHEAT EARS REVERSE (1909–1958)

Victor D. Brenner designed this cent which was issued to commemorate the 100th anniversary of Abraham Lincoln's birth. The designer's initials V.D.B. appear on the reverse of a limited quantity of cents of 1909. Later in the year they were removed from the dies but restored in 1918 as very small incuse letters beneath the shoulder. The Lincoln type was the first cent to have the motto IN GOD WE TRUST.

G-4 GOOD—Date worn but apparent. Lines in wheat heads missing. Full rims.
VG-8 VERY GOOD—Half of lines visible in upper wheat heads.
F-12 FINE—Wheat lines worn but visible.
VF-20 VERY FINE—Lincoln's cheekbone and jawbone worn but separated. No worn spots on wheat heads.
EF-40 EXTREMELY FINE—Slight wear. All details sharp.
AU-50 ABOUT UNCIRCULATED—Slight wear on cheek and jaw and on wheat stalks.
MS-60 UNCIRCULATED—No trace of wear. Light blemishes or discoloration.
MS-63 CHOICE UNCIRCULATED—No trace of wear. Slight blemishes. Red-brown color.
MS-65 GEM UNCIRCULATED—No trace of wear. Barely noticeable blemishes. Nearly full red color.
PF-63 CHOICE PROOF—Reflective surfaces with only a few blemishes in secondary focal places. No major flaws.

Location of mintmark S or D on obverse of Lincoln cent.

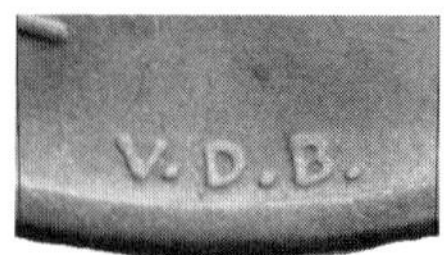
Designer's Initials V.D.B. (1909 Only)

No V.D.B. on Reverse (1909–1958)

Brilliant Uncirculated coins are worth more than prices shown. Spotted, cleaned, or discolored pieces are worth less.

	Mintage	G-4	VG-8	F-12	VF-20	EF-40	AU-50	MS-60	MS-63
1909, V.D.B.	27,995,000	$4.00	$4.25	$4.50	$5.00	$6.00	$6.25	$7	$9
1909, V.D.B. **(a)**	(1,194)								1,200
1909S, V.D.B.	484,000	350.00	375.00	420.00	550.00	675.00	750.00	900	1,100
1909	72,702,618	0.60	0.75	0.90	1.30	1.75	3.25	8	14
1909 **(a)**	(2,352)								225
1909S	1,825,000	40.00	45.00	55.00	75.00	100.00	125.00	150	200
1910	146,801,218	0.05	0.10	0.15	0.20	0.75	2.50	9	13
1910 **(a)**	(4,083)								150
1910S	6,045,000	5.00	6.00	7.00	8.00	15.00	30.00	40	55
1911	101,177,787	0.05	0.10	0.25	0.40	1.00	3.00	10	25
1911 **(a)**	(2,411)								175
1911D	12,672,000	1.75	2.25	3.75	8.00	17.00	30.00	45	65
1911S	4,026,000	10.00	11.00	12.00	16.00	27.00	45.00	90	135
1912	68,153,060	0.10	0.25	0.50	1.50	2.50	8.00	17	25
1912 **(a)**	(2,145)								150
1912D	10,411,000	2.50	2.75	3.50	7.50	23.00	35.00	70	115
1912S	4,431,000	6.00	7.50	8.50	11.00	25.00	37.00	70	100
1913	76,532,352	0.10	0.20	0.40	1.25	6.00	10.00	15	25
1913 **(a)**	(2,848)								160
1913D	15,804,000	0.75	1.00	1.50	3.50	12.00	20.00	50	90
1913S	6,101,000	3.00	4.00	5.00	6.00	17.00	35.00	75	125
1914	75,238,432	0.10	0.25	0.50	1.50	5.00	15.00	25	35
1914 **(a)**	(1,365)								180
1914D **(b)**	1,193,000	90.00	110.00	170.00	225.00	375.00	700.00	1,000	1,800
1914S	4,137,000	6.00	7.00	9.00	13.00	32.00	75.00	140	230
1915	29,092,120	0.35	0.70	1.40	4.00	20.00	30.00	45	60
1915 **(a)**	(1,050)								275
1915D	22,050,000	0.35	0.50	0.65	2.00	8.00	20.00	40	55
1915S	4,833,000	3.50	4.00	5.00	10.00	22.00	55.00	90	140
1916	131,833,677	0.03	0.05	0.10	0.30	1.00	5.00	10	15
1916 **(a)**	(1,050)								400
1916	35,956,000	0.08	0.13	0.40	0.75	5.00	10.00	35	50
1916S	22,510,000	0.30	0.40	0.75	1.50	6.00	15.00	38	70
1917	196,429,785	0.03	0.05	0.10	0.25	0.60	3.00	10	15
1917D	55,120,000	0.08	0.10	0.25	1.00	6.00	14.00	35	45
1917S	32,620,000	0.08	0.10	0.25	0.50	2.75	12.00	35	60

a. Matte Proof. **b.** Beware of altered date or mintmark. No V.D.B. on shoulder of genuine 1914-D cent.

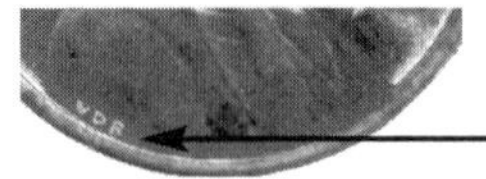

Designer's initials placed on Lincoln's shoulder next to rim, starting 1918.

Brilliant Uncirculated coins before 1934 are worth more than prices shown. Spotted, cleaned, or discolored pieces are worth less.

	Mintage	G-4	VG-8	F-12	VF-20	EF-40	AU-50	MS-60	MS-63
1918	288,104,634	$0.03	$0.05	$0.10	$0.20	$1.00	$3.00	$6.00	$15.00
1918D	47,830,000	0.08	0.13	0.35	1.00	6.00	9.00	32.00	65.00
1918S	34,680,000	0.08	0.13	0.35	0.80	3.00	15.00	35.00	75.00
1919	392,021,000	0.03	0.04	0.05	0.15	0.75	1.50	5.00	14.00
1919D	57,154,000	0.04	0.06	0.10	0.40	2.00	15.00	28.00	50.00
1919S	139,760,000	0.04	0.06	0.10	0.30	1.35	7.00	18.00	42.00
1920	310,165,000	0.03	0.04	0.05	0.15	0.50	1.50	6.00	12.00
1920D	49,280,000	0.04	0.06	0.10	0.30	3.00	12.00	33.00	50.00
1920S	46,220,000	0.04	0.06	0.10	0.30	2.00	15.00	42.00	100.00
1921	39,157,000	0.05	0.08	0.15	0.35	1.50	6.00	22.00	38.00
1921S	15,274,000	0.35	0.50	0.70	1.50	12.00	35.00	50.00	100.00
1922D	7,160,000	3.50	4.50	5.00	8.00	14.00	25.00	42.00	60.00
1922, No D **(c)**	*	270.00	325.00	375.00	525.00	1,200.00	2,200.00	4,200.00	15,000.00
1923	74,723,000	0.03	0.04	0.05	0.15	1.00	2.50	7.00	14.00
1923S	8,700,000	0.50	0.60	0.75	2.00	14.00	35.00	100.00	225.00
1924	75,178,000	0.03	0.04	0.06	0.15	1.50	3.50	15.00	25.00
1924D	2,520,000	8.00	10.00	13.00	19.00	42.00	85.00	150.00	225.00
1924S	11,696,000	0.40	0.50	0.80	1.10	7.00	29.00	55.00	110.00
1925	139,949,000	0.03	0.04	0.05	0.15	0.50	2.00	5.00	10.00
1925D	22,580,000	0.04	0.06	0.10	0.30	3.00	11.00	27.00	38.00
1925S	26,380,000	0.04	0.06	0.10	0.25	3.00	14.00	40.00	75.00
1926	157,088,000	0.03	0.04	0.05	0.15	0.50	2.00	5.00	8.00
1926D	28,020,000	0.04	0.06	0.10	0.30	2.50	9.00	35.00	50.00
1926S	4,550,000	0.85	1.25	2.00	2.50	7.00	20.00	60.00	125.00
1927	144,440,000	0.03	0.04	0.05	0.20	0.50	1.00	5.00	10.00
1927D	27,170,000	0.04	0.06	0.10	0.25	1.00	4.00	25.00	40.00
1927S	14,276,000	0.25	0.30	0.50	1.00	4.00	11.00	35.00	70.00
1928	134,116,000	0.03	0.04	0.05	0.15	0.50	1.00	4.50	10.00
1928D	31,170,000	0.04	0.06	0.10	0.25	0.85	4.00	15.00	34.00
1928S	17,266,000	0.06	0.10	0.25	0.50	1.50	5.00	34.00	55.00
1929	185,262,000	0.03	0.04	0.05	0.15	0.35	1.50	4.00	6.00
1929D	41,730,000	0.04	0.06	0.10	0.25	1.00	2.00	12.00	15.00
1929S	50,148,000	0.03	0.05	0.10	0.15	0.60	1.75	7.00	11.00
1930	157,415,000	0.03	0.04	0.05	0.15	0.25	0.75	2.00	3.50
1930D	40,100,000	0.04	0.06	0.10	0.25	0.60	1.00	5.00	10.00
1930S	24,286,000	0.03	0.05	0.10	0.15	0.40	2.00	3.50	5.00
1931	19,396,000	0.15	0.20	0.30	0.40	0.60	2.00	10.00	15.00
1931D	4,480,000	1.00	1.25	1.50	2.00	4.00	10.00	30.00	40.00
1931S	866,000	35.00	45.00	47.00	50.00	55.00	60.00	65.00	80.00
1932	9,062,000	0.40	0.50	0.60	1.00	1.25	3.50	10.00	13.00
1932D	10,500,000	0.25	0.35	0.40	0.50	0.85	3.00	10.00	15.00
1933	14,360,000	0.25	0.35	0.45	0.60	1.10	3.50	10.00	15.00
1933D	6,200,000	0.60	0.75	1.00	1.25	1.75	4.00	12.00	15.00
1934	219,080,000	0.03	0.03	0.03	0.03	0.10	1.00	3.00	4.00
1934D	28,446,000	0.04	0.06	0.08	0.10	0.25	1.25	7.50	14.00
1935	245,388,000	0.03	0.03	0.03	0.04	0.06	0.20	2.00	3.00
1935D	47,000,000	0.03	0.03	0.03	0.04	0.20	0.50	3.00	4.00
1935S	38,702,000	0.03	0.04	0.04	0.04	0.12	1.25	4.00	6.00
1936	309,632,000	0.03	0.03	0.03	0.04	0.06	0.25	1.00	3.00
1936, PF-63	(5,569)								85.00
1936D	40,620,000	0.03	0.03	0.03	0.04	0.08	0.20	1.00	3.00
1936S	29,130,000	0.03	0.03	0.03	0.04	0.10	0.20	1.00	3.00

* Included in number above. **c.** 1922 cents with a weak or missing mintmark were made from extremely worn dies that originally struck normal 1922-D cents. Three different die pairs were involved; two of them produced "Weak D" coins. One die pair (no. 2, identified by a "strong reverse") is acknowledged as striking "No D" coins. Weak D cents are worth considerably less. Beware of removed mintmark.

	Mintage	G-4	VG-8	F-12	VF-20	EF-40	MS-60	MS-63	MS-65	PF-63
1937 . . .(9,320)	309,170,000	$0.02	$0.02	$0.02	$0.03	$0.05	$0.20	$50.00	$3.00	
1937, Proof										$34
1937D	50,430,000	0.02	0.02	0.02	0.03	0.06	0.30	0.80	4.00	
1937S	34,500,000	0.03	0.03	0.03	0.04	0.06	0.30	0.80	4.00	
1938 . .(14,734)	156,682,000	0.02	0.02	0.02	0.03	0.05	0.30	0.75	2.00	
1938, Proof										25
1938D	20,010,000	0.02	0.03	0.04	0.06	0.15	0.50	1.00	5.00	
1938S	15,180,000	0.06	0.08	0.10	0.12	0.15	0.30	1.00	4.00	
1939 . .(13,520)	316,466,000	0.02	0.02	0.02	0.03	0.03	0.20	0.30	2.50	
1939, Proof										23
1939D	15,160,000	0.06	0.08	0.10	0.12	0.15	0.35	1.00	4.00	
1939S	52,070,000	0.03	0.03	0.03	0.04	0.10	0.30	1.00	4.00	
1940 . .(15,872)	586,810,000	0.02	0.02	0.02	0.03	0.03	0.20	0.30	2.00	
1940, Proof										16
1940D	81,390,000	0.02	0.02	0.02	0.03	0.03	0.20	0.40	2.00	
1940S	112,940,000	0.02	0.02	0.02	0.03	0.04	0.20	0.40	2.75	
1941 . .(21,100)	887,018,000	0.02	0.02	0.02	0.03	0.03	0.20	0.30	2.00	
1941, Proof										15
1941D	128,700,000	0.02	0.02	0.02	0.03	0.03	0.40	0.80	3.00	
1941S	92,360,000	0.02	0.02	0.02	0.03	0.04	0.35	0.80	5.00	
1942 . .(32,600)	657,796,000	0.02	0.02	0.02	0.03	0.03	0.10	0.15	1.00	
1942, Proof										15
1942D	206,698,000	0.02	0.02	0.02	0.03	0.03	0.10	0.15	2.00	
1942S	85,590,000	0.02	0.02	0.02	0.03	0.10	1.00	2.00	8.00	

Variety 2 – Zinc-Coated Steel (1943)

	Mintage	F-12	VF-20	EF-40	MS-60	MS-63	MS-65
1943	684,628,670	$0.05	$0.10	$0.15	$0.30	$0.70	$2
1943D	217,660,000	0.05	0.10	0.15	0.35	1.25	3
1943S	191,550,000	0.06	0.12	0.20	0.60	1.50	5

Variety 1 (Bronze) Resumed (1944–1958)

	Mintage	VF-20	EF-40	MS-63	MS-65
1944	1,435,400,000	$0.02	$0.03	$0.15	$0.50
1944D	430,578,000	0.02	0.03	0.20	0.50
1944D, D Over S	*	75.00	90.00	225.00	600.00
1944S	282,760,000	0.02	0.03	0.15	1.50
1945	1,040,515,000	0.02	0.03	0.20	0.50
1945D	266,268,000	0.02	0.03	0.15	0.50
1945S	181,770,000	0.02	0.03	0.10	2.00
1946	991,655,000	0.02	0.03	0.10	0.50
1946D	315,690,000	0.02	0.03	0.15	1.00
1946S	198,100,000	0.02	0.03	0.15	1.25
1947	190,555,000	0.02	0.03	0.25	0.50
1947D	194,750,000	0.02	0.02	0.12	0.50

* Included in number above.

1944-D, D Over S

1955, Doubled-Die Error

	Mintage	VF-20	EF-40	MS-63	MS-65
1947S	99,000,000	$0.02	$0.03	$0.15	$1.50
1948	317,570,000	0.02	0.02	0.15	0.50
1948D	172,637,500	0.02	0.02	0.12	0.60
1948S	81,735,000	0.02	0.03	0.20	1.50
1949	217,775,000	0.02	0.02	0.30	0.75
1949D	153,132,500	0.02	0.02	0.20	0.75

Chart continued on next page.

		Mintage	VF-20	EF-40	MS-63	MS-65	PF-65
1949S		64,290,000	0.03	0.05	0.50	2.00	
1950	(51,386)	272,635,000	0.02	0.02	0.25	0.50	$30.00
1950D		334,950,000	0.02	0.02	0.10	0.50	
1950S		118,505,000	0.02	0.03	0.25	0.80	
1951	(57,500)	284,576,000	0.02	0.02	0.25	0.80	35.00
1951D		625,355,000	0.02	0.02	0.10	0.50	
1951S		136,010,000	0.02	0.03	0.30	0.60	
1952	(81,980)	186,775,000	0.02	0.02	0.15	0.60	25.00
1952D		746,130,000	0.02	0.02	0.15	0.60	
1952S		137,800,004	0.02	0.03	0.50	1.50	
1953	(128,800)	256,755,000	0.02	0.03	0.10	0.50	25.00
1953D		700,515,000	0.02	0.02	0.10	0.50	
1953S		181,835,000	0.02	0.03	0.12	0.50	
1954	(233,300)	71,640,050	0.03	0.05	0.10	0.50	11.00
1954D		251,552,500	0.02	0.02	0.05	0.30	
1954S		96,190,000	0.02	0.03	0.05	0.30	
1955, Doubled-Die Obverse			500.00	700.00 **(a)**	1,400.00	5,000.00	
1955	(378,200)	330,958,200	0.02	0.02	0.06	0.30	10.00
1955D		563,257,500	0.02	0.02	0.05	0.25	
1955S		44,610,000	0.10	0.15	0.15	0.50	
1956	(669,384)	420,745,000	0.02	0.02	0.05	0.25	1.75
1956D		1,098,201,100	0.02	0.02	0.05	0.30	
1957	(1,247,952)	282,540,000	0.02	0.02	0.05	0.30	1.75
1957D		1,051,342,000	0.02	0.02	0.03	0.30	
1958	(875,652)	252,525,000	0.02	0.02	0.03	0.30	2.00
1958D		800,953,300	0.02	0.02	0.03	0.30	

* Included in regular mintage. **a.** Value for MS-60 Uncirculated is $1,000.

LINCOLN, MEMORIAL REVERSE (1959 TO DATE)

Small Date

Large Date

		Mintage	MS-63	MS-65	PF-65
1959	(1,149,291)	609,715,000	$0.01	$0.10	$1.00
1959D		1,279,760,000	0.01	0.10	
1960, Large Date	(1,691,602)	586,405,000	0.01	0.10	0.50
1960, Small Date	*	*	1.00	2.50	9.00
1960D, Large Date		1,580,884,000	0.01	0.10	
1960D, Small Date		*	0.02	0.10	
1961	(3,028,244)	753,345,000	0.01	0.10	0.50
1961D		1,753,266,700	0.01	0.10	
1962	(3,218,019)	606,045,000	0.01	0.10	0.50
1962D		1,793,148,140	0.01	0.10	
1963	(3,075,645)	754,110,000	0.01	0.10	0.50
1963D		1,774,020,400	0.01	0.10	
1964	(3,950,762)	2,648,575,000	0.01	0.10	0.50
1964D		3,799,071,500	0.01	0.10	
1965		1,497,224,900	0.02	0.12	
1966		2,188,147,783	0.04	0.12	
1967		3,048,667,100	0.03	0.12	
1968		1,707,880,970	0.02	0.12	
1968D		2,886,269,600	0.01	0.10	
1968S	(3,041,506)	258,270,001	0.02	0.10	0.50
1969		1,136,910,000	0.05	0.20	
1969D		4,002,832,200	0.03	0.10	
1969S	(2,934,631)	544,375,000	0.03	0.10	0.50
1969S Doubled-Die Obverse		*	—	—	

* Included in number above.

Small Date, Numbers Aligned at Top

Large Date, Low 7 in Date

Enlarged Detail of 1972 Doubled-Die Error

1969-S, Doubled-Die Error

		Mintage	MS-63	MS-65	PF-65
1970		1,898,315,000	$0.05	$0.10	
1970D		2,891,438,900	0.02	0.10	
1970S, Small Date (High 7)	(2,632,810)	690,560,004	13.00	22.00	$25.00
1970S, Large Date (Low 7)		*	0.03	0.10	0.25
1971		1,919,490,000	0.05	0.20	
1971D		2,911,045,600	0.03	0.20	
1971S	(3,220,733)	525,133,459	0.03	0.20	0.25
1972, Doubled-Die Obverse		**	190.00	300.00	
1972		2,933,255,000	0.01	0.05	
1972D		2,665,071,400	0.02	0.10	
1972S	(3,260,996)	376,939,108	0.02	0.10	0.25
1973		3,728,245,000	0.01	0.10	
1973D		3,549,576,588	0.01	0.10	
1973S	(2,760,339)	317,177,295	0.02	0.10	0.25
1974		4,232,140,523	0.01	0.10	
1974D		4,235,098,000	0.01	0.10	
1974S	(2,612,568)	409,426,660	0.03	0.10	0.25
1975		5,451,476,142	0.01	0.10	
1975D		4,505,275,300	0.01	0.10	
1974S	(2,845,450)				1.50
1976		4,674,292,426	0.01	0.10	
1976D		4,221,592,455	0.02	0.10	
1976S	(4,149,730)				1.25
1977		4,469,930,000	0.01	0.10	
1977D		4,194,062,300	0.01	0.10	
1977S	(3,251,152)				1.00
1978		5,558,605,000	0.01	0.10	
1978D		4,280,233,400	0.01	0.10	
1978S	(3,127,781)				1.00
1979		6,018,515,000	0.01	0.10	
1979D		4,139,357,254	0.01	0.10	
1979S, Filled S	(3,677,175)				1.50
1979S, Clear S *	*				1.75
1980		7,414,705,000	0.01	0.10	
1980D		5,140,098,660	0.01	0.10	
1980S	(3,554,806)				1.00
1981		7,491,750,000	0.01	0.10	
1981D		5,373,235,677	0.01	0.10	
1981S, Filled S	(4,063,083)				1.50
1981S, Clear S *	*				20.00
1982, Large Date		10,712,525,000	0.01	0.10	
1982, Small Date		*	0.02	0.12	
1982D, Large Date		6,012,979,368	0.01	0.10	
1982S	(3,857,479)				1.60

* Included in number above. ** Included in number below.

Large Date

Small Date

1995, Doubled Die showing strong doubling on word "LIBERTY".

Copper-Plated Zinc (1982 to Date)

	Mintage	MS-63	MS-65	PF-65
1982, Large Date	*	$0.01	$0.05	
1982, Small Date	*	0.01	0.05	
1982D, Large Date	*	0.05	0.50	
1982D, Small Date	*	0.01	0.05	
1983	7,752,355,000	0.01	0.05	
1983D	6,467,199,428	0.01	0.05	
1983S	(3,279,126)	0.01	0.05	$1.10
1984	8,151,079,000	0.01	0.05	
1984, Doubled Ear	**	50.00	100.00	
1984D	5,569,238,906	0.01	0.05	
1984S	(3,065,110)			1.10
1985	5,648,489,887	0.01	0.05	
1985D	5,287,339,926	0.01	0.05	
1985S	(3,362,821)			1.25
1986	4,491,395,493	0.01	0.05	
1986D	4,442,866,698	0.01	0.05	
1986S	(3,010,497)			2.00
1987	4,682,466,931	0.01	0.05	
1987D	4,879,389,514	0.01	0.05	
1987S	(4,227,728)			1.10
1988	6,092,810,000	0.01	0.05	
1988D	5,253,740,443	0.01	0.05	
1988S	(3,262,948)			3.25
1989	7,261,535,000	0.01	0.05	
1989D	5,345,467,111	0.01	0.05	
1989S	(3,220,194)			3.00
1990	6,851,765,000	0.01	0.05	
1990D	4,922,894,533	0.01	0.05	
1990S	(3,299,559)			2.00
1990, Pf, No S	**			—
1991	5,165,940,000	0.01	0.05	
1991D	4,158,446,076	0.01	0.05	
1991S	(2,867,787)			10.00
1992	4,648,905,000	0.01	0.05	
1992, Close AM **(a)**	**	—	—	
1992D	4,448,673,300	0.01	0.05	
1992D, Close AM **(a)**	**	—	—	
1992S	(4,176,560)			1.10
1993	5,684,705,000	0.01	0.05	
1993D	6,426,650,571	0.01	0.05	
1993S	(3,394,792)			2.00
1994	6,500,850,000	0.01	0.05	
1994D	7,131,765,000	0.01	0.05	
1994S	(3,269,923)			2.00
1995	6,411,440,000	$0.01	$0.05	
1995, DblDie Obv	**	4.00	18.00	
1995D	7,128,560,000	0.01	0.05	
1995S	(2,797,481)			$2.00
1996	6,612,465,000	0.01	0.05	
1996D	6,510,795,000	0.01	0.05	
1996S	(2,525,265)			1.25
1997	4,622,800,000	0.01	0.05	
1997D	4,576,555,000	0.01	0.05	
1997S	(2,796,678)			2.00
1998	5,032,155,000	0.01	0.05	
1998, Wide AM **(a)**	**	2.00	4.00	
1998D	5,225,353,500	0.01	0.05	
1998S	(2,086,507)			2.00
1999	5,237,600,000	0.01	0.05	
1999, Wide AM **(a)**	**		—	
1999D	6,360,065,000	0.01	0.05	
1999S	(3,347,966)			1.00
1999S, Close AM	**			—
2000	5,503,200,000	0.01	0.05	
2000, Wide AM **(a)**	**	2.00	2.50	
2000D	8,774,220,000	0.01	0.05	
2000S	(4,047,993)			1.00
2001	4,959,600,000	0.01	0.05	
2001D	5,374,990,000	0.01	0.05	
2001S	(3,184,606)			1.00
2002	3,260,800,000	0.01	0.05	
2002D	4,028,055,000	0.01	0.05	
2002S	(3,211,995)			1.00
2003	3,300,000,000	0.01	0.05	
2003D	3,548,000,000	0.01	0.05	
2003S	(3,298,439)			1.00
2004	3,379,600,000	0.01	0.05	
2004D	3,456,400,000	0.01	0.05	
2004S	(2,965,422)			1.00
2005	*3,935,600,000*	0.01	0.05	
2005D	*3,764,450,500*	0.01	0.05	
2005S	*(3,344,679)*			1.00
2006	*4,290,000,000*	0.01	0.05	
2006D	*3,944,000,000*	0.01	0.05	
2006S	*(2,923,105)*			1.00
2007		0.01	0.05	
2007D		0.01	0.05	
2007S				1.00

* Included in previous page's mintages. ** Included in number above. **a.** Varieties were made using Proof dies that have a wide space between AM in AMERICA. The letters nearly touch on other Uncirculated cents.

TWO-CENT PIECE (1864–1873)

The Act of April 22, 1864, which changed the weight and composition of the cent, included a provision for the bronze two-cent piece. The weight was specified as 96 grains, the alloy being the same as for the cent. There are two varieties for the first year of issue, 1864: the Small Motto and the Large Motto. The differences are illustrated in the closeups below.

1864, Small Motto

1864, Large Motto

On the obverse the D in GOD is narrow on the Large Motto variety. The stem to the leaf shows plainly on the Small Motto variety.

G-4 GOOD—At least part of IN GOD visible.
VG-8 VERY GOOD—WE weakly visible
F-12 FINE—Complete motto visible. The word WE weak.
EF-40 EXTREMELY FINE—The word WE bold.
AU-50 ABOUT UNCIRCULATED—Traces of wear visible on leaf tips, arrow points, and the word WE.
MS-60 UNCIRCULATED—No trace of wear. Light blemishes.
MS-63 UNCIRCULATED—Some distracting contact marks or blemishes in prime focal areas. Some impairment of luster possible.
PF-63 CHOICE PROOF—Reflective surfaces with only a few blemishes in secondary focal places. No major flaws.

Brilliant red choice Uncirculated and Proof coins are worth more than prices shown. Cleaned or discolored pieces are worth less.

	Mintage	G-4	VG-8	F-12	VF-20	EF-40	AU-50	MS-60	MS-63	PF-63
1864, All kinds	19,847,500									
1864, Small Motto		$55	$70	$100	$200	$325	$400	$525	$750	$10,000
1864, Large Motto *(100+)*		8	9	12	16	23	32	55	90	325
1865 *(500+)*	13,640,000	8	9	12	16	23	32	55	90	275
1866 *(725+)*	3,177,000	8	9	12	16	23	32	55	90	275
1867 *(625+)*	2,938,750	8	9	12	16	23	32	55	90	275
1868 *(600+)*	2,803,750	8	9	14	18	25	37	65	110	275
1869 *(600+)*	1,546,500	9	10	14	19	32	60	100	110	275
1870 *(1,000+)*	861,250	11	13	19	25	45	80	125	150	375
1871 *(960+)*	721,250	13	15	22	30	65	90	165	190	400
1872 *(950+)*	65,000	120	160	180	230	350	400	500	800	600
1873 *(1,000+)*							700			1,000

SILVER THREE-CENT PIECES (TRIMES) (1851–1873)

This smallest of United States silver coins was authorized by Congress March 3, 1851. The first three-cent silver pieces had no lines bordering the six-pointed star. From 1854 through 1858 there were three lines, while issues of the last 15 years show only two lines. Issues from 1854 through 1873 have an olive sprig over the III and a bundle of three arrows beneath.

G-4 GOOD—Star worn smooth. Legend and date readable.
VG-8 VERY GOOD—Outline of shield defined. Legend and date clear.
F-12 FINE—Only star points worn smooth.
VF-20 VERY FINE—Only partial wear on star ridges.
EF-40 EXTREMELY FINE—Ridges on star points visible.
AU-50 ABOUT UNCIRCULATED—Trace of wear visible at each star point. Center of shield possibly weak.
MS-60 UNCIRCULATED—No trace of wear. Light blemishes.
MS-63 CHOICE UNCIRCULATED—Some distracting contact marks or blemishes in prime focal areas. Some impairment of luster possible.
PF-63 CHOICE PROOF—Reflective surfaces with only a few blemishes in secondary focal places. No major flaws.

Mintmark location.

No Outline Around Star

Well-struck specimens command higher prices.

	Mintage	G-4	VG-8	F-12	VF-20	EF-40	AU-50	MS-60	MS-63	PF-63
1851	5,447,400	$13	$16	$18	$24	$33	$70	$90	$150	—
1851O	720,000	16	20	25	47	75	110	180	260	
1852	18,663,500	13	16	18	24	33	70	85	150	—
1853	11,400,000	13	16	18	24	33	70	85	150	

Three Outlines to Star, Large Date

	Mintage	G-4	VG-8	F-12	VF-20	EF-40	AU-50	MS-60	MS-63	PF-63
1854	671,000	$14	$17	$20	$26	$55	$115	$175	$325	$6,500
1855	139,000	16	28	30	50	100	135	275	450	2,200
1856	1,458,000	13	16	20	26	50	100	150	320	1,800
1857	1,042,000	13	16	20	26	50	100	150	320	1,600
1858 *(300+)*	1,603,700	13	16	20	26	50	90	150	320	1,200

Two Outlines to Star, Small Date

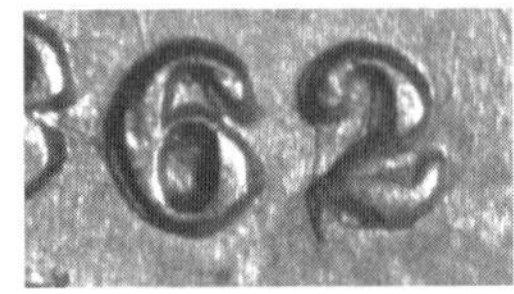

1862, 2 Over 1

	Mintage	G-4	VG-8	F-12	VF-20	EF-40	AU-50	MS-60	MS-63	PF-63
1859 (800)	364,200	$13	$16	$20	$26	$35	$75	$90	$175	$275
1860 (1,000)	286,000	13	16	20	26	35	75	90	175	275
1861 (1,000)	497,000	13	16	20	26	35	75	90	175	275
1862, 2 Over 1	*	13	16	20	26	35	90	110	225	
1862 (550)	343,000	13	16	20	26	35	75	90	175	285
1863 (460)	21,000				150	200	275	350	550	320
1864 (470)	12,000				150	200	275	350	550	310

* Included in number below.

	Mintage	VF-20	EF-40	AU-50	MS-60	MS-63	PF-63
1865	(500)....8,000	$175	$200	$300	$375	$525	$315
1866	(725)...22,000	150	175	275	350	500	315
1867	(625)....4,000	175	200	300	375	525	315
1868	(600)....3,500	175	200	300	375	600	315
1869	(600)....4,500	175	200	300	375	500	315
1870	(1,000)....3,000	175	200	300	375	500	325
1871	(960)....3,400	175	200	300	375	500	325
1872	(950)....1,000	200	225	300	375	600	350
1873, Proof only	(600)........	400				600	

NICKEL THREE-CENT PIECES (1865–1889)

The three-cent pieces struck in nickel composition were designed to replace the silver three-cent coins. Composition is 75% copper and 25% nickel. All were coined at Philadelphia and have plain edges.

G-4 GOOD—Date and legends complete though worn. III smooth.
VG-8 VERY GOOD—III half worn. Rims complete.
VF-20 VERY FINE—Three-quarters of hair details visible.
EF-40 EXTREMELY FINE—Slight, even wear.
AU-50 ABOUT UNCIRCULATED—Slight wear on hair curls, above forehead, and on wreath and numeral III.
MS-60 UNCIRCULATED—No trace of wear. Light blemishes.
MS-63 CHOICE UNCIRCULATED—Some distracting contact marks or blemishes in prime focal areas. Some impairment of luster possible.
PF-63 CHOICE PROOF—Reflective surfaces with only a few blemishes in secondary focal places. No major flaws.

Brilliant choice Uncirculated and Proof coins are worth more than prices shown. Spotted, cleaned, or discolored pieces are worth less.

	Mintage	G-4	VG-8	F-12	VF-20	EF-40	AU-50	MS-60	MS-63	PF-63
1865	*(500+)* 11,382,000	$7	$9	$10	$12	$15	$25	$50	$90	$650
1866	*(725+)* ..4,801,000	7	9	10	12	15	25	50	90	160
1867	*(625+)* ..3,915,000	7	9	10	12	15	25	50	90	160
1868	*(600+)* ..3,252,000	7	9	10	12	15	25	50	90	160
1869	*(600+)*..1,604,000	7	9	10	12	15	25	50	90	160
1870	*(1,000+)* ..1,335,000	7	9	10	12	15	25	50	90	160
1871	*(960+)* ...604,000	7	9	10	12	15	25	50	100	160
1872	*(950+)* ...862,000	7	9	10	12	15	25	50	100	160
1873	*(1,100+)* ...390,000	7	9	10	12	15	25	50	90	160
1874	*(700+)*...790,000	8	10	11	13	17	27	60	110	160
1875	*(700+)* ...228,000	9	11	12	14	20	32	80	110	160
1876	*(1,150+)* ...162,000	9	11	12	15	22	38	110	125	175
1877, Pf only	*(510+)*				550	600				900
1878, Pf only	(2,350)				250	375				475
1879	(3,200) 38,000	20	25	30	40	60	75	130	200	200
1880	(3,955) 21,000	40	45	50	60	70	85	150	180	200
1881	(3,575)..1,077,000	7	9	10	12	15	25	50	90	160
1882	(3,100) 22,200	35	45	50	60	80	100	150	200	225
1883	(6,609) 4,000	75	85	100	135	160	180	200	375	235
1884	(3,942) 1,700	150	165	180	250	275	300	400	550	275
1885	(3,790) 1,000	175	200	225	275	325	350	450	550	275
1886, Pf only	(4,290)				175	200				250
1887	(2,960) 5,001	120	140	150	160	175	225	250	275	250
1887, 7/6	*				175	200				275
1888	(4,582) 36,501	20	23	27	35	45	60	140	175	185
1889	(3,436) 18,125	35	50	60	75	85	100	150	200	185

* Included in number above.

SHIELD (1866–1883)

The Shield type nickel was made possible by the Act of May 16, 1866. Its weight was set at 77-16/100 grains with the same composition as the nickel three-cent piece.

G-4 GOOD—All letters in motto readable.
VG-8 VERY GOOD—Motto clear and stands out. Rims slightly worn but even. Part of shield lines visible.
F-12 FINE—Half of each olive leaf worn smooth.
EF-40 EXTREMELY FINE—Slight wear to leaf tips and cross over shield.
AU-50 ABOUT UNCIRCULATED—Traces of light wear on only the high design points. Half of mint luster present.
MS-60 UNCIRCULATED—No trace of wear. Light blemishes.
MS-63 CHOICE UNCIRCULATED—Some distracting blemishes in prime focal areas. Impaired luster possible.
PF-63 CHOICE PROOF—Reflective surfaces. Only a few blemishes in secondary focal areas. No major flaws.

Brilliant choice Uncirculated and Proof coins are worth more than prices shown. Spotted, cleaned, or discolored pieces are worth less.

	Mintage	G-4	VG-8	F-12	EF-40	AU-50	MS-60	MS-63	PF-63
1866, Rays ......*(600+)*	14,742,500	$10	$16	$18	$80	$100	$125	$180	$1,250
1867, Rays ....*(25+)*	2,019,000	13	19	25	90	125	225	275	15,000
1867, No Rays ...*(600+)*	28,890,500	9	10	11	20	25	70	120	210

Without Rays (1867–1883)

Typical Example of 1883, 3 Over 2
Other varieties exist.

	Mintage	G-4	VG-8	F-12	EF-40	AU-50	MS-60	MS-63	PF-63
1868 ....*(600+)*	28,817,000	$9	$10	$11	$20	$25	$70	$120	$210
1869 ....*(600+)*	16,395,000	9	10	11	20	25	70	120	210
1870 ....*(1,000+)*	4,806,000	9	10	11	20	25	70	120	210
1871 ....*(960+)*	561,000	22	28	40	85	110	150	175	235
1872 ....*(950+)*	6,036,000	10	11	13	24	50	90	125	210
1873, Close 3 .*(1,100+)*	436,050	10	11	13	30	55	100	175	210
1873, Open 3	4,113,950	9	10	11	25	50	90	125	
1874 ....*(700+)*	3,538,000	10	11	13	24	50	90	130	210
1875 ....*(700+)*	2,097,000	12	14	20	40	55	100	140	225
1876 ....*(1,150+)*	2,530,000	12	14	20	40	55	100	120	210
1877, Pf only ...*(510+)*				400	850				1,250
1878, Pf only ..(2,350)				275	450				650
1879 ....(3,200)	25,900	175	225	275	325	350	400	450	400
1880 ....(3,955)	16,000	190	240	290	500	800	1,600	2,500	450
1881 ....(3,575)	68,800	125	150	175	250	275	350	450	300
1882 ....(3,100)	11,472,900	8	9	10	19	25	60	100	175
1883 ....(5,419)	1,451,500	8	9	10	19	25	65	100	180
1883, 3 Over 2	*		60	80	175	250	375	500	

* Included in number above.

LIBERTY HEAD (1883–1912)

In 1883 the design was changed to the familiar "Liberty head." This type first appeared without the word CENTS on the coin, merely a large letter V. These "CENTS-less" coins were goldplated by fraudsters and passed as $5 pieces. Later in that year the word CENTS was added.

G-4 GOOD—No details in head. LIBERTY obliterated.
VG-8 VERY GOOD—Some letters in LIBERTY legible.
F-12 FINE—All letters in LIBERTY legible.
VF-20 VERY FINE—LIBERTY bold, including letter L.
EF-40 EXTREMELY FINE—LIBERTY sharp. Corn grains at bottom of wreath visible on reverse.
AU-50 ABOUT UNCIRCULATED—Traces of light wear on only high points of design. Half of mint luster present.
MS-60 UNCIRCULATED—No trace of wear. Contact marks possible. Surface may be spotted, or luster faded.
MS-63 CHOICE UNCIRCULATED—No trace of wear. Light blemishes.
PF-63 CHOICE PROOF—Reflective surfaces. Only a few blemishes in secondary focal areas. No major flaws.

Variety 1, Without CENTS (1883 Only)

Brilliant choice Uncirculated and Proof coins are worth more than prices shown; spotted or cleaned coins, less.

	Mintage	G-4	VG-8	F-12	VF-20	EF-40	AU-50	MS-60	MS-63	PF-63
1883, Without CENTS . . . .(5,219). . .	5,474,300	$2.25	$2.75	$3.10	$4.00	$4.75	$6.25	$18.00	$26.00	$165.00

Variety 2, With CENTS (1883–1913)

Mintmark Location

	Mintage	G-4	VG-8	F-12	VF-20	EF-40	AU-50	MS-60	MS-63	PF-63
1883, W/CENTS (6,783)	16,026,200	$5.00	$6.00	$10	$16	$35	$45	$75	$100	$140
1884 . . . . (3,942)	11,270,000	6.00	10.00	12	20	35	45	100	130	130
1885 . . . . (3,790)	1,472,700	230.00	275.00	325	450	550	700	850	1,100	700
1886 . . . . (4,290)	3,326,000	90.00	125.00	200	250	300	350	400	500	375
1887 . . . . (2,960)	15,260,692	4.00	7.00	11	20	40	45	75	125	150
1888 . . . . (4,582)	10,167,901	9.00	12.00	18	40	45	50	125	175	150
1889 . . . . (3,336)	15,878,025	2.50	4.00	8	12	25	30	75	125	140
1890 . . . . (2,740)	16,256,532	2.50	4.00	8	12	25	30	75	125	140
1891 . . . . (2,350)	16,832,000	2.50	4.00	8	12	25	30	75	125	140
1892 . . . . (2,745)	11,696,897	2.50	4.00	8	12	25	30	75	125	140
1893 . . . . (2,195)	13,368,000	2.50	4.00	8	12	30	35	80	135	140
1894 . . . . (2,632)	5,410,500	6.00	10.00	40	70	110	150	180	210	140
1895 . . . . (2,062)	9,977,822	1.50	2.50	7	10	25	30	75	130	140
1896 . . . . (1,862)	8,841,058	2.00	5.00	9	12	22	25	75	140	140
1897 . . . . (1,938)	20,426,797	2.00	5.00	9	12	22	24	50	125	140
1898 . . . . (1,795)	12,530,292	2.00	5.00	9	12	22	24	50	125	140
1899 . . . . (2,031)	26,027,000	0.75	1.00	3	6	14	22	50	110	140
1900 . . . . (2,262)	27,253,733	0.75	1.00	3	6	14	20	40	100	125
1901 . . . . (1,985)	26,478,228	0.75	1.00	3	6	14	20	40	90	125
1902 . . . . (2,018)	31,487,561	0.75	1.00	3	6	14	20	40	90	125
1903 . . . . (1,790)	28,004,935	0.75	1.00	2	4	11	20	40	90	125
1904 . . . . (1,817)	21,403,167	0.75	1.00	2	4	11	20	40	90	125
1905 . . . . (2,152)	29,825,124	0.75	1.00	2	4	11	20	40	90	125
1906 . . . . (1,725)	38,612,000	0.75	1.00	2	4	11	20	40	90	125
1907 . . . . (1,475)	39,213,325	0.75	1.00	2	4	11	20	40	90	125
1908 . . . . (1,620)	22,684,557	0.75	1.00	2	4	11	20	40	90	125
1909 . . . . (4,763)	11,585,763	0.75	1.00	2	4	11	20	40	90	125
1910 . . . . (2,405)	30,166,948	0.75	1.00	2	4	11	20	40	90	125
1911 . . . . (1,733)	39,557,639	0.75	1.00	2	4	11	20	40	90	125
1912 . . . . (2,145)	26,234,569	0.75	1.00	2	4	11	20	40	90	125
1912D	8,474,000	1.00	1.50	4	13	35	85	135	150	
1912S	238,000	60.00	75.00	100	175	375	600	700	900	
1913 Liberty Head *(5 known)*									2,000,000	

INDIAN HEAD OR BUFFALO (1913–1938)

The Buffalo nickel was designed by James E. Fraser, whose initial F is below the date. He modeled the bison after Black Diamond in the New York Central Park Zoo.

G-4 GOOD—Legends and date readable. Buffalo's horn does not show.
VG-8 VERY GOOD—Horn worn nearly flat.
F-12 FINE—Horn and tail smooth but partially visible. Obverse rim intact.
VF-20 VERY FINE—Much of horn visible. Indian's cheekbone worn.
EF-40 EXTREMELY FINE—Horn lightly worn. Slight wear on Indian's hair ribbon.
AU-50 ABOUT UNCIRCULATED—Traces of light wear on high points of design. Half of mint luster present.
MS-60 UNCIRCULATED—No trace of wear. May have several blemishes.
MS-63 CHOICE UNCIRCULATED—No trace of wear. Light blemishes.
MATTE PF-63 CHOICE PROOF—Crisp surfaces. Only a few blemishes in secondary focal areas. No major flaws.

Variety 1 – FIVE CENTS on Raised Ground (1913)

Brilliant choice Uncirculated coins are worth more than prices shown. Spotted, cleaned, weakly struck, or discolored pieces are worth less.

	Mintage	G-4	VG-8	F-12	VF-20	EF-40	AU-50	MS-60	MS-63	MATTE PF-63
1913, Var 1 . .(1,520)	30,992,000	$4	$5	$6	$8	$11	$12	$21	$30	$750
1913D, Variety 1	5,337,000	6	8	9	12	18	22	35	45	
1913S, Variety 1	2,105,000	15	22	24	28	40	50	70	90	

Variety 2 – FIVE CENTS in Recess (1913–1938)

Mintmark Below FIVE CENTS

1916, Doubled-Die Obverse

1918-D, 8 Over 7

	Mintage	G-4	VG-8	F-12	VF-20	EF-40	AU-50	MS-60	MS-63	MATTE PF-63
1913, Var 2 . . . . . .(1,514)	29,857,186	$4.25	$5.50	$6.50	$7.50	$11	$15	$22	$32	$600
1913D, Var 2 . .	4,156,000	45.00	55.00	70.00	85.00	120	130	150	175	
1913S, Var 2 . .	1,209,000	115.00	145.00	170.00	235.00	315	340	415	565	
1914 . .(1,275)	20,664,463	10.00	11.00	12.00	14.00	16	22	35	50	675
1914D	3,912,000	35.00	45.00	60.00	95.00	130	170	225	325	
1914S	3,470,000	12.00	14.00	18.00	35.00	50	80	95	240	
1915 . .(1,050)	20,986,220	2.50	2.50	4.00	5.00	12	30	45	50	700
1915D	7,569,000	8.00	10.00	18.00	35.00	75	85	140	175	
1915S	1,505,000	15.00	22.00	32.00	65.00	125	180	265	420	
1916 . . . .(600)	63,497,466	2.00	2.50	3.00	3.50	5	10	28	35	900
1916, DblDie Obv	*	1,000.00	1,800.00	3,600.00	5,600.00	8,500	14,000	33,000	70,000	
1916D	13,333,000	6.00	9.00	10.00	22.00	45	60	90	135	
1916S	11,860,000	350.00	6.00	9.00	22.00	45	65	100	165	
1917	51,424,019	2.00	250.00	3.00	4.00	7	16	30	60	
1917D	9,910,000	7.00	10.00	14.00	42.00	75	110	175	375	
1917S	4,193,000	9.00	13.00	20.00	50.00	85	135	225	575	
1918	32,086,314	1.50	2.00	2.50	6.00	16	22	60	135	

* Included in number above.

	Mintage	G-4	VG-8	F-12	VF-20	EF-40	AU-50	MS-60	MS-63
1918D, 8 Over 7	*	$550.00	$650.00	$1,300.00	$2,500.00	$4,500.00	$6,000	$15,000	$32,000
1918D	8,362,000	7.00	12.00	16.00	70.00	130.00	175	235	600
1918S	4,882,000	5.00	12.00	15.00	45.00	90.00	150	210	1,500
1919	60,868,000	0.50	0.55	0.80	2.00	7.00	15	32	60
1919D **(a)**	8,006,000	5.00	9.00	20.00	70.00	130.00	160	325	750
1919S **(a)**	7,521,000	4.00	8.00	14.00	70.00	130.00	160	325	900
1920	63,093,000	0.45	0.60	1.25	2.50	6.00	15	32	70
1920D **(a)**	9,418,000	3.00	6.00	12.00	65.00	150.00	175	300	800
1920S	9,689,000	1.50	3.00	9.00	50.00	120.00	150	230	750
1921	10,663,000	0.80	2.00	3.00	10.00	25.00	35	70	140
1921S	1,557,000	30.00	80.00	85.00	315.00	465.00	520	865	1,200
1923	35,715,000	0.45	0.60	0.80	4.00	7.50	18	32	80
1923S **(a)**	6,142,000	3.00	3.50	8.00	80.00	160.00	180	235	550
1924	21,620,000	0.40	0.60	0.80	4.00	9.00	25	40	80
1924D	5,258,000	3.50	4.00	10.00	40.00	120.00	140	190	500
1924S	1,437,000	8.00	18.00	40.00	240.00	725.00	825	1,200	2,200

* Included in number below. **a.** Uncirculated pieces with full, sharp details are worth considerably more.

1937-D, "3-Legged" Variety

1938-D, D Over S

Brilliant choice Uncirculated coins are worth more than prices shown. Spotted, cleaned, weakly struck, or discolored pieces are worth less.

	Mintage	G-4	VG-8	F-12	VF-20	EF-40	AU-50	MS-60	MS-63	PF-63
1925	35,565,100	$1.00	$1.25	$2.00	$4.00	$9.00	$16.00	$26	$47	
1925D	4,450,000	4.00	7.00	18.00	60.00	90.00	125.00	230	325	
1925S	6,256,000	2.00	6.00	10.00	50.00	90.00	125.00	230	1,200	
1926	44,693,000	0.35	0.45	0.60	3.00	5.00	12.00	22	32	
1926D	5,638,000	3.00	6.00	10.00	50.00	90.00	140.00	160	235	
1926S	970,000	9.00	15.00	35.00	250.00	500.00	1,300.00	2,000	4,000	
1927	37,981,000	0.50	0.45	0.60	1.50	6.00	10.00	24	36	
1927D	5,730,000	0.85	2.00	2.50	15.00	40.00	50.00	85	160	
1927S	3,430,000	0.60	0.90	1.75	18.00	45.00	75.00	250	1,100	
1928	23,411,000	0.40	0.45	0.60	2.00	5.00	10.00	22	30	
1928D	6,436,000	0.45	0.85	1.75	6.00	20.00	23.00	28	48	
1928S	6,936,000	0.60	0.75	1.25	5.00	15.00	50.00	125	300	
1929	36,446,000	0.35	0.40	0.60	2.00	5.00	10.00	16	35	
1929D	8,370,000	0.45	0.60	0.80	3.00	15.00	18.00	32	65	
1929S	7,754,000	0.40	0.60	0.75	0.90	5.00	12.00	25	45	
1930	22,849,000	0.40	0.50	0.70	0.80	4.00	10.00	16	35	
1930S	5,435,000	0.40	0.50	0.70	0.80	6.00	15.00	25	60	
1931S	1,200,000	7.00	8.00	8.80	9.25	15.00	25.00	28	45	
1934	20,213,003	0.35	0.45	0.55	0.75	3.00	9.00	16	30	
1934D	7,480,000	0.35	0.45	0.55	1.25	7.00	20.00	30	55	
1935	58,264,000	0.35	0.45	0.55	0.75	1.25	4.00	10	22	
1935D	12,092,000	0.35	0.45	0.55	0.75	3.00	18.00	20	35	
1935S	10,300,000	0.35	0.45	0.55	0.75	2.00	7.50	15	36	
1936 . . .(4,420)	118,997,000	0.35	0.45	0.55	0.75	1.25	4.00	10	23	$650
1936D	24,814,000	0.45	0.60	0.75	1.50	6.00	12.00	15	18	
1936S	14,930,000	0.35	0.45	0.55	0.75	1.25	4.50	11	16	
1937. . .(5,769)	79,480,000	0.35	0.45	0.55	0.75	1.25	2.75	13	16	550
1937D	17,826,000	0.35	0.45	0.55	0.75	1.25	4.00	11	16	
1937D, 3-Legged	*	200.00	325.00	400.00	450.00	550.00	700.00	1,200	2,750	
1937S	5,635,000	0.35	0.45	0.55	0.75	1.25	4.00	11	20	
1938D	7,020,000	0.35	0.45	0.55	0.75	1.25	4.00	11	15	
1938D, D Over S	*			4.00	5.00	8.00	12.00	25	35	

* Included in number above.

JEFFERSON (1938 TO DATE)

This nickel was originally designed by Felix Schlag. He won an award of $1,000 in a competition with some 390 artists. It established the definite public approval of portrait and pictorial rather than symbolic devices on our coinage. On October 8, 1942, the wartime five-cent piece composed of copper (56%), silver (35%), and manganese (9%) was introduced to eliminate nickel, a critical war material. A larger mintmark was placed above the dome. The letter P (Philadelphia) was used for the first time, indicating the change of alloy. The designer's initials FS were added below the bust starting in 1966. The mintmark position was moved to the obverse starting in 1968.

VG-8 VERY GOOD—Second porch pillar from right nearly gone, other three still visible but weak.
F-12 FINE—Jefferson's cheekbone worn flat. Hair lines and eyebrow faint. Second pillar weak, especially at bottom.
VF-20 VERY FINE—Second pillar plain and complete on both sides.
EF-40 EXTREMELY FINE—Cheekbone, hair lines, eyebrow slightly worn but well defined. Base of triangle above pillars visible but weak.
MS-63 SELECT UNCIRCULATED—No trace of wear. Slight blemishes.
MS-65 CHOICE UNCIRCULATED—No trace of wear. Barely noticeable blemishes.
PF 65 GEM PROOF—Brilliant surfaces. No noticeable blemishes or flaws. May have a few barely noticeable marks or hairlines.

Mintmark Located at Right of Building

Wartime Silver

Mintmark, Starting 1968

Uncirculated pieces with fully struck steps are valued higher.

	Mintage	VG-8	F-12	VF-20	EF-40	MS-63	MS-65	PF-65
1938. . . . . (19,365)	19,496,000	$0.07	$0.10	$0.20	$0.25	$1.10	$5.00	$50
1938D	5,376,000	0.25	0.35	0.75	1.00	2.25	7.00	
1938S	4,105,000	0.40	0.60	0.85	1.50	2.75	8.00	
1939. . . . . (12,535)	120,615,000	0.08	0.10	0.12	0.25	1.00	2.00	50
1939D	3,514,000	1.20	1.60	2.25	4.00	35.00	50.00	
1939S	6,630,000	0.25	0.30	0.50	1.25	12.00	20.00	
1940. . . . . (14,158)	176,485,000			0.05	0.10	1.00	2.00	45
1940D	43,540,000			0.05	0.10	1.25	3.50	
1940S	39,690,000			0.05	0.10	1.25	3.50	
1941. . . . . (18,720)	203,265,000			0.05	0.10	0.50	2.00	45
1941D	53,432,000			0.05	0.10	1.25	3.00	
1941S	43,445,000			0.05	0.10	1.50	3.50	
1942. . . . . (29,600)	49,789,000			0.05	0.10	1.25	4.00	45
1942D	13,938,000	0.10	0.15	0.25	1.00	15.00	23.00	

Wartime Silver Alloy (1942–1945)

	Mintage	VG-8	F-12	VF-20	EF-40	MS-63	MS-65	PF-65
1942P . . . . (27,600)	57,873,000	$0.20	$0.20	$0.25	$0.40	$4	$8.00	$100
1942S	32,900,000	0.20	0.20	0.25	0.40	4	9.00	
1943P, 3 Over 2	*		15.00	20.00	35.00	130	320.00	
1943P	271,165,000	0.20	0.20	0.25	0.35	3	6.00	
1943D	15,294,000	0.20	0.30	0.35	0.50	5	7.00	
1943S	104,060,000	0.20	0.20	0.25	0.35	3	6.00	
1944P	119,150,000	0.20	0.30	0.25	0.35	5	8.50	
1944D	32,309,000	0.20	0.20	0.25	0.35	5	8.00	
1944S	21,640,000	0.20	0.20	0.25	0.35	4	8.00	
1945P	119,408,100	0.20	0.20	0.25	0.35	3	8.00	
1945D	37,158,000	0.20	0.20	0.25	0.35	3	7.00	
1945S	58,939,000	0.20	0.20	0.25	0.35	3	7.00	

* Included in number below.

Prewar Composition, Mintmark Style Resumed (1946–1967)

	Mintage	VF-20	EF-40	MS-63	MS-65	PF-65
1946	161,116,000	$0.05	$0.05	$0.50	$2.50	
1946D	45,292,200	0.05	0.05	0.50	2.50	
1946S	13,560,000	0.05	0.06	0.25	1.75	
1947	95,000,000	0.05	0.05	0.35	1.75	
1947D	37,822,000	0.05	0.05	0.35	1.75	
1947S	24,720,000	0.05	0.06	0.35	1.75	
1948	89,348,000	0.05	0.05	0.35	1.75	
1948D	44,734,000	0.05	0.06	0.50	2.00	
1948S	11,300,000	0.05	0.06	0.50	2.00	
1949	60,652,000	0.05	0.06	1.25	2.75	
1949D	36,498,000	0.05	0.05	0.50	2.00	
1949D, D Over S	*	18.00	30.00	120.00	160.00	
1949S	9,716,000	0.05	0.10	0.40	2.00	
1950 (51,386)	9,796,000	0.05	0.10	0.50	2.50	$25.00
1950D	2,630,030	2.00	2.25	8.00	11.00	
1951 (57,500)	28,552,000	0.05	0.06	1.25	3.00	22.00
1951D	20,460,000	0.05	0.06	2.00	3.50	
1951S	7,776,000	0.05	0.10	0.50	2.50	
1952 (81,980)	63,988,000	0.05	0.05	0.35	1.75	17.50
1952D	30,638,000	0.05	0.05	2.00	3.00	
1952S	20,572,000	0.05	0.05	0.55	1.50	
1953 (128,800)	46,644,000	0.05	0.05	0.10	0.35	16.00
1953D	59,878,600	0.05	0.05	0.10	0.35	
1953S	19,210,900	0.05	0.05	0.25	0.50	
1954 (233,300)	47,684,050	0.05	0.05	0.50	1.00	8.50
1954D	117,183,060	0.05	0.05	0.20	0.50	
1954S	29,384,000	0.05	0.05	0.50	1.00	
1954S, S Over D	*	2.50	5.00	20.00	35.00	
1955 (378,200)	7,888,000	0.06	0.08	0.40	0.50	6.00

* Included in number above.

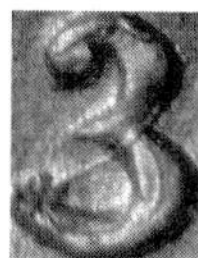

1943, 3 Over 2

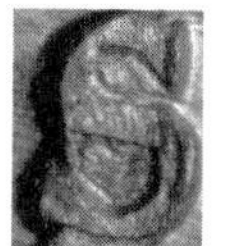

1954-S, S Over D

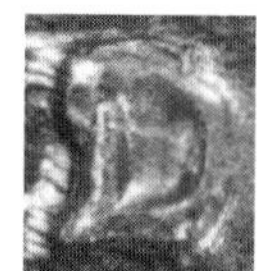

1955-D, D Over S (a)

	Mintage	VF-20	EF-40	MS-63	MS-65	PF-65
1955D	74,464,100	$0.05	$0.05	$0.20	$40.00	
1955D, D Over S **(a)**	*	3.00	5.00	30.00	35.00	
1956 (669,384)	35,216,000		0.05	0.10	0.40	$1.00
1956D	67,222,940		0.05	0.10	0.40	
1957 (1,247,952)	38,408,000		0.05	0.10	0.40	1.00
1957D	136,828,900		0.05	0.20	0.60	
1958 (875,652)	17,088,000		0.05	0.20	0.60	1.50
1958D	168,249,120		0.05	0.10	0.40	
1959 (1,149,291)	27,248,000		0.05	0.10	0.20	0.75
1959D	160,738,240		0.05	0.10	0.20	
1960 (1,691,602)	55,416,000		0.05	0.10	0.20	0.75
1960D	192,582,180		0.05	0.10	0.20	
1961 (3,028,144)	73,640,100		0.05	0.10	0.20	0.75
1961D	229,342,760		0.05	0.10	0.20	
1962 (3,218,019)	97,384,000		0.05	0.10	0.20	0.75
1962D	280,195,720		0.05	0.10	0.25	
1963 (3,075,645)	175,776,000		0.05	0.10	0.20	0.75
1963D	276,829,460		0.05	0.10	0.20	
1964 (3,950,762)	1,024,672,000		0.05	0.10	0.20	0.75
1964D	1,787,297,160		0.05	0.10	0.20	
1965	136,131,380		0.05	0.10	0.20	

* Included in number above. **a.** Varieties exist. Values are for the variety illustrated.

Chart continues on next page.

1966 Through 2003

	Mintage	MS-63	MS-65	PF-65
1966	156,208,283	$0.10	$0.20	
1967	107,325,800	0.10	0.20	
1968D	91,227,880	0.10	0.20	
1968S	(3,041,506)			
	100,396,004	0.10	0.20	$0.75
1969D	202,807,500	0.10	0.20	
1969S	(2,934,631)			
	120,165,000	0.10	0.20	0.75
1970D	515,485,380	0.10	0.20	
1970S	(2,632,810)			
	238,832,004	0.10	0.20	0.75
1971	106,884,000	0.25	0.50	
1971D	316,144,800	$0.10	$0.20	
1971S	(3,220,733)			$1.00
1972	202,036,000	0.10	0.20	
1972D	351,694,600	0.10	0.20	
1972S	(3,260,996)			1.00
1973	384,396,000	0.10	0.20	
1973D	261,405,000	0.10	0.20	
1973S	(2,760,339)			1.00
1974	601,752,000	0.10	0.20	
1974D	277,373,000	0.10	0.20	
1974S	(2,612,568)			1.00

	Mintage	MS-65	PF-65
1975	181,772,000	$0.35	
1975D	401,875,300	0.20	
1975S	(2,845,450)		$0.85
1976	367,124,000	0.20	
1976D	563,964,147	0.20	
1976S	(4,149,730)		0.85
1977	585,376,000	0.20	
1977D	297,313,422	0.50	
1977S	(3,251,152)		0.75
1978	391,308,000	0.20	
1978D	313,092,780	0.20	
1978S	(3,127,781)		0.75
1979	463,188,000	0.20	
1979D	325,867,672	0.20	
1979S, Filled S	(3,677,175)		0.75
1979S, Clear S	*		1.00
1980P	593,004,000	0.20	
1980D	502,323,448	0.20	
1980S	(3,554,806)		0.75
1981P	657,504,000	0.20	
1981D	364,801,843	0.20	
1981S	(4,063,083)		0.85
1982P	292,355,000	2.00	
1982D	373,726,544	1.50	
1982S	(3,857,479)		1.00
1983P	561,615,000	2.00	
1983D	536,726,276	1.25	
1983S	(3,279,126)		1.00
1984P	746,769,000	1.25	
1984D	517,675,146	0.20	
1984S	(3,065,110)		1.50
1985P	647,114,962	0.25	
1985D	459,747,446	0.25	
1985S	(3,362,821)		1.25
1986P	536,883,483	0.25	
1986D	361,819,140	0.60	
1986S	(3,010,497)		2.50
1987P	371,499,481	0.20	
1987D	410,590,604	0.20	
1987S	(4,227,728)		1.00
1988P	771,360,000	0.20	
1988D	663,771,652	0.20	
1988S	(3,262,948)		2.00
1989P	898,812,000	0.20	
1989D	570,842,474	$0.20	
1989S	(3,220,194)		$1.50
1990P	661,636,000	0.20	
1990D	663,938,503	0.20	
1990S	(3,299,559)		1.75
1991P	614,104,000	0.20	
1991D	436,496,678	0.20	
1991S	(2,867,787)		2.00
1992P	399,552,000	1.00	
1992D	450,565,113	0.20	
1992S	(4,176,560)		1.50
1993P	412,076,000	0.20	
1993D	406,084,135	0.20	
1993S	(3,394,792)		1.50
1994P	722,160,000	0.20	
1994D	715,762,110	0.20	
1994S	(3,269,923)		1.50
1995P	774,156,000	0.40	
1995D	888,112,000	0.20	
1995S	(2,797,481)		2.00
1996P	829,332,000	0.20	
1996D	817,736,000	0.20	
1996S	(2,525,265)		1.00
1997P	470,972,000	0.20	
1997D	466,640,000	0.20	
1997S	(2,796,678)		1.75
1998P	688,272,000	0.20	
1998D	635,360,000	0.20	
1998S	(2,086,507)		1.75
1999P	1,212,000,000	0.20	
1999D	1,066,720,000	0.20	
1999S	(3,347,966)		2.00
2000P	846,240,000	0.20	
2000D	1,509,520,000	0.20	
2000S	(4,047,993)		1.75
2001P	675,704,000	0.20	
2001D	627,680,000	0.20	
2001S	(3,184,606)		1.75
2002P	539,280,000	0.20	
2002D	691,200,000	0.20	
2002S	(3,211,995)		1.50
2003P	441,840,000	0.20	
2003D	383,040,000	0.20	
2003S	(3,298,439)		1.50

* Included in number above.

"Westward Journey" Nickels

The Westward Journey Nickel Series™ (2004–2006) commemorates the bicentennial of the Louisiana Purchase and the journey of Meriwether Lewis and William Clark to explore that vast territory. **2004**—*Obverse*: traditional portrait of Jefferson. *Reverses*: Louisiana Purchase / Peace Medal reverse, by Mint sculptor Norman E. Nemeth. Keelboat reverse, by Mint sculptor Al Maletsky. **2005**—*Obverse*: new portrait of Jefferson, designed by Joe Fitzgerald after a 1789 marble bust by Jean-Antoine Houdon, and rendered by Mint sculptor Don Everhart. *Reverses*: American Bison reverse, designed by Jamie Franki and produced by Norman E. Nemeth. "Ocean in View" reverse, designed by Joe Fitzgerald and produced by Mint sculptor Donna Weaver. **2006**—*Obverse*: facing portrait of Jefferson, designed by Jamie Franki and sculpted by Donna Weaver. *Reverse*: traditional depiction of Monticello.

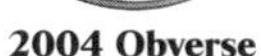
2004 Obverse

Peace Medal

Keelboat

2005 Obverse

American Bison

Ocean in View

2006 Obverse

Monticello

	Mintage	MS-65	PF-65
2004P, Peace Medal	361,440,000	$0.25	
2004D, Peace Medal	372,000,000	0.25	
2004S, Peace Medal	(2,965,422)		$1.10
2004P, Keelboat	366,720,000	0.25	
2004D, Keelboat	344,880,000	0.25	
2004S, Keelboat	(2,965,422)		1.10
2005P, American Bison	*448,320,000*	0.25	
2005D, American Bison	*487,680,000*	0.25	
2005S, American Bison	*(3,344,679)*		1.10
2005P, Ocean in View	*394,080,000*	0.25	
2005D, Ocean in View	*411,120,000*	0.25	
2005S, Ocean in View	*(3,344,679)*		1.10
2006P, Monticello	*693,120,000*	0.25	
2006D, Monticello	*809,280,000*	0.25	
2006S, Monticello	*(2,923,105)*		1.10
2007P		0.20	
2007D		0.20	
2007S			1.10

The half dime types present the same general characteristics as larger United States silver coins. Authorized by the Act of April 2, 1792, they were not coined until February, 1795, although dated 1794. At first the weight was 20.8 grains, and fineness .8924. By the Act of January 18, 1837, the weight was slightly reduced to 20-5/8 grains and the fineness changed to .900. Finally, the weight was reduced to 19.2 grains by the Act of February 21, 1853.

FLOWING HAIR (1794–1795)

AG-3 ABOUT GOOD—Details clear enough to identify.
G-4 GOOD—Eagle, wreath, bust outlined but lack details.
VG-8 VERY GOOD—Some details on face. All lettering legible.
F-12 FINE—Hair ends visible. Hair at top smooth.
VF-20 VERY FINE—Hair lines at top visible. Hair about ear defined.
EF-40 EXTREMELY FINE—Hair above forehead and at neck well defined but shows some wear.
AU-50 ABOUT UNCIRCULATED—Slight wear on high waves of hair, near ear and face, and on head and tips of eagle's wings.
MS-60 UNCIRCULATED—No trace of wear. Light blemishes.
MS-63 CHOICE UNCIRCULATED—Some distracting marks or blemishes in prime focal areas. Some impairment of luster possible.

Weakly struck Uncirculated coins are worth less than values shown.

	Mintage	AG-3	G-4	VG-8	F-12	VF-20	EF-40	AU-50	MS-60	MS-63
1794	86,416	$300	$550	$700	$1,000	$1,500	$2,500	$4,500	$8,000	$14,000
1795	*	200	475	575	750	1,200	2,100	3,200	6,500	10,000

* Included in number above.

DRAPED BUST (1796–1797)

AG-3 ABOUT GOOD—Details clear enough to identify.
G-4 GOOD—Date, stars, LIBERTY readable. Bust of Liberty outlined, but no details.
VG-8 VERY GOOD—Some details visible.
F-12 FINE—Hair and drapery lines worn, but visible.
VF-20 VERY FINE—Only left side of drapery indistinct.
EF-40 EXTREMELY FINE—Details visible in all hair lines.
AU-50 ABOUT UNCIRCULATED—Slight wear on bust, shoulder, and hair; wear on eagle's head and top of wings.
MS-60 UNCIRCULATED—No trace of wear. Light blemishes.
MS-63 CHOICE UNCIRCULATED—Some distracting marks or blemishes in prime focal areas. Impaired luster possible.

Small Eagle Reverse (1796–1797)

	Mintage	AG-3	G-4	VG-8	F-12	VF-20	EF-40	AU-50	MS-60	MS-63
1796, 6 Over 5	10,230	$275	$500	$600	$1,000	$1,600	$2,800	$5,500	$10,500	$20,000
1796	*	225	475	550	900	1,400	2,750	4,500	6,250	13,000
1796, LIKERTY	*	225	475	550	900	1,400	2,750	4,500	6,500	15,000
1797, 15 Stars	44,527	225	475	550	900	1,400	2,500	4,000	6,250	12,000
1797, 16 Stars	*	225	475	550	800	1,400	2,500	4,000	6,250	12,000
1797, 13 Stars	*	275	500	600	1,000	1,600	3,250	5,000	12,000	17,000

* Included in number above.

Heraldic Eagle Reverse (1800–1805)

1800 LIBEKTY

	Mintage	AG-3	G-4	VG-8	F-12	VF-20	EF-40	AU-50	MS-60	MS-63
1800	24,000	$150	$300	$450	$700	$1,000	$1,500	$3,000	$4,500	$9,500
1800, LIBEKTY	16,000	150	300	450	700	1,000	1,500	3,000	4,500	9,500
1801	27,760	150	300	500	800	1,100	1,700	3,500	6,000	10,500
1802	3,060	8,000	12,000	15,000	27,000	50,000	70,000	—	—	—
1803	37,850	175	400	500	850	1,150	1,750	3,750	6,200	10,500
1805	15,600	175	400	500	850	1,500	2,600	7,500	—	—

CAPPED BUST (1829–1837)

G-4 GOOD—Bust of Liberty outlined, no detail. Date and legend legible.
VG-8 VERY GOOD—Complete legend and date plain. At least three letters of LIBERTY on edge of cap show clearly.
F-12 FINE—All letters in LIBERTY visible.
VF-20 VERY FINE—Full rims. Ear and shoulder clasp show plainly.
EF-40 EXTREMELY FINE—Ear very distinct; eyebrow and hair well defined.
AU-50 ABOUT UNCIRCULATED—Traces of light wear on many of the high points. At least half of mint luster still present.
MS-60 UNCIRCULATED—No trace of wear. Light blemishes.
MS-63 CHOICE UNCIRCULATED—No trace of wear. Light blemishes. Attractive mint luster.

	Mintage	G-4	VG-8	F-12	VF-20	EF-40	AU-50	MS-60	MS-63
1829	1,230,000	$15	$20	$25	$40	$75	$100	$175	$400
1830	1,240,000	15	20	25	40	75	100	175	400
1831	1,242,700	15	20	25	40	75	100	175	400
1832	965,000	15	20	25	40	75	100	175	400
1833	1,370,000	15	20	25	40	75	100	175	400
1834	1,480,000	15	20	25	40	75	100	175	400
1835	2,760,000	15	20	25	40	75	100	175	400
1836	1,900,000	15	20	25	40	75	100	175	400
1837, Small 5c	871,000	19	25	35	65	110	185	475	1,000
1837, Large 5c	*	15	20	25	40	75	100	175	400

* Included in number above.

LIBERTY SEATED (1837–1873)

G-4 GOOD—LIBERTY on shield smooth. Date and letters legible.
VG-8 VERY GOOD—At least three letters in LIBERTY visible.
F-12 FINE—Entire LIBERTY visible, weak spots.
VF-20 VERY FINE—Entire LIBERTY strong and even.
EF-40 EXTREMELY FINE—LIBERTY and scroll edges distinct.
AU-50 ABOUT UNCIRCULATED—Traces of light wear on many of the high points. At least half of mint luster still present.
MS-60 UNCIRCULATED—No trace of wear. Light blemishes.
MS-63 CHOICE UNCIRCULATED—No trace of wear. Light blemishes. Attractive mint luster.

Variety 1 – No Stars on Obverse (1837–1838)

See next page for chart.

	Mintage	G-4	VG-8	F-12	VF-20	EF-40	AU-50	MS-60	MS-63
1837	1,405,000	$15	$20	$30	$60	$100	$175	$400	$500
1838O, No Stars	70,000	35	60	100	200	325	500	850	3,400

Variety 2 – Stars on Obverse (1838–1853)

From 1838 through 1859 the mintmark is located above the bow on the reverse. Large, medium, or small mintmark varieties occur for several dates.

	Mintage	G-4	VG-8	F-12	VF-20	EF-40	AU-50	MS-60	MS-63
1838	2,255,000	$7	$8	$11	$14	$30	$65	$150	$180
1839	1,069,150	7	8	11	14	30	65	150	180
1839O	1,034,039	9	11	13	20	35	65	185	800
1840	1,344,085	7	8	11	14	30	65	150	180
1840O	935,000	9	11	13	20	35	85	275	950
1841	1,150,000	7	8	11	14	30	65	100	125
1841O	815,000	8	10	15	20	45	115	325	650
1842	815,000	7	8	13	16	32	65	90	125
1842O	350,000	13	15	27	75	210	375	525	850
1843	1,165,000	7	8	11	14	30	65	90	130
1844	430,000	7	8	11	14	30	65	90	130
1844O	220,000	30	45	85	225	475	1,300	2,300	6,000
1845	1,564,000	7	8	11	14	30	65	90	130
1846	27,000	100	150	275	350	950	1,800	5,000	9,000
1847	1,274,000	7	8	11	14	30	65	110	220
1848	668,000	7	8	11	14	30	65	100	130
1848O	600,000	9	11	15	23	45	110	190	270
1849, 9 Over 6	*	10	12	16	23	45	110	200	600
1849, 9 Over 8	*	10	13	22	25	50	120	270	700
1849, Normal Date	1,309,000	7	8	11	14	30	65	100	200
1849O	140,000	12	17	33	90	200	400	1,000	1,900
1850	955,000	7	8	11	15	35	60	90	145
1850O	690,000	8	10	13	21	45	135	325	700
1851	781,000	7	8	11	15	35	60	90	125
1851O	860,000	8	10	12	18	45	100	225	350
1852	1,000,500	7	8	11	14	28	60	90	125
1852O	260,000	12	17	27	55	110	210	385	775
1853, No Arrows	135,000	14	18	27	55	110	175	325	475
1853O, No Arrows	160,000	80	125	160	275	600	1,100	2,500	5,500

* Included in number below.

Variety 3 – Arrows at Date (1853–1855)

As on the dimes, quarters, and halves, arrows were placed at the sides of the date for a short period starting in 1853 to denote the reduction of weight.

	Mintage	G-4	VG-8	F-12	VF-20	EF-40	AU-50	MS-60	MS-63	PF-63
1853	13,210,020	$7	$8	$10	$14	$30	$55	$110	$130	
1853O	2,200,000	8	9	12	19	32	70	135	400	
1854	5,740,000	7	8	10	14	30	60	110	140	$4,000
1854O	1,560,000	8	9	11	18	30	70	135	350	
1855	1,750,000	7	8	10	14	30	55	110	130	3,500
1855O	600,000	7	10	11	24	80	110	275	475	

Variety 2 Resumed (1856–1859: Weight Standard of 1853)

1858 Over Inverted Date

	Mintage	G-4	VG-8	F-12	VF-20	EF-40	AU-50	MS-60	MS-63	PF-63
1856	4,880,000	$7	$8	$9	$12	$25	$50	$80	$120	$2,000
1856O	1,100,000	7	8	10	20	40	100	210	450	
1857	7,280,000	7	8	9	12	25	50	80	120	1,500
1857O	1,380,000	7	8	10	16	30	80	175	210	
1858	3,500,000	7	8	9	12	25	50	80	120	750
1858, Over Inverted Date	*	15	20	30	50	95	150	300	600	
1858O	1,660,000	7	8	10	18	28	60	125	180	
1859	340,000	8	9	12	20	50	90	130	150	650
1859O	560,000	8	9	12	20	50	90	130	150	

* Included in number above.

Variety 4 – Legend on Obverse (1860–1873)

	Mintage	G-4	VG-8	F-12	VF-20	EF-40	AU-50	MS-60	MS-63	PF-63
1860 (1,000)	799,000	$7	$8	$10	$12	$19	$30	$75	$100	$320
1860O	1,060,000	7	8	10	12	19	35	100	135	
1861 (1,000)	3,360,000	7	8	10	12	19	30	75	100	320
1862 (550)	1,492,000	9	12	18	20	25	40	110	125	320
1863 (460)	18,000	60	70	95	125	200	270	300	400	350
1863S	100,000	11	15	18	21	60	160	350	450	
1864 (470)	48,000	110	170	200	275	400	500	550	600	350
1864S	90,000	18	20	35	50	110	180	310	700	
1865 (500)	13,000	100	125	180	210	275	300	400	600	350
1865S	120,000	11	15	18	22	60	200	450	800	
1866 (725)	10,000	100	115	150	200	300	320	375	600	320
1866S	120,000	10	15	18	22	60	180	200	400	
1867 (625)	8,000	175	200	250	300	350	400	475	620	350
1867S	120,000	9	13	18	25	60	140	210	500	
1868 (600)	88,600	20	25	40	70	120	200	300	400	350
1868S	280,000	7	9	11	13	19	40	125	250	
1869 (600)	208,000	7	9	11	13	19	60	120	150	320
1869S	230,000	7	9	11	13	19	50	150	350	
1870 (1,000)	535,000	7	9	10	11	19	30	70	120	320
1870S *(unique)*								—		
1871 (960)	1,873,000	7	9	10	11	19	30	70	120	320
1871S	161,000	8	11	15	25	40	75	135	210	
1872 (950)	2,947,000	7	9	10	11	19	30	70	120	320
1872S	837,000	7	9	10	11	19	30	70	120	
1873 (600)	7,126,000	7	9	10	11	19	30	70	120	320
1873S	324,000	7	9	10	11	19	30	70	120	

The designs of the dimes, first coined in 1796, followed closely those of the half dimes up through the Liberty Seated type. The dimes in each instance weigh twice as much as the half dimes.

DRAPED BUST (1796–1807)
Small Eagle Reverse (1796–1797)

AG-3 ABOUT GOOD—Details clear enough to identify.
G-4 GOOD—Date legible. Bust outlined, but no detail.
VG-8 VERY GOOD—All but deepest drapery folds worn smooth. Hair lines nearly gone and curls lacking in detail.
F-12 FINE—All drapery lines visible. Hair partly worn.
VF-20 VERY FINE—Only left side of drapery indistinct.
EF-40 EXTREMELY FINE—Hair well outlined with details visible.
AU-50 ABOUT UNCIRCULATED—Traces of light wear on many of the high points. At least half of mint luster still present.
MS-60 UNCIRCULATED—No trace of wear. Light blemishes.
MS-63 CHOICE UNCIRCULATED—Some distracting marks or blemishes in prime focal areas. Impaired luster possible.

1797, 16 Stars

1797, 13 Stars

	Mintage	AG-3	G-4	VG-8	F-12	VF-20	EF-40	AU-50	MS-60	MS-63
1796	22,135	$375	$700	$1,000	$1,300	$2,000	$3,400	$4,500	$6,500	$14,000
1797, All kinds	25,261									
1797, 16 Stars		375	700	1,000	1,300	2,100	3,500	5,000	7,000	16,000
1797, 13 Stars		375	700	1,000	1,300	2,100	3,500	5,000	7,000	15,000

Heraldic Eagle Reverse (1798–1807)

	Mintage	AG-3	G-4	VG-8	F-12	VF-20	EF-40	AU-50	MS-60	MS-63
1798, All kinds	27,550									
1798, 98 Over 97, 16 Stars on Reverse		$125	$275	$400	$475	$700	$1,250	$2,100	$3,200	$7,000
1798, 98 Over 97, 13 Stars on Reverse		250	800	1,000	1,500	3,000	4,000	—	—	
1798		125	225	250	425	600	1,100	1,600	2,500	7,000
1800	21,760	125	225	250	425	600	1,100	1,600	2,700	7,000
1801	34,640	125	250	275	500	900	1,800	3,200	5,000	14,000
1802	10,975	160	325	450	800	1,200	2,500	4,000	12,000	
1803	33,040	110	225	300	400	600	1,500	3,500	5,500	
1804	8,265	250	500	800	1,200	2,000	5,000	12,000	17,500	
1805	120,780	100	200	225	350	500	900	1,100	2,800	4,200
1807	165,000	100	200	225	350	500	900	1,100	2,800	4,200

CAPPED BUST (1809–1837)

G-4 GOOD—Date, letters, and stars discernible. Bust outlined, no details.
VG-8 VERY GOOD—Legends and date plain. Some letters in LIBERTY visible.
F-12 FINE—Clear LIBERTY. Ear and shoulder clasp visible. Part of rim visible on both sides.
VF-20 VERY FINE—LIBERTY distinct. Full rim. Ear and clasp plain and distinct.
EF-40 EXTREMELY FINE—LIBERTY sharp. Ear distinct. Hair above eye well defined.
AU-50 ABOUT UNCIRCULATED—Traces of light wear on only the high points of the design. Half of mint luster present.
MS-60 UNCIRCULATED—No trace of wear. Light blemishes.
MS-63 CHOICE UNCIRCULATED—Some distracting marks or blemishes in prime focal areas. Impaired luster possible.

Variety 1 – Wide Border (1809–1828)

	Mintage	G-4	VG-8	F-12	VF-20	EF-40	AU-50	MS-60	MS-63
1809	51,065	$55	$85	$150	$250	$500	$800	$1,900	$2,900
1811/9	65,180	40	60	125	225	500	800	1,700	2,750
1814	421,500	13	16	28	70	200	275	500	1,200
1820	942,587	13	16	25	60	200	275	500	1,200
1821	1,186,512	13	16	25	60	200	275	500	1,200
1822	100,000	175	300	425	700	1,400	2,300	5,000	8,500
1823, 3 Over 2, All kinds	440,000								
1823, 3 Over 2, Small E's		13	16	25	60	200	275	550	1,100
1823, 3 Over 2, Large E's		13	16	25	60	200	275	550	1,100

1823, 3 Over 2

1824, 4 Over 2

1828, Large Date

1828, Small Date

	Mintage	G-4	VG-8	F-12	VF-20	EF-40	AU-50	MS-60	MS-63
1824, 4 Over 2	510,000	$14	$18	$40	$140	$300	$600	$1,000	$1,800
1825	*	13	16	20	50	175	275	500	1,100
1827	1,215,000	13	16	20	50	175	275	500	1,100
1828, Large Date, Curl Base 2	125,000	16	30	50	140	300	600	1,000	1,800

* Included in number above.

Variety 2 – Modified Design (1828–1837)

1829, Small 10c

1829, Large 10c

1830, 30 Over 29

	Mintage	G-4	VG-8	F-12	VF-20	EF-40	AU-50	MS-60	MS-63
1828, Sm Date, Square Base 2	*	$13	$18	$30	$65	$200	$325	$625	$1,100
1829, Small 10c	770,000	12	14	16	35	120	175	400	750
1829, Medium 10c	*	12	14	16	35	120	175	350	650
1829, Large 10c	*	12	16	22	50	135	200	400	675
1830, 30 Over 29	510,000	17	25	45	90	250	275	500	1,100
1830, Large 10c	*	12	14	16	35	120	175	350	675
1830, Small 10c	*	12	14	16	35	120	175	350	675
1831	771,350	12	14	16	35	120	175	350	675
1832	522,500	12	14	16	35	120	175	350	675
1833	485,000	12	14	16	35	120	175	350	675
1834	635,000	12	14	16	35	120	175	350	675
1835	1,410,000	12	14	16	35	120	175	350	675
1836	1,190,000	12	14	16	35	120	175	350	675
1837	359,500	12	14	16	35	120	175	350	675

* Included in number above.

LIBERTY SEATED (1837–1891)

Variety 1 – No Stars on Obverse (1837–1838)

G-4 GOOD—LIBERTY on shield smooth. Date and letters legible.
F-12 FINE—LIBERTY visible, weak spots.
VF-20 VERY FINE—LIBERTY strong and even.
EF-40 EXTREMELY FINE—LIBERTY and scroll edges distinct.
AU-50 ABOUT UNCIRCULATED—Wear on Liberty's shoulder and hair high points; slight wear on eagle's breast, tail, and wing tips.
MS-60 UNCIRCULATED—No trace of wear. Light blemishes.
MS-63 CHOICE UNCIRCULATED—Some distracting contact marks or blemishes in prime focal areas. Impaired luster possible.

No Drapery From Elbow
No Stars on Obverse

Mintmarks on Liberty Seated dimes on reverse, within or below the wreath. Size of mintmark varies on many dates.

	Mintage	G-4	F-12	VF-20	EF-40	AU-50	MS-60	MS-63
1837	682,500	$15	$35	$125	$220	$325	$600	$850
1838O	406,034	20	60	160	300	550	1,300	3,000

Variety 2 – Stars on Obverse (1838–1853)

No Drapery From Elbow, Tilted Shield (1838–1840)

1838, Small Stars

1838, Large Stars

Drapery From Elbow, Upright Shield (1840–1891)

Obverse

Reverse

	Mintage	G-4	F-12	VF-20	EF-40	AU-50	MS-60	MS-63
1838, All kinds	1,992,500							
1838, Small Stars		$9	$18	$35	$70	$175	$400	$600
1838, Large Stars		8	11	14	40	100	150	350
1838, Partial Drapery		9	18	35	75	210	425	1,000
1839	1,053,115	8	11	14	40	100	150	350
1839O	1,323,000	9	13	16	45	120	175	500
1840, No Drapery	981,500	8	11	14	40	100	150	350
1840O, No Drapery	1,175,000	9	13	20	50	120	475	950
1840, Drapery	377,500	13	30	55	125	170	425	2,200
1841	1,622,500	8	11	14	20	50	135	250
1841O	2,007,500	9	13	15	28	90	425	900
1842	1,887,500	8	11	14	20	50	135	250
1842O	2,020,000	9	13	17	100	500	1,300	2,600
1843	1,370,000	8	11	14	20	50	135	250
1843O	150,000	16	45	100	250	800	2,000	—
1844	72,500	100	225	350	600	800	1,300	4,000
1845	1,755,000	8	11	14	20	50	135	275
1845O	230,000	9	20	80	185	475	1,300	—
1846	31,300	30	75	150	400	900	1,800	6,500
1847	245,000	9	16	27	55	120	400	1,000
1848	451,500	8	11	16	35	60	210	400
1849	839,000	8	11	14	20	50	150	425
1849O	300,000	8	17	50	110	300	1,000	2,400

	Mintage	G-4	F-12	VF-20	EF-40	AU-50	MS-60	MS-63
1850	1,931,500	$8	$11	$14	$20	$50	$125	$300
1850O	510,000	9	13	33	65	150	425	975
1851	1,026,500	8	11	14	20	50	160	325
1851O	400,000	9	17	35	100	175	1,000	1,400
1852	1,535,500	8	11	14	20	50	150	300
1852O	430,000	10	20	50	100	175	800	1,300
1853, No Arrows	95,000	20	40	75	135	175	350	400

Variety 3 – Arrows at Date (1853–1855)

Arrows at Date (1853–1855)

Small Date, Arrows Removed (1856–1860)

	Mintage	G-4	F-12	VF-20	EF-40	AU-50	MS-60	MS-63	PF-63
1853, With Arrows	12,078,010	$7	$8	$12	$22	$60	$150	$300	
1853O	1,100,000	7	8	17	45	120	475	1,200	
1854	4,470,000	7	8	12	22	60	150	300	$5,250
1854O	1,770,000	7	8	13	35	75	285	500	
1855	2,075,000	7	8	12	22	60	175	400	5,250

Variety 2 Resumed (1856–1860)

	Mintage	G-4	F-12	VF-20	EF-40	AU-50	MS-60	MS-63	PF-63
1856, All kinds	5,780,000								
1856, Large Date		$7	$8	$11	$18	$40	$140	$275	
1856, Small Date		7	8	11	18	40	140	275	$1,800
1856O	1,180,000	7	8	11	24	90	300	650	
1856S	70,000	35	125	200	400	625	1,350	—	
1857	5,580,000	7	8	10	18	40	135	275	1,800
1857O	1,540,000	7	8	11	18	70	190	275	
1858 *(300+)*	1,540,000	7	8	10	18	40	135	275	900
1858O	290,000	8	15	35	75	125	300	450	
1858S	60,000	35	90	150	325	600	1,350		
1859 *(800+)*	429,200	7	8	11	25	50	135	275	700
1859O	480,000	7	9	18	37	100	180	375	
1859S	60,000	35	110	175	450	850	2,000		
1860S	140,000	12	20	50	125	350	950	1,800	

Variety 4 – Legend on Obverse (1860–1873)

	Mintage	G-4	F-12	VF-20	EF-40	AU-50	MS-60	MS-63	PF-63
1860 (1,000)	606,000	$7	$8	$10	$18	$40	$135	$250	$400
1860O	40,000	155	350	675	1,500	2,400	5,500	—	
1861 (1,000)	1,883,000	7	8	10	18	40	100	180	400
1861S	172,500	13	40	80	160	210	600	1,800	
1862 (550)	847,000	7	8	10	16	25	100	120	350
1862S	180,750	11	21	50	100	125	600	1,000	
1863 (460)	14,000	100	200	300	350	400	550	600	400
1863S	157,500	11	20	40	70	125	450	1,200	

Chart continues on next page.

	Mintage	G-4	F-12	VF-20	EF-40	AU-50	MS-60	MS-63	PF-63
1864 . . . .(470)	11,000	$80	$170	$210	$350	$425	$550	$600	$400
1864S	230,000	8	17	32	60	110	500	550	
1865 . . . .(500)	10,000	75	200	250	310	375	525	600	400
1865S	175,000	8	17	32	100	250	800	1,900	
1866 . . . .(725)	8,000	120	235	375	400	600	700	800	400
1866S	135,000	11	20	40	100	135	550	1,100	
1867 . . . .(625)	6,000	175	275	400	475	550	675	800	450
1867S	140,000	9	20	40	100	220	600	900	
1868 . . . .(600)	464,000	7	8	16	31	60	175	375	300
1868S	260,000	7	13	30	50	75	185	450	
1869 . . . .(600)	256,000	7	13	25	40	70	185	400	300
1869S	450,000	7	11	17	35	65	185	375	
1870 . . . .(1,000)	470,500	7	8	11	18	40	110	200	300
1870S	50,000	100	150	200	280	350	750	1,000	
1871 . . . .(960)	906,750	7	8	11	15	65	140	180	300
1871CC	20,100	450	1,200	1,700	3,800	5,000	—	—	
1871S	320,000	7	8	11	15	65	110	200	
1872 . . . .(950)	2,395,500	7	8	11	13	35	75	110	300
1872CC	35,480	200	575	1,400	2,800	7,000	—	—	
1872S	190,000	10	35	50	95	175	500	1,000	
1873, Close 3 (1,100)	1,506,900	7	8	11	13	30	100	125	300
1873, Open 3	60,000	9	20	30	60	90	195	550	
1873CC *(unique)*	12,400							—	

Variety 5 – Arrows at Date (1873–1874)

In 1873, the dime was increased in weight from 2.49 grams to 2.50 grams. Arrows at the date in 1873 and 1874 indicate this change.

	Mintage	G-4	F-12	VF-20	EF-40	AU-50	MS-60	MS-63	PF-63
1873 . . . .(800)	2,377,700	$7	$11	$22	$55	$120	$275	$450	$700
1873CC	18,791	400	1,400	3,000	7,000	12,000	—	—	
1873S	455,000	8	16	28	65	175	450	950	
1874 . . . .(700)	2,939,300	7	11	22	55	125	285	450	700
1874CC	10,817	1,100	2,500	5,500	8,500	13,500	—		
1874S	240,000	11	27	45	90	220	400	900	

Variety 4 Resumed (1875–1891)

	Mintage	G-4	F-12	VF-20	EF-40	AU-50	MS-60	MS-63	PF-63
1875 . . . .(700)	10,350,000	$6	$7	$9	$13	$30	$75	$110	$250
1875CC	4,645,000	6	7	10	15	32	125	185	
1875S	9,070,000	6	7	9	13	30	75	110	
1876 . . . .(1,150)	1,145,000	6	7	9	13	30	75	110	250
1876CC	8,270,000	6	7	9	15	32	100	175	
1876S	10,420,000	6	7	9	13	30	75	110	
1877 . . . .(510)	7,310,000	6	7	9	13	30	75	110	275
1877CC	7,700,000	6	7	9	13	30	100	160	
1877S	2,340,000	6	7	9	13	30	75	110	
1878 . . . .(800)	1,677,200	6	7	9	13	30	80	110	250
1878CC	200,000	20	50	75	150	200	450	700	
1879 . . . .(1,100)	14,000	70	120	180	210	275	325	350	250
1880 . . . .(1,355)	36,000	50	100	125	175	225	275	350	250
1881 . . . .(975)	24,000	50	100	125	175	225	300	350	250
1882 . . . .(1,100)	3,910,000	6	7	9	13	30	75	110	250

	Mintage	G-4	F-12	VF-20	EF-40	AU-50	MS-60	MS-63	PF-63
1883	(1,039)....7,674,673	$6	$7	$9	$13	$30	$75	$110	$250
1884	(875)....3,365,505	6	7	9	13	30	75	110	250
1884S	564,969	9	13	20	35	110	325	575	
1885	(930)....2,532,497	6	7	9	13	30	75	110	250
1885S	43,690	150	325	600	1,000	2,000	2,600	4,000	
1886	(886)....6,376,684	6	7	9	13	30	75	110	250
1886S	206,524	10	20	30	50	90	275	500	
1887	(710)...11,283,229	6	7	9	13	30	75	110	250
1887S	4,454,450	6	7	9	13	30	75	110	
1888	(832)....5,495,655	6	7	9	13	30	75	110	250
1888S	1,720,000	6	7	9	15	40	120	300	
1889	(711)....7,380,000	6	7	9	13	30	75	110	250
1889S	972,678	7	10	20	35	60	200	400	
1890	(590)....9,910,951	6	7	9	13	30	75	110	250
1890S	1,423,076	7	9	17	30	60	135	275	
1891	(600)...15,310,000	6	7	9	13	30	75	110	275
1891O	4,540,000	6	7	9	15	40	110	150	
1891S	3,196,116	6	7	9	13	35	100	125	

BARBER OR LIBERTY HEAD (1892–1916)

This type was designed by Charles E. Barber, chief engraver of the Mint. His initial B is at the truncation of the neck. He also designed the quarters and half dollars of the same period.

G-4 GOOD—Date and letters plain. LIBERTY obliterated.
VG-8 VERY GOOD—Some letters visible in LIBERTY.
F-12 FINE—Letters in LIBERTY visible, though some weak.
VF-20 VERY FINE—Letters of LIBERTY evenly plain.
EF-40 EXTREMELY FINE—All letters in LIBERTY sharp, distinct. Headband edges distinct.
AU-50 ABOUT UNCIRCULATED—Slight traces of wear on hair cheekbone and on leaf tips in wreath.
MS-60 UNCIRCULATED—No trace of wear. Light blemishes.
MS-63 CHOICE UNCIRCULATED—Some distracting blemishes in prime focal areas. Impaired luster possible.

Mintmark location is on reverse, below wreath.

	Mintage	G-4	VG-8	F-12	VF-20	EF-40	AU-50	MS-60	MS-63	PF-63
1892	(1,245)... 12,120,000	$2	$4.00	$9	$14	$16	$35	$80	$120	$275
1892O	3,841,700	5	7.00	15	24	35	45	100	175	
1892S	990,710	35	45.00	85	125	160	180	240	400	
1893, 3 Over 2	*					120	160	350	1,000	500
1893	(792)....3,339,940	4	6.00	10	15	24	35	100	140	275
1893O	1,760,000	15	25.00	65	80	90	125	175	350	
1893S	2,491,401	7	14.00	18	25	40	75	150	375	
1894	(972)....1,330,000	8	20.00	55	75	90	100	175	350	275
1894O	720,000	35	50.00	100	160	220	350	850	1,450	
1894S	24							600,000		
1895	(880).....690,000	40	45.00	100	275	300	350	400	800	300
1895O	440,000	175	200.00	450	700	1,350	1,600	3,200	4,500	
1895S	1,120,000	20	30.00	75	100	125	150	275	600	
1896	(762)....2,000,000	4	10.00	28	35	50	60	110	275	275
1896O	610,000	35	75.00	160	200	280	325	600	1,350	
1896S	575,056	40	70.00	150	200	275	300	500	800	
1897	(731)...10,868,533	1	1.25	3	5	12	22	80	125	275
1897O	666,000	35	50.00	140	180	250	320	500	900	
1897S	1,342,844	8	16.00	50	75	85	125	250	600	

* Included in number below.

Chart continues on next page.

	Mintage	G-4	VG-8	F-12	VF-20	EF-40	AU-50	MS-60	MS-63	PF-63
1898 (735)	16,320,000	$1.00	$1.25	$3	$6.00	$12.00	$30	$65	$95	$275
1898O	2,130,000	3.00	4.00	30	60.00	80.00	120	260	600	
1898S	1,702,507	2.00	5.00	16	25.00	40.00	75	180	600	
1899 (846)	19,580,000	1.00	1.25	3	6.00	12.50	30	65	95	275
1899O	2,650,000	4.50	6.00	35	45.00	70.00	100	210	550	
1899S	1,867,493	4.50	4.00	8	16.00	20.00	55	160	400	
1900 (912)	17,600,000	1.00	1.25	3	6.00	12.00	30	65	90	275
1900O	2,010,000	8.00	20.00	45	50.00	120.00	160	320	500	
1900S	5,168,270	1.75	2.00	5	7.00	13.00	35	120	220	
1901 (813)	18,859,665	1.00	1.25	3	6.00	12.00	32	65	90	275
1901O	5,620,000	1.50	1.75	5	9.00	30.00	50	250	450	
1901S	593,022	42.00	70.00	185	250.00	300.00	340	650	900	
1902 (777)	21,380,000	0.90	1.00	2	4.00	12.00	30	65	90	275
1902O	4,500,000	1.50	2.00	6	12.00	25.00	50	180	450	
1902S	2,070,000	3.00	6.00	18	30.00	45.00	70	180	450	
1903 (755)	19,500,000	0.90	1.00	2	4.00	12.00	30	65	90	275
1903O	8,180,000	1.50	2.00	6	8.00	18.00	35	150	285	
1903S	613,300	40.00	60.00	200	250.00	400.00	500	750	1,000	
1904 (670)	14,600,357	0.90	1.00	2	4.00	12.00	30	65	90	275
1904S	800,000	20.00	35.00	75	100.00	150.00	250	425	850	
1905 (727)	14,551,623	0.90	1.00	2	4.00	12.00	30	65	90	275
1905O	3,400,000	1.25	3.00	13	25.00	50.00	75	150	250	
1905S	6,855,199	0.90	2.00	4	7.00	18.00	40	140	200	
1906 (675)	19,957,731	0.90	1.00	2	5.00	12.00	30	65	90	275
1906D	4,060,000	0.90	2.00	4	8.00	13.00	32	95	200	
1906O	2,610,000	2.00	5.00	20	35.00	45.00	65	120	175	
1906S	3,136,640	1.50	2.00	5	10.00	16.00	50	125	200	
1907 (575)	22,220,000	0.90	1.00	2	4.00	12.00	30	65	90	275
1907D	4,080,000	0.90	2.50	5	8.00	18.00	60	150	450	
1907O	5,058,000	0.90	3.50	15	18.00	24.00	40	120	190	
1907S	3,178,470	1.25	2.50	6	12.00	20.00	45	200	400	
1908 (545)	10,600,000	0.90	1.00	2	4.00	12.00	30	65	90	275
1908D	7,490,000	0.90	1.50	4	6.00	14.00	35	70	150	
1908O	1,789,000	1.50	5.00	22	35.00	50.00	75	160	300	
1908S	3,220,000	0.90	3.00	6	8.00	16.00	75	175	350	
1909 (650)	10,240,000	0.90	1.00	2	3.50	12.00	30	65	90	275
1909D	954,000	3.50	10.00	35	50.00	75.00	100	275	600	
1909O	2,287,000	1.50	3.00	6	10.00	20.00	60	120	275	
1909S	1,000,000	3.00	8.50	40	50.00	100.00	165	275	650	
1910 (551)	11,520,000	0.90	1.00	2	3.50	12.00	30	65	90	275
1910D	3,490,000	1.00	3.00	5	6.00	18.00	45	125	250	
1910S	1,240,000	0.90	5.00	25	35.00	60.00	90	250	400	
1911 (543)	18,870,000	1.25	1.75	2	3.50	12.00	30	65	90	275
1911D	11,209,000	0.90	1.00	2	3.50	12.00	30	65	90	
1911S	3,520,000	1.00	3.00	8	8.00	16.00	45	120	220	
1912 (700)	19,349,300	0.90	1.00	2	3.50	12.00	30	65	90	275
1912D	11,760,000	0.90	1.00	2	3.50	12.00	30	65	90	
1912S	3,420,000	0.90	3.00	5	8.00	16.00	50	100	165	
1913 (622)	19,760,000	0.90	1.00	2	3.50	12.00	30	65	90	275
1913S	510,000	8.50	17.00	45	80.00	125.00	175	275	400	
1914 (425)	17,360,230	0.90	1.00	2	3.50	12.00	30	65	90	275
1914D	11,908,000	0.90	1.00	2	3.50	12.00	30	65	90	
1914S	2,100,000	0.90	2.10	6	8.00	12.00	30	100	190	
1915 (450)	5,620,000	0.90	1.00	2	3.50	12.00	30	65	90	275
1915S	960,000	2.00	2.50	20	22.00	35.00	75	160	300	
1916	18,490,000	0.90	1.00	2	3.50	12.00	30	65	90	
1916S	5,820,000	0.90	1.00	2	3.50	12.00	30	65	90	

WINGED LIBERTY HEAD OR MERCURY (1916–1945)

Although this coin is commonly called the *Mercury* dime, the main device is in fact a representation of Liberty. The wings crowning her cap are intended to symbolize liberty of thought. The designer's monogram AW is at the right of the neck.

G-4 GOOD—Letters and date clear. Lines and bands in fasces obliterated.
VG-8 VERY GOOD—Half of sticks discernible in fasces.
F-12 FINE—All sticks in fasces defined. Diagonal bands worn nearly flat.
VF-20 VERY FINE—Diagonal bands definitely visible.
EF-40 EXTREMELY FINE—Only slight wear on diagonal bands. Braids and hair before ear clearly visible.
AU-50 ABOUT UNCIRCULATED—Slight trace of wear. Most mint luster present.
MS-63 CHOICE UNCIRCULATED—No trace of wear. Light blemishes. Attractive mint luster.
MS-65 GEM UNCIRCULATED—Only light, scattered marks that are not distracting. Strong luster, good eye appeal.

Mintmark location is on reverse, left of fasces.

Uncirculated values shown are for average pieces with minimum blemishes; those with sharp strikes and split bands on reverse are worth much more.

	Mintage	G-4	VG-8	F-12	VF-20	EF-40	MS-60	MS-63	MS-65
1916	22,180,080	$1.50	$2.10	$3.50	$4.25	$5.50	$18	$24	$50
1916D	264,000	475.00	625.00	1,150.00	1,550.00	2,575.00	8,600	9,500	17,000
1916S	10,450,000	3.00	4.00	5.00	6.00	10.00	20	35	125
1917	55,230,000	0.80	0.90	1.25	3.00	4.00	15	26	85
1917D	9,402,000	2.25	3.25	5.00	8.00	22.00	65	180	700
1917S	27,330,000	0.80	0.90	3.00	3.50	6.00	30	90	275
1918	26,680,000	0.80	0.85	3.00	6.00	13.00	40	90	225
1918D	22,674,800	0.80	0.85	3.00	6.00	12.00	55	150	375
1918S	19,300,000	0.80	0.85	2.00	5.00	8.50	45	150	375
1919	35,740,000	0.80	0.85	2.00	3.00	6.00	30	75	175
1919D	9,939,000	0.80	0.90	4.00	12.00	20.00	90	275	1,000
1919S	8,850,000	0.80	0.85	3.00	8.00	20.00	120	285	650
1920	59,030,000	0.80	0.85	1.50	3.50	5.00	27	40	150
1920D	19,171,000	0.80	0.85	2.00	6.00	11.00	85	220	450
1920S	13,820,000	0.80	0.85	2.00	6.00	10.00	65	175	650
1921	1,230,000	30.00	40.00	80.00	175.00	300.00	650	1,100	1,850
1921D	1,080,000	35.00	70.00	100.00	200.00	400.00	675	1,200	1,850
1923	50,130,000	0.80	0.85	1.50	3.00	4.00	15	25	65
1923S	6,440,000	0.80	0.85	4.00	8.00	32.00	80	220	600
1924	24,010,000	0.80	0.85	2.00	3.00	7.00	23	60	120
1924D	6,810,000	0.80	0.85	3.50	8.00	26.00	95	280	600
1924S	7,120,000	0.80	0.85	3.00	5.00	24.00	90	290	625
1925	25,610,000	0.80	0.85	2.00	3.00	4.50	28	45	125
1925D	5,117,000	2.50	3.25	6.00	22.00	60.00	180	425	950
1925S	5,850,000	0.80	0.85	3.00	7.00	30.00	90	275	800
1926	32,160,000	0.80	0.85	1.50	3.00	4.50	25	35	130
1926D	6,828,000	0.80	0.85	3.00	6.00	17.00	60	150	350
1926S	1,520,000	3.00	5.00	12.00	32.00	140.00	425	850	1,800
1927	28,080,000	0.80	0.85	1.50	3.00	4.00	13	32	80
1927D	4,812,000	0.80	0.85	3.00	12.00	35.00	110	225	725
1927S	4,770,000	0.80	0.85	2.00	4.00	15.00	120	275	800
1928	19,480,000	0.80	0.85	2.00	3.00	4.50	25	30	70
1928D	4,161,000	0.80	0.85	4.00	10.00	24.00	85	180	475
1928S	7,400,000	0.80	0.85	2.00	2.50	8.00	35	160	265
1929	25,970,000	0.80	0.85	2.00	2.25	3.00	13	20	40
1929D	5,034,000	0.80	0.85	2.00	4.00	8.00	17	22	40
1929S	4,730,000	0.80	0.85	2.00	2.50	5.00	18	25	60
1930	6,770,000	0.80	0.85	2.00	2.50	4.00	15	25	60
1930S	1,843,000	1.00	1.50	3.00	3.80	8.00	30	65	110
1931	3,150,000	0.80	0.85	2.00	3.00	5.00	20	40	80
1931D	1,260,000	4.00	5.00	7.00	11.00	18.00	48	75	150

Chart continues on next page.

	Mintage	VG-8	F-12	VF-20	EF-40	MS-60	MS-63	MS-65	PF-63
1931S	1,800,000	$2.50	$3.00	$5.00	$8.50	$38.00	$75	$150	
1934	24,080,000	0.80	0.80	0.80	0.90	10.00	15	25	
1934D	6,772,000	0.80	0.80	0.80	0.90	20.00	30	45	
1935	58,830,000	0.80	0.80	0.80	0.90	6.50	9	18	
1935D	10,477,000	0.80	0.80	0.80	0.90	20.00	25	50	
1935S	15,840,000	0.80	0.80	0.80	0.90	12.00	16	25	
1936 (4,130)	87,500,000	0.80	0.80	0.80	0.90	5.00	12	16	$1,200
1936D	16,132,000	0.80	0.80	0.80	0.90	14.00	20	30	
1936S	9,210,000	0.80	0.80	0.80	0.90	12.00	15	18	
1937 (5,756)	56,860,000	0.80	0.80	0.80	0.90	4.00	9	15	425
1937D	14,146,000	0.80	0.80	0.80	0.90	14.00	16	24	
1937S	9,740,000	0.80	0.80	0.80	0.90	12.00	15	22	
1938 (8,728)	22,190,000	0.80	0.80	0.80	0.90	7.00	9	15	250
1938D	5,537,000	0.80	0.80	0.80	0.90	9.00	10	16	
1938S	8,090,000	0.80	0.80	0.80	0.90	8.00	9	15	
1939 (9,321)	67,740,000	0.80	0.80	0.80	0.90	4.50	8	12	225
1939D	24,394,000	0.80	0.80	0.80	0.90	4.50	8	14	
1939S	10,540,000	0.80	0.80	0.80	0.90	12.00	15	25	
1940 (11,827)	65,350,000	0.80	0.80	0.80	0.90	4.50	7	15	210
1940D	21,198,000	0.80	0.80	0.80	0.90	4.50	9	16	
1940S	21,560,000	0.80	0.80	0.80	0.90	4.50	8	16	
1941 (16,557)	175,090,000	0.80	0.80	0.80	0.90	4.50	7	15	200
1941D	45,634,000	0.80	0.80	0.80	0.90	4.50	9	16	
1941S	43,090,000	0.80	0.80	0.80	1.00	4.50	8	16	
1942, 2 Over 1	*	275.00	375.00	400.00	450.00	1,200.00	2,200	7,500	
1942 (22,329)	205,410,000	0.80	0.80	0.80	0.90	4.50	7	15	200
1942D, 2 Over 1	*	275.00	375.00	400.00	450.00	1,200.00	2,400	4,200	
1942D	60,740,000	0.80	0.80	0.80	0.90	5.50	9	16	
1942S	49,300,000	0.80	0.80	0.80	0.90	6.50	9	16	
1943	191,710,000	0.80	0.80	0.80	0.90	4.50	6	15	
1943D	71,949,000	0.80	0.80	0.80	0.90	5.50	7	16	
1943S	60,400,000	0.80	0.80	0.80	0.90	5.50	7	15	
1944	231,410,000	0.80	0.80	0.80	0.90	4.50	6	15	
1944D	62,224,000	0.80	0.80	0.80	0.90	4.50	6	15	
1944S	49,490,000	0.80	0.80	0.80	0.90	4.50	6	15	
1945	159,130,000	0.80	0.80	0.80	0.90	4.50	6	15	
1945D	40,245,000	0.80	0.80	0.80	0.90	4.50	6	16	
1945S	41,920,000	0.80	0.80	0.80	0.90	4.50	7	16	
1945S, Micro S Mintmark	*	0.80	0.80	0.80	0.90	9.00	15	42	

* Included in regular mintage.

ROOSEVELT (1946 TO DATE)

John R. Sinnock (whose initials JS are at the truncation of the neck) designed this dime showing a portrait of Franklin D. Roosevelt. The design has heavier lettering and a more modernistic character than preceding types.

VF-20 EXTREMELY FINE—Moderate wear on high points of design. All major details are clear.

EF-40 EXTREMELY FINE—All lines of torch, flame, and hair very plain.

MS-63 CHOICE UNCIRCULATED—Some distracting contact marks or blemishes in prime focal areas. Impaired luster possible.

MS-65 GEM UNCIRCULATED—Only light, non-distracting scattered marks. Strong luster, good eye appeal.

PF-65 GEM PROOF—Nearly perfect.

Mintmark on reverse (1946–1964).

Mintmark on obverse starting 1968.

Silver Coinage (1946–1964)

	Mintage	VF-20	EF-40	MS-63	MS-65	PF-65
1946	255,250,000	$0.80	$0.80	$1.50	$6.00	
1946D	61,043,500	0.80	0.80	1.50	7.00	
1946S	27,900,000	0.80	0.80	2.25	10.00	

	Mintage	VF-20	EF-40	MS-63	MS-65	PF-65
1947	121,520,000	$0.80	$0.80	$3.00	$6.00	
1947D	46,835,000	0.80	0.80	3.25	6.00	
1947S	34,840,000	0.80	0.80	3.00	6.00	
1948	74,950,000	0.80	0.80	2.00	6.00	
1948D	52,841,000	0.80	0.80	3.00	6.00	
1948S	35,520,000	0.80	0.80	2.75	6.00	
1949	30,940,000	0.80	0.80	12.50	16.00	
1949D	26,034,000	0.80	0.80	5.00	9.00	
1949S	13,510,000	0.80	0.80	20.00	25.00	
1950 (51,386)	50,130,114	0.80	0.80	6.00	7.00	$25
1950D	46,803,000	0.80	0.80	3.00	6.00	
1950S	20,440,000	0.80	0.80	18.00	22.00	
1951 (57,500)	103,880,102	0.80	0.80	1.25	5.00	25
1951D	56,529,000	0.80	0.80	1.25	5.00	
1951S	31,630,000	0.80	0.80	6.00	10.00	
1952 (81,980)	99,040,093	0.80	0.80	1.00	5.00	16
1952D	122,100,000	0.80	0.80	1.00	3.00	
1952S	44,419,500	0.80	0.80	4.00	6.00	
1953 (128,800)	53,490,120	0.80	0.80	1.50	4.00	16
1953D	136,433,000	0.80	0.80	1.50	4.00	
1953S	39,180,000	0.80	0.80	1.25	4.00	
1954 (233,300)	114,010,203	0.80	0.80	1.25	4.00	10
1954D	106,397,000	0.80	0.80	1.25	4.00	
1954S	22,860,000	0.80	0.80	1.25	4.00	
1955 (378,200)	12,450,181	0.80	0.80	1.25	5.00	8
1955D	13,959,000	0.80	0.80	1.25	4.00	
1955S	18,510,000	0.80	0.80	1.25	4.00	
1956 (669,384)	108,640,000	0.80	0.80	1.25	4.00	2
1956D	108,015,100	0.80	0.80	1.00	3.50	
1957 (1,247,952)	160,160,000	0.80	0.80	1.00	3.50	2
1957D	113,354,330	0.80	0.80	1.25	3.25	
1958 (875,652)	31,910,000	0.80	0.80	1.00	4.00	2
1958D	136,564,600	0.80	0.80	1.00	4.00	
1959 (1,149,291)	85,780,000	0.80	0.80	1.00	3.50	2
1959D	164,919,790	0.80	0.80	1.00	3.50	
1960 (1,691,602)	70,390,000	0.80	0.80	1.00	3.50	2
1960D	200,160,400	0.80	0.80	0.90	3.00	
1961 (3,028,244)	93,730,000	0.80	0.80	0.90	3.00	2
1961D	209,146,550	0.80	0.80	0.90	3.00	
1962 (3,218,019)	72,450,000	0.80	0.80	0.90	3.00	2
1962D	334,948,380	0.80	0.80	0.90	3.00	
1963 (3,075,645)	123,650,000	0.80	0.80	0.90	3.00	2
1963D	421,476,530	0.80	0.80	0.90	3.00	
1964 (3,950,762)	929,360,000	0.80	0.80	0.90	3.00	2
1964D	1,357,517,180	0.80	0.80	0.90	3.00	

Clad Coinage and Silver Proofs (1965 to Date)

	Mintage	MS-63	MS-65	PF-65
1965	1,652,140,570	$0.15	$0.75	
1966	1,382,734,540	0.15	0.65	
1967	2,244,007,320	0.15	0.50	
1968	424,470,400	0.15	0.50	
1968D	480,748,280	0.15	0.50	
1968S	(3,041,506)			$0.50
1969	145,790,000	0.25	0.50	
1969D	563,323,870	0.15	0.20	
1969S	(2,394,631)			0.50
1970	345,570,000	0.15	0.25	
1970D	754,942,100	0.15	0.25	
1970S	(2,632,810)			0.50
1971	162,690,000	0.18	0.30	
1971D	377,914,240	0.16	0.20	
1971S	(3,220,733)			0.50
1972	431,540,000	$0.15	$0.25	
1972D	330,290,000	0.15	0.25	
1972S	(3,260,996)			$0.50
1973	315,670,000	0.15	0.25	
1973D	455,032,426	0.15	0.25	
1973S	(2,760,339)			0.50
1974	470,248,000	0.15	0.25	
1974D	571,083,000	0.15	0.25	
1974S	(2,612,568)			0.50
1975	585,673,900	0.15	0.25	
1975D	313,705,300	0.15	0.25	
1975S	(2,845,450)			0.60
1976	568,760,000	1.50	0.25	
1976D	695,222,774		0.15	
1976S	(4,149,730)			0.50

Chart continues on next page.

	Mintage	MS-63	MS-65	PF-65
1977	796,930,000	$0.15	$0.25	
1977D	376,607,228	0.15	0.25	
1977S	(3,251,152)			$0.50
1978	663,980,000		0.15	
1978D	282,847,540		0.15	
1978S	(3,127,781)			0.40
1979	315,440,000	0.15	0.25	
1979D	390,921,184	0.15	0.25	
1979S, Filled S	(3,677,175)			0.50
1979S, Clear S	*			0.75
1980P	735,170,000	0.15	0.25	
1980D	719,354,321	0.15	0.25	
1980S	(3,554,806)			0.40
1981P	676,650,000	0.15	0.25	
1981D	712,284,143	0.15	0.25	
1981S	(4,063,083)			0.40
1982, No Mintmark		85.00	115.00	
1982P	519,475,000	1.50	2.00	
1982D	542,713,584	0.60	1.10	
1982S	(3,857,479)			0.60
1983P	647,025,000	1.25	1.50	
1983D	730,129,224	0.35	0.60	
1983S	(3,279,126)			0.50
1984P	856,669,000	0.15	0.25	
1984D	704,803,976	0.20	0.35	
1984S	(3,065,110)			0.75
1985P	705,200,962	0.15	0.25	
1985D	587,979,970	0.15	0.25	
1985S	(3,362,821)			0.50
1986P	682,649,693	0.25	0.35	
1986D	473,326,970	0.25	0.35	
1986S	(3,010,497)			1.00
1987P	762,709,481	0.15	0.35	
1987D	653,203,402	0.15	0.35	
1987S	(4,227,728)			0.60
1988P	1,030,550,000	0.12	0.20	
1988D	962,385,489	0.12	0.20	
1988S	(3,262,948)			1.00
1989P	1,298,400,000	0.10	0.20	
1989D	896,535,597	0.10	0.20	
1989S	(3,220,194)			1.00
1990P	1,034,340,000	0.10	0.20	
1990D	839,995,824	0.10	0.20	
1990S	(3,299,559)			1.00
1991P	927,220,000	0.10	0.20	
1991D	601,241,114	0.12	0.20	
1991S	(2,867,787)			1.20
1992P	593,500,000	0.10	0.15	
1992D	616,273,932	0.10	0.15	
1992S	(2,858,981)			2.00
1992S, Silver	(1,317,579)			3.00
1993P	766,180,000	0.10	0.15	
1993D	750,110,166	0.10	0.15	
1993S	(2,633,439)			2.00
1993S, Silver	(761,353)			2.50
1994P	1,189,000,000	0.10	0.15	

* Included in number above.

	Mintage	MS-63	MS-65	PF-65
1994D	1,303,268,110	$0.10	$0.15	
1994S	(2,484,594)			$2.00
1994S, Silver	(785,329)			2.50
1995P	1,125,500,000	0.10	0.20	
1995D	1,274,890,000	0.15	0.25	
1995S	(2,117,496)			3.00
1995S, Silver	(679,985)			4.00
1996P	1,421,163,000	0.10	0.20	
1996D	1,400,300,000	0.10	0.20	
1996W	1,457,000	6.00		
1996S	(1,750,244)			2.00
1996S, Silver	(775,021)			3.00
1997P	991,640,000	0.10	0.15	
1997D	979,810,000	0.10	0.15	
1997S	(2,055,000)			3.00
1997S, Silver	(741,678)			10.00
1998P	1,163,000,000	0.10	0.15	
1998D	1,172,250,000	0.10	0.15	
1998S	(2,086,507)			2.00
1998S, Silver	(878,792)			3.00
1999P	2,164,000,000	0.10	0.15	
1999D	1,397,750,000	0.10	0.15	
1999S	(2,543,401)			1.00
1999S, Silver	(804,565)			3.50
2000P	1,842,500,000	0.10	0.15	
2000D	1,818,700,000	0.10	0.15	
2000S	(3,082,572)			1.00
2000S, Silver	(965,421)			2.00
2001P	1,369,590,000	0.10	0.15	
2001D	1,412,800,000	0.10	0.15	
2001S	(2,294,909)			0.50
2001S, Silver	(889,697)			2.00
2002P	1,187,500,000	0.10	0.15	
2002D	1,379,500,000	0.10	0.15	
2002S	(2,319,766)			0.75
2002S, Silver	(892,229)			1.50
2003P	1,085,500,000	0.10	0.15	
2003D	986,500,000	0.10	0.15	
2003S	(2,172,684)			0.50
2003S, Silver	(1,125,755)			1.50
2004P	1,328,000,000	0.10	0.15	
2004D	1,159,500,000	0.10	0.15	
2004S	(1,789,488)			0.50
2004S, Silver	(1,175,934)			0.50
2005P	*1,412,000,000*	0.10	0.15	
2005D	*1,423,500,000*	0.10	0.15	
2005S	*(2,275,000)*			0.50
2005S, Silver	*(1,069,679)*			1.50
2006P	*1,381,000,000*	0.10	0.15	
2006D	*1,447,000,000*	0.10	0.15	
2006S	*(1,934,965)*			0.50
2006S, Silver	*(988,140)*			1.50
2007P		0.10	0.15	
2007D		0.10	0.15	
2007S				0.50
2007S, Silver				1.50

LIBERTY SEATED (1875–1878)

The twenty-cent piece was a short-lived coin authorized by the Act of March 3, 1875. The edge of the coin is plain. Most of the 1876-CC coins were melted at the Mint and never released. The mintmark is on the reverse below the eagle.

G-4 GOOD—LIBERTY on shield obliterated. Letters and date legible.
VG-8 VERY GOOD—One or two letters in LIBERTY barely visible. Other details bold.
F-12 FINE—Some letters of LIBERTY possibly visible.
VF-20 VERY FINE—LIBERTY readable, but partly weak.
EF-40 EXTREMELY FINE—LIBERTY mostly sharp. Only slight wear on high points of coin.
AU-50 ABOUT UNCIRCULATED—Slight trace of wear on breast, head, and knees.
MS-60 UNCIRCULATED—No trace of wear. Light blemishes.
MS-63 CHOICE UNCIRCULATED—Some distracting blemishes in prime focal areas. Some impairment of luster possible.
PF-63 CHOICE PROOF—Reflective surfaces with only a few blemishes in secondary focal places. No major flaws.

	Mintage	G-4	VG-8	F-12	VF-20	EF-40	AU-50	MS-60	MS-63	PF-63
1875 .....(2,790)	36,910	$55	$60	$75	$125	$180	$225	$325	$600	$1,100
1875CC	133,290	65	70	125	175	250	300	500	950	
1875S	1,155,000	50	55	65	85	125	155	275	600	
1876 .....(1,260)	14,640	65	80	110	160	220	250	425	700	1,200
1876CC	10,000							70,000		
1877 ....(350)					1,000	1,200				2,200
1878 ....(600)					900	1,000				1,800

Authorized in 1792, this denomination was not issued until four years later. The first type weighed 104 grains which remained standard until modified to 103-1/8 grains by the Act of January 18, 1837. As with the dime and half dime, the weight was reduced and arrows placed at the date in 1853. Rays were placed in the field of the reverse during that year only.

DRAPED BUST (1796–1807)

AG-3 ABOUT GOOD—Details clear enough to identify.
G-4 GOOD—Date readable. Bust outlined, but no detail.
VG-8 VERY GOOD—All but deepest drapery folds worn smooth. Hairlines nearly gone and curls lacking in detail.
F-12 FINE—All drapery lines visible. Hair partly worn.
VF-20 VERY FINE—Only left side of drapery indistinct.
EF-40 EXTREMELY FINE—Hair well outlined and detailed.
AU-50 ABOUT UNCIRCULATED—Slight trace of wear on shoulder and highest waves of hair.
MS-60 UNCIRCULATED—No trace of wear. Light blemishes.
MS-63 CHOICE UNCIRCULATED—Some distracting contact marks or blemishes in prime focal areas. Impaired luster possible.

Small Eagle Reverse (1796)

	Mintage	AG-3	G-4	VG-8	F-12	VF-20	EF-40	AU-50	MS-60	MS-63
1796	6,146	$2,750	$5,000	$6,500	$12,000	$18,000	$22,000	$30,000	$42,000	$60,000

Heraldic Eagle Reverse (1804–1807)

	Mintage	AG-3	G-4	VG-8	F-12	VF-20	EF-40	AU-50	MS-60	MS-63
1804	6,738	$500	$1,200	$1,500	$2,000	$3,000	$5,500	$12,000	$20,000	$45,000
1805	121,394	50	110	140	210	425	850	1,500	2,600	5,000
1806, 6 Over 5	*	50	110	140	210	425	950	1,600	2,850	8,000
1806	206,124	50	110	140	210	425	850	1,500	2,600	5,000
1807	220,643	50	110	140	210	425	850	1,500	2,600	5,000

* Included in number below.

CAPPED BUST (1815–1838)
Variety 1 – Large Diameter (1815–1828)

AG-3 ABOUT GOOD—Details clear enough to identify.
G-4 GOOD—Date, letters, stars legible. Hair under Liberty's headband smooth. Cap lines worn smooth.
VG-8 VERY GOOD—Rim well defined. Main details visible. Full LIBERTY on cap. Hair above eye nearly smooth.
F-12 FINE—All hair lines visible, but only partial detail visible in drapery. Shoulder clasp distinct.
VF-20 VERY FINE—All details visible, but some wear evident. Clasp and ear sharp.
EF-40 EXTREMELY FINE—All details distinct. Hair well outlined.
AU-50 ABOUT UNCIRCULATED—Slight trace of wear on tips of curls and above the eye, and on the wing and claw tips.
MS-60 UNCIRCULATED—No trace of wear. Light blemishes.
MS-63 CHOICE UNCIRCULATED—Some distracting contact marks or blemishes in prime focal areas. Impaired luster possible.

	Mintage	AG-3	G-4	VG-8	F-12	VF-20	EF-40	AU-50	MS-60	MS-63
1815	89,235	$15	$35	$45	$65	$175	$500	$650	$1,200	$2,300
1818, 8 Over 5	*	15	35	45	65	175	475	650	1,400	2,500
1818, Normal Date	361,174	15	35	40	60	150	450	625	1,100	2,300
1819	144,000	15	35	40	60	150	450	625	1,100	2,300
1820	127,444	15	35	40	60	150	450	625	1,100	2,300
1821	216,851	15	35	40	60	150	450	625	1,100	2,300
1822	64,080	15	35	45	75	175	475	675	1,300	2,800
1822, 25 Over 50c	*	275	650	1,300	2,200	3,000	5,000	9,000	16,000	
1823, 3 Over 2	17,800	2,750	5,500	8,500	15,000	20,000	30,000			
1824, 4 Over 2	**	25	40	60	120	300	800	1,900	4,500	
1825	168,000	15	35	40	55	150	450	625	1,200	2,300
1827, Original (Curl Base 2 in 25c)	4,000									100,000
1827, Restrike (Square Base 2 in 25c)	*									50,000
1828	102,000	15	35	40	55	150	425	700	1,300	2,600
1828, 25 Over 50c	*	30	60	110	225	450	800	1,500	3,800	

* Included in regular mintage. ** Included in 1825 mintage.

Variety 2 – Reduced Diameter (1831–1838)

G-4 GOOD—Bust of Liberty well defined. Hair under headband smooth. Date, letters, stars legible. Scant rims.
VG-8 VERY GOOD—Details apparent but worn on high spots. Rims strong. Full LIBERTY.
F-12 FINE—All hair lines visible. Drapery partly worn. Shoulder clasp distinct.
VF-20 VERY FINE—Only top spots worn. Clasp sharp. Ear distinct.
EF-40 EXTREMELY FINE—Hair details and clasp bold and clear.
AU-50 ABOUT UNCIRCULATED—Slight trace of wear on hair around forehead, on cheek, and at top and bottom tips of eagle's wings and left claw.
MS-60 UNCIRCULATED—No trace of wear. Light blemishes.
MS-63 CHOICE UNCIRCULATED—Some distracting contact marks or blemishes in prime focal areas. Impaired luster possible.

	Mintage	G-4	VG-8	F-12	VF-20	EF-40	AU-50	MS-60	MS-63
1831	398,000	$30	$35	$40	$65	$150	$275	$475	$1,500
1832	320,000	30	35	40	65	150	275	475	1,500
1833	156,000	30	35	50	70	185	300	650	2,000
1834	286,000	30	35	40	65	150	275	475	1,500
1835	1,952,000	30	35	40	65	150	275	475	1,500
1836	472,000	30	35	40	65	150	275	475	1,500
1837	252,400	30	35	40	65	150	275	475	1,500
1838	366,000	30	35	40	65	150	275	475	1,500

LIBERTY SEATED (1838–1891)

G-4 GOOD—Scant rim. LIBERTY on shield worn off. Date and letters legible.
VG-8 VERY GOOD—Rim fairly defined, at least three letters in LIBERTY evident.
F-12 FINE—LIBERTY complete, but partly weak.
VF-20 VERY FINE—LIBERTY strong.
EF-40 EXTREMELY FINE—Complete LIBERTY and edges of scroll. Clasp clear.
AU-50 ABOUT UNCIRCULATED—Slight wear on Liberty's knees and breast and on eagle's neck, wing tips, and claws.
MS-60 UNCIRCULATED—No trace of wear. Light blemishes.
MS-63 CHOICE UNCIRCULATED—Some distracting contact marks or blemishes in prime focal areas. Impaired luster possible.

Variety 1 – No Motto Above Eagle (1838–1853)

Mintmark location is on reverse, below eagle.

Small Date

Large Date

	Mintage	G-4	VG-8	F-12	VF-20	EF-40	AU-50	MS-60	MS-63
1838	466,000	$10	$13	$20	$35	$110	$220	$625	$1,750
1839	491,146	10	13	20	35	110	220	625	1,750
1840	188,127	9	12	21	32	70	110	400	1,100
1840O	425,200	11	15	27	45	125	225	650	2,000
1841	120,000	18	30	45	65	110	125	425	850
1841O	452,000	10	12	19	32	80	120	350	700
1842, Small Date (Proof only)									28,000
1842, Large Date	88,000	30	40	75	130	175	250	750	15,000
1842O, Small Date	*	145	225	450	750	1,400	3,250	6,500	
1842O, Large Date	769,000	10	11	17	31	70	125	650	1,800
1843	645,600	9	10	16	22	40	60	225	600
1843O	968,000	10	13	20	45	100	275	900	2,200
1844	421,200	9	10	16	22	40	60	225	600
1844O	740,000	10	11	18	32	80	120	550	1,400
1845	922,000	9	10	16	22	40	60	225	625
1846	510,000	9	10	16	22	40	60	225	600
1847	734,000	9	10	16	22	40	60	225	600
1847O	368,000	12	17	27	50	110	275	800	2,300
1848	146,000	11	17	28	50	80	125	450	1,100
1849	340,000	10	12	20	27	70	100	400	700
1849O	**(a)**	150	250	435	850	1,500	2,200	5,000	—
1850	190,800	13	17	25	35	65	100	400	750
1850O	412,000	13	17	25	35	65	180	550	1,100
1851	160,000	15	20	28	50	85	100	400	725
1851O	88,000	65	100	200	300	650	1,100	2,900	
1852	177,060	16	21	30	55	90	110	375	650
1852O	96,000	80	120	175	300	600	1,500	3,500	9,000
1853, Recut Date, No Arrows or Rays	44,200	110	140	175	275	500	750	1,300	2,000

* Included in number below. **a.** Mintage for 1849-O included with 1850-O.

Variety 2 – Arrows at Date, Rays Around Eagle (1853)

1853, 3 Over 4

	Mintage	G-4	VG-8	F-12	VF-20	EF-40	AU-50	MS-60	MS-63
1853	15,210,020	$9	$12	$15	$20	$65	$125	$450	$950
1853, 3 Over 4	*	20	35	55	110	160	250	900	2,500
1853O	1,332,000	9	12	17	30	115	450	1,200	4,250

* Included in number above.

Variety 3 – Arrows at Date, No Rays (1854–1855)

	Mintage	G-4	VG-8	F-12	VF-20	EF-40	AU-50	MS-60	MS-63
1854	12,380,000	$9	$11	$14	$18	$35	$100	$250	$700
1854O	1,484,000	9	11	16	20	40	110	325	850
1855	2,857,000	9	11	14	18	35	100	275	700
1855O	176,000	17	25	45	110	150	340	1,200	3,500
1855S	396,400	17	25	35	60	125	300	850	2,000

Variety 1 Resumed (1856–1865; Weight Standard of 1853)

	Mintage	G-4	VG-8	F-12	VF-20	EF-40	AU-50	MS-60	MS-63	PF-63
1856	7,264,000	$9	$11	$14	$19	$27	$60	$170	$300	$2,600
1856O	968,000	9	11	14	21	40	100	500	825	
1856S	286,000	15	20	35	80	160	300	1,000	3,750	
1857	9,644,000	9	11	14	19	26	60	150	300	1,800
1857O	1,180,000	9	11	14	19	37	110	500	1,200	
1857S	82,000	25	40	70	150	250	400	1,200	3,250	
1858 . . . . *(300+)*	7,368,000	9	11	14	19	26	60	150	300	1,000
1858O	520,000	9	11	14	25	50	150	650	2,750	
1858S	121,000	19	32	50	100	200	600	4,000	—	
1859 . . . . (800)	1,343,200	9	11	14	19	26	60	150	425	625
1859O	260,000	9	14	20	26	50	150	500	1,600	
1859S	80,000	35	55	90	150	550	4,000	—	—	
1860 . . . (1,000)	804,400	9	11	14	19	26	60	175	300	550
1860O	388,000	9	11	14	20	32	150	450	850	
1860S	56,000	65	100	150	325	1,000	3,000	—	—	
1861 . . . (1,000)	4,853,600	9	11	14	19	26	60	175	350	550
1861S	96,000	20	37	85	175	400	2,000	—	—	
1862 . . . . (550)	932,000	9	11	14	19	26	60	175	350	550
1862S	67,000	19	26	50	100	200	400	1,000	3,500	
1863 . . . . (460)	191,600	14	18	30	45	70	120	300	425	550
1864 . . . . (470)	93,600	30	35	45	70	110	180	300	600	550
1864S	20,000	110	160	275	400	850	1,600	—	—	
1865 . . . . (500)	58,800	25	30	45	70	110	180	350	600	550
1865S	41,000	30	40	60	140	225	450	1,200	1,900	

Variety 4 – Motto Above Eagle (1866–1873)

	Mintage	G-4	VG-8	F-12	VF-20	EF-40	AU-50	MS-60	MS-63	PF-63
1866 . . . . . . (725)	16,800	$150	$200	$225	$350	$550	$700	$850	$1,200	$425
1866S	28,000	75	110	200	350	500	900	1,600	2,500	
1867 . . . . . . (625)	20,000	80	100	175	210	260	350	500	1,100	425
1867S	48,000	75	100	160	210	300	425	1,750	—	
1868 . . . . . . (600)	29,400	40	60	80	100	125	210	400	700	425
1868S	96,000	30	40	50	90	200	350	1,100	2,800	
1869 . . . . . . (600)	16,000	90	110	170	200	275	400	600	1,100	425
1869S	76,000	30	45	80	125	225	450	1,000	2,000	
1870 . . . . (1,000)	86,400	20	25	40	60	90	175	400	500	425

Chart continues on next page.

	Mintage	G-4	VG-8	F-12	VF-20	EF-40	AU-50	MS-60	MS-63	PF-63
1870CC	8,340	$1,000	$1,750	$3,500	$6,000	$10,000	$20,000	—		
1871 . . .(960)	118,200	11	16	22	40	60	125	$225	$425	$400
1871CC	10,890	700	1,300	2,000	6,000	9,000	16,000	—		
1871S	30,900	100	150	200	300	450	850	1,300	2,000	
1872 . . .(950)	182,000	11	16	22	40	60	100	300	700	400
1872CC	22,850	200	350	600	1,100	2,000	4,000	10,000		
1872S	83,000	225	425	525	650	1,000	1,850	3,000		
1873 . . .(650)	212,600	11	16	22	35	50	90	200	425	400
1873CC	4,000				—			—		

Variety 5 – Arrows at Date (1873–1874)

	Mintage	G-4	VG-8	F-12	VF-20	EF-40	AU-50	MS-60	MS-63	PF-63
1873 . . .(540)	1,271,160	$10	$11	$16	$35	$90	$175	$425	$700	$800
1873CC	12,462	600	1,000	1,800	3,250	8,000	11,000	25,000	40,000	
1873S	156,000	11	14	23	45	110	200	600	1,000	
1874 . . .(700)	471,200	10	11	16	35	90	175	450	750	800
1874S	392,000	11	13	20	45	110	175	450	750	

Variety 4 Resumed (1875–1891)

1877-S, S Over Horizontal S

	Mintage	G-4	VG-8	F-12	VF-20	EF-40	AU-50	MS-60	MS-63	PF-63
1875 . . . .(700)	4,292,800	$9	$11	$14	$18	$25	$60	$125	$200	$350
1875CC	140,000	25	35	65	125	200	300	700	1,100	
1875S	680,000	10	16	23	35	70	125	275	500	
1876 . . .(1,150)	17,816,000	9	11	14	19	25	60	125	200	350
1876CC	4,944,000	11	16	18	23	35	75	200	400	
1876S	8,596,000	9	11	14	18	25	60	125	200	
1877 . . . .(510)	10,911,200	9	11	14	18	25	60	125	200	350
1877CC	4,192,000	10	16	18	23	35	75	200	350	
1877S	8,996,000	9	11	14	19	25	60	125	200	
1877S, S Over Horizontal S	*	11	16	35	50	90	125	300	500	
1878 . . . .(800)	2,260,000	9	11	14	19	25	60	125	200	350
1878CC	996,000	11	16	20	30	55	95	250	400	
1878S	140,000	30	55	80	100	175	275	600	1,000	
1879 . . .(1,100)	13,600	40	50	75	80	100	135	200	375	350
1880 . . .(1,355)	13,600	40	50	75	80	100	135	200	375	350
1881 . . . .(975)	12,000	50	65	85	100	120	190	225	400	400
1882 . . .(1,100)	15,200	45	50	80	100	110	150	275	375	350
1883 . . .(1,039)	14,400	45	50	80	100	110	150	275	375	350
1884 . . . .(875)	8,000	90	100	120	125	150	200	350	450	350

* Included in number above.

	Mintage	G-4	VG-8	F-12	VF-20	EF-40	AU-50	MS-60	MS-63	PF-63
1885 . . . . . (930)	13,600	$40	$50	$75	$100	$110	$200	$300	$400	$350
1886 . . . . . (886)	5,000	95	110	150	175	275	375	475	500	400
1887 . . . . . (710)	10,000	80	90	100	125	175	200	300	400	350
1888 . . . . . (832)	10,001	70	80	90	135	200	225	300	375	350
1888S	1,216,000	9	11	14	18	25	65	150	275	
1889 . . . . . (711)	12,000	50	60	90	110	120	200	325	425	450
1890 . . . . . (590)	80,000	20	25	35	50	80	125	275	375	350
1891 . . . . . (600)	3,920,000	8	9	11	15	22	65	150	250	350
1891O	6,800	50	65	110	325	475	525	1,600	2,200	
1891S	2,216,000	9	11	14	18	25	65	150	275	

BARBER OR LIBERTY HEAD (1892–1916)

Like other silver coins of this type, the quarter dollars minted from 1892 to 1916 were designed by Charles E. Barber. His initial B is found at the truncation of the neck of Miss Liberty.

G-4 GOOD—Date and legends legible. LIBERTY worn off headband.
VG-8 VERY GOOD—Some letters in LIBERTY legible.
F-12 FINE—LIBERTY completely legible but not sharp.
VF-20 VERY FINE—All letters in LIBERTY evenly plain.
EF-40 EXTREMELY FINE—LIBERTY bold, and its ribbon distinct.
AU-50 ABOUT UNCIRCULATED—Slight trace of wear above forehead, on cheek, and on eagle's head, wings, and tail.
MS-60 UNCIRCULATED—No trace of wear. Light blemishes.
MS-63 CHOICE UNCIRCULATED—Some distracting contact marks or blemishes in prime focal areas. Impaired luster possible.
PF-63 CHOICE PROOF—Reflective surfaces with only a few blemishes in secondary focal places. No major flaws.

	Mintage	G-4	VG-8	F-12	VF-20	EF-40	AU-50	MS-60	MS-63	PF-63
1892 . . . (1,245)	8,236,000	$2.25	$3.00	$9	$13	$27	$50	$115	$125	$300
1892O	2,460,000	3.00	5.00	11	18	35	60	150	200	
1892S	964,079	10.00	18.00	30	40	70	130	200	425	
1893 . . . . (792)	5,444,023	2.25	3.00	9	13	30	50	115	165	300
1893O	3,396,000	3.00	4.00	10	14	35	60	160	220	
1893S	1,454,535	6.00	10.00	20	40	70	130	200	500	
1894 . . . . (972)	3,432,000	2.25	2.50	10	15	30	60	110	200	300
1894O	2,852,000	2.50	3.00	10	20	35	90	160	300	
1894S	2,648,821	3.00	3.50	11	20	35	90	160	300	
1895 . . . . (880)	4,440,000	2.25	2.50	10	14	30	60	110	200	300
1895O	2,816,000	3.00	5.00	15	27	45	90	185	400	
1895S	1,764,681	5.00	8.00	20	35	47	110	225	450	
1896 . . . . (762)	3,874,000	2.50	3.00	9	14	32	60	125	200	300
1896O	1,484,000	10.00	18.00	50	110	150	275	450	750	
1896S	188,039	275.00	450.00	700	1,200	1,900	2,600	3,200	7,000	
1897 . . . . (731)	8,140,000	2.25	3.00	9	13	28	50	90	125	300
1897O	1,414,800	5.00	12.00	40	100	130	275	425	750	
1897S	542,229	15.00	22.00	90	120	130	275	425	750	
1898 . . . . (735)	11,100,000	2.25	2.50	9	13	30	50	90	125	300
1898O	1,868,000	5.00	9.00	22	55	110	150	300	650	
1898S	1,020,592	4.00	7.00	15	20	35	90	200	600	
1899 . . . . (846)	12,624,000	2.25	2.50	9	13	26	50	90	125	300
1899O	2,644,000	3.00	5.00	9	16	32	100	200	400	
1899S	708,000	5.00	12.00	18	35	45	125	225	550	
1900 . . . . (912)	10,016,000	2.25	2.50	9	13	25	60	90	125	300
1900O	3,416,000	4.00	9.00	20	30	50	150	250	400	
1900S	1,858,585	2.50	4.00	11	16	30	50	175	450	

Chart continues on next page.

	Mintage	G-4	VG-8	F-12	VF-20	EF-40	AU-50	MS-60	MS-63	PF-63
1901 (813)	8,892,000	$2.25	$3.00	$8.00	$14	$30	$60	$100	$120	$300
1901O	1,612,000	18.00	25.00	55.00	100	175	250	400	900	
1901S	72,664	2,750.00	4,000.00	6,000.00	7,500	10,000	13,000	18,000	23,000	
1902 (777)	12,196,967	2.25	2.50	8.00	14	30	50	90	125	300
1902O	4,748,000	2.50	3.00	12.00	25	50	90	200	600	
1902S	1,524,612	4.50	7.00	18.00	30	60	100	220	475	
1903 (755)	9,759,309	2.25	2.50	8.00	14	30	50	90	175	300
1903O	3,500,000	3.00	4.00	11.00	20	32	100	150	600	
1903S	1,036,000	4.00	6.00	14.00	25	45	100	210	400	
1904 (670)	9,588,143	2.25	2.50	8.00	14	25	50	90	125	300
1904O	2,456,000	3.00	4.00	16.00	30	90	175	350	600	
1905 (727)	4,967,523	2.50	3.50	8.50	14	30	50	90	150	300
1905O	1,230,000	4.00	10.00	35.00	60	110	160	200	550	
1905S	1,884,000	2.75	4.00	16.00	22	42	90	175	500	
1906 (675)	3,655,760	2.50	3.00	8.00	14	25	50	90	125	300
1906D	3,280,000	2.50	3.00	9.00	15	26	60	110	200	
1906O	2,056,000	2.50	3.00	12.00	17	30	90	135	250	
1907 (575)	7,132,000	2.50	3.00	8.00	14	25	50	90	125	300
1907D	2,484,000	2.50	3.00	9.00	15	26	60	125	350	
1907O	4,560,000	2.50	3.00	8.00	14	25	55	100	250	
1907S	1,360,000	4.00	5.00	16.00	22	50	100	200	400	
1908 (545)	4,232,000	2.50	3.00	8.00	14	25	50	90	125	300
1908D	5,788,000	2.50	3.00	8.00	14	25	50	110	200	
1908O	6,244,000	2.25	2.50	8.00	14	25	50	100	125	
1908S	784,000	6.00	13.00	35.00	60	150	200	350	550	
1909 (650)	9,268,000	2.25	2.50	8.00	14	25	50	90	125	300
1909D	5,114,000	2.25	2.50	8.00	14	25	60	110	160	
1909O	712,000	6.00	13.00	30.00	70	125	225	400	850	
1909S	1,348,000	2.25	2.50	10.00	16	30	90	150	350	
1910 (551)	2,244,000	2.25	2.50	8.00	14	25	60	90	150	300
1910D	1,500,000	2.25	2.50	15.00	18	35	110	175	400	
1911 (543)	3,720,000	2.25	2.50	8.00	14	25	50	90	125	300
1911D	933,600	2.25	2.50	30.00	90	130	225	325	600	
1911S	988,000	2.25	2.50	18.00	20	50	120	175	350	
1912 (700)	4,400,000	2.25	2.50	8.00	14	25	50	90	125	300
1912S	708,000	2.25	2.50	15.00	18	35	100	175	400	
1913 (613)	484,000	6.00	9.00	25.00	67	185	210	550	600	375
1913D	1,450,800	2.25	4.00	11.00	17	35	75	140	185	
1913S	40,000	500.00	800.00	1,600.00	2,500	3,000	3,750	4,500	5,500	
1914 (380)	6,244,230	2.25	2.50	8.00	14	25	50	90	125	375
1914D	3,046,000	2.25	2.50	8.00	14	25	50	90	125	
1914S	264,000	30.00	40.00	75.00	120	200	300	450	675	
1915 (450)	3,480,000	2.25	2.50	8.00	14	25	50	90	125	375
1915D	3,694,000	2.25	2.50	8.00	14	25	50	90	125	
1915S	704,000	2.25	2.50	9.00	15	32	90	125	200	
1916	1,788,000	2.25	2.50	8.00	14	25	50	90	125	
1916D	6,540,800	2.25	2.50	8.00	14	25	50	90	125	

STANDING LIBERTY (1916–1930)

This design is by Hermon A. MacNeil, whose initial M is above and to the right of the date. Liberty bears a shield of protection in her left arm, while the right hand holds the olive branch of peace. There was a modification in 1917. The reverse had a new arrangement of stars and the eagle was higher. After 1924 the date was "recessed," thereby giving it greater protection from the effects of circulation.

G-4 GOOD—Date and lettering legible. Top of date worn. Liberty's right leg and toes worn off. Much wear evident on left leg and drapery lines.
VG-8 VERY GOOD—Distinct date. Toes faintly visible. Drapery lines visible above Liberty's left leg.
F-12 FINE—High curve of right leg flat from thigh to ankle. Only slight wear evident on left leg. Drapery lines over right thigh seen only at sides of leg.
VF-20 VERY FINE—Garment line across right leg worn, but visible at sides.
EF-40 EXTREMELY FINE—Flattened only at high spots. Liberty's toes are sharp. Drapery lines across right leg evident.
AU-50 ABOUT UNCIRCULATED—Slight trace of wear on head, kneecap, shield's center, and highest point on eagle's body.
MS-60 UNCIRCULATED—No trace of wear, but contact marks, surface spots, or faded luster possible.
MS-63 CHOICE UNCIRCULATED—No trace of wear. Light blemishes. Attractive mint luster.

Variety 1 – No Stars Below Eagle (1916–1917)

Mintmark location is on obverse, to left of date.

	Mintage	G-4	VG-8	F-12	VF-20	EF-40	AU-50	MS-60	MS-63
1916	52,000	$1,800	$2,500	$4,000	$6,000	$7,500	$8,000	$10,000	$12,500
1917, Variety 1	8,740,000	13	18	26	32	50	100	140	180
1917D, Variety 1	1,509,200	13	18	26	32	55	110	150	200
1917S, Variety 1	1,952,000	16	21	28	40	75	125	170	250

Variety 2 – Stars Below Eagle (1917–1930)

Pedestal Date (1917–1924)

1918-S, 8 Over 7

	Mintage	G-4	VG-8	F-12	VF-20	EF-40	AU-50	MS-60	MS-63
1917, Variety 2	13,880,000	$11	$13	$16	$18	$27	$55	$100	$140
1917D, Variety 2	6,224,400	15	21	30	35	50	75	125	175
1917S, Variety 2	5,552,000	15	21	30	35	50	75	125	175
1918	14,240,000	8	9	15	17	25	50	100	145
1918D	7,380,000	13	15	25	30	40	75	125	200
1918S, Normal Date	11,072,000	9	11	17	20	30	50	120	175
1918S, 8 Over 7	*	800	900	1,600	2,500	3,500	7,000	10,000	20,000
1919	11,324,000	18	22	27	35	40	60	100	125
1919D	1,944,000	50	70	100	150	225	300	375	800
1919S	1,836,000	50	70	100	150	300	350	500	900
1920	27,860,000	8	10	15	20	25	40	100	125
1920D	3,586,400	25	30	40	45	65	100	125	450
1920S	6,380,000	9	12	16	20	30	50	110	400
1921	1,916,000	85	110	160	200	275	400	500	750
1923	9,716,000	8	10	15	17	20	35	100	150
1923S	1,360,000	150	200	225	350	450	550	700	900
1924	10,920,000	8	10	12	15	20	45	100	150
1924D	3,112,000	25	35	50	65	100	125	150	175
1924S	2,860,000	12	15	20	25	60	125	150	500

* Included in number above.

Recessed Date (1925–1930)

	Mintage	G-4	VG-8	F-12	VF-20	EF-40	AU-50	MS-60	MS-63
1925	12,280,000	$2.25	$2.50	$3	$6	$16	$35	$70	$140
1926	11,316,000	2.25	2.50	3	6	16	35	70	140
1926D	1,716,000	2.25	4.00	8	16	26	50	100	170
1926S	2,700,000	2.25	2.50	6	11	50	125	200	400
1927	11,912,000	2.25	2.50	3	6	16	35	70	140
1927D	976,000	6.00	8.00	13	30	65	90	160	200
1927S	396,000	12.00	16.00	40	140	600	1,600	2,500	4,200
1928	6,336,000	2.25	2.50	3	6	16	35	70	135
1928D	1,627,600	2.25	2.50	3	6	16	35	70	135
1928S	2,644,000	2.25	2.50	3	6	16	35	70	140
1929	11,140,000	2.25	2.50	3	6	16	35	70	140
1929D	1,358,000	2.25	2.50	3	6	16	35	70	140
1929S	1,764,000	2.25	2.50	3	6	16	35	70	140
1930	5,632,000	2.25	2.50	3	6	16	35	70	135
1930S	1,556,000	2.25	2.50	3	6	16	35	70	135

WASHINGTON (1932 TO DATE)

This type was intended to be a commemorative issue marking the 200th anniversary of Washington's birth. John Flanagan, a New York sculptor, was the designer. The initials JF are found at the base of the neck. The mintmark is on the reverse below the wreath for coins from 1932 to 1964. Starting in 1968, the mintmark was moved to the obverse at the right of the ribbon.

F-12 FINE—Hair lines about Washington's ear visible. Tiny feathers on eagle's breast faintly visible.
VF-20 VERY FINE—Most hair details visible. Wing feathers clear.
EF-40 EXTREMELY FINE—Hair lines sharp. Wear spots confined to top of eagle's legs and center of breast.
MS-60 UNCIRCULATED—No trace of wear, but many contact marks, surface spotting, or faded luster possible.
MS-63 CHOICE UNCIRCULATED—No trace of wear. Light blemishes. Attractive mint luster.
MS-64 UNCIRCULATED—A few scattered contact marks. Good eye appeal and attractive luster.
MS-65 GEM UNCIRCULATED—Only light, scattered contact marks that are not distracting. Strong luster, good eye appeal.
PF-65 GEM PROOF—Hardly any blemishes, and no flaws.

Since 1968, the mintmark has been on obverse at the right of the ribbon.

Silver Coinage (1932–1964)

	Mintage	VG-8	F-12	VF-20	EF-40	MS-60	MS-63	MS-65	PF-65
1932	5,404,000	$2	$2.50	$3.00	$4.00	$13	$23	$200	
1932D	436,800	75	90.00	120.00	175.00	525	2,000	14,500	
1932S	408,000	75	90.00	100.00	120.00	275	700	3,750	
1934	31,912,052	2	2.00	2.25	3.00	9	17	45	
1934D	3,527,200	2	2.00	2.25	10.00	100	175	650	
1935	32,484,000	2	2.00	2.00	2.50	9	15	45	
1935D	5,780,000	2	2.00	2.50	8.00	100	140	400	
1935S	5,660,000	2	2.00	2.50	5.00	40	60	140	
1936 (3,837)	41,300,000	2	2.00	2.00	2.50	8	16	40	$850
1936D	5,374,000	2	2.50	5.00	18.00	180	350	675	
1936S	3,828,000	2	2.00	2.00	4.00	40	75	200	
1937 (5,542)	19,696,000	2	2.00	2.00	2.00	8	15	48	325
1937D	7,189,600	2	2.00	2.00	3.25	25	45	70	
1937S	1,652,000	2	2.00	3.00	10.00	70	100	150	
1938 (8,045)	9,472,000	2	2.00	2.00	3.50	30	50	120	200
1938S	2,832,000	2	2.00	2.00	4.00	35	60	125	
1939 (8,795)	33,540,000	2	2.00	2.00	2.25	5	12	25	175
1939D	7,092,000	2	2.00	2.00	2.75	14	20	50	
1939S	2,628,000	2	2.00	2.00	5.00	45	65	150	

	Mintage	F-12	VF-20	EF-40	MS-60	MS-63	MS-65	PF-65
1940 (11,246)	35,704,000	$2	$2.00	$2.00	$5.00	$12	$30.00	$150.00
1940D	2,797,600	2	2.50	7.50	50.00	80	140.00	
1940S	8,244,000	2	2.00	2.50	7.00	13	25.00	
1941 (15,287)	79,032,000	2	2.00	2.00	2.50	6	20.00	100.00
1941D	16,714,800	2	2.00	2.00	12.00	22	25.00	
1941S	16,080,000	2	2.00	2.00	7.50	18	25.00	
1942 (21,123)	102,096,000	2	2.00	2.00	2.50	4	10.00	100.00
1942D	17,487,200	2	2.00	2.50	6.00	12	20.00	
1942S	19,384,000	2	2.00	3.25	27.00	45	95.00	
1943	99,700,000	2	2.00	2.00	2.50	4	20.00	
1943D	16,095,600	2	2.00	2.00	8.00	16	20.00	
1943S	21,700,000	2	2.00	2.50	8.00	19	25.00	
1944	104,956,000	2	2.00	2.00	2.50	4	18.00	
1944D	14,600,800	2	2.00	2.00	4.00	10	18.00	
1944S	12,560,000	2	2.00	2.00	5.00	12	18.00	
1945	74,372,000	2	2.00	2.00	2.50	3	18.00	
1945D	12,341,600	2	2.00	2.00	4.00	12	20.00	
1945S	17,004,001	2	2.00	2.00	3.00	5	15.00	
1946	53,436,000	2	2.00	2.00	2.50	3	16.00	
1946D	9,072,800	2	2.00	2.00	2.50	3	15.00	
1946S	4,204,000	2	2.00	2.00	2.50	3	16.00	
1947	22,556,000	2	2.00	2.00	2.50	5	15.00	
1947D	15,338,400	2	2.00	2.00	2.50	4	15.00	
1947S	5,532,000	2	2.00	2.00	2.50	4	15.00	
1948	35,196,000	2	2.00	2.00	2.50	3	15.00	
1948D	16,766,800	2	2.00	2.00	2.50	5	30.00	
1948S	15,960,000	2	2.00	2.00	2.50	4	18.00	
1949	9,312,000	2	2.00	2.00	10.00	18	30.00	
1949D	10,068,400	2	2.00	2.00	6.00	11	22.00	
1950 (51,386)	24,920,126	2	2.00	2.00	2.50	4	13.00	30.00
1950D	21,075,600	2	2.00	2.00	2.50	4	13.00	
1950D, D Over S	*		25.00	75.00	125.00	200	950.00	
1950S	10,284,004	2	2.00	2.00	5.00	6	25.00	
1950S, S Over D	*		25.00	80.00	140.00	200	400.00	
1951 (57,500)	43,448,102	2	2.00	2.00	2.50	3	14.00	27.50
1951D	35,354,800	2	2.00	2.00	2.50	3	14.00	
1951S	9,048,000	2	2.00	2.00	5.00	12	18.00	
1952 (81,980)	38,780,093	2	2.00	2.00	2.50	3	11.00	25.00
1952D	49,795,200	2	2.00	2.00	2.50	3	16.00	
1952S	13,707,800	2	2.00	2.00	5.00	10	16.00	
1953 (128,800)	18,536,120	2	2.00	2.00	2.50	3	16.00	22.00
1953D	56,112,400	2	2.00	2.00	2.50	3	15.00	
1953S	14,016,000	2	2.00	2.00	2.50	3	12.00	
1954 (233,300)	54,412,203	2	2.00	2.00	2.50	4	13.00	12.00
1954D	42,305,500	2	2.00	2.00	2.50	3	17.00	
1954S	11,834,722	2	2.00	2.00	2.50	3	15.00	
1955 (378,200)	18,180,181	2	2.00	2.00	2.50	3	12.00	12.00
1955D	3,182,400	2	2.00	2.00	2.50	3	20.00	
1956 (669,384)	44,144,000	2	2.00	2.00	2.50	3	8.00	4.00
1956D	32,334,500	2	2.00	2.00	2.50	3	10.00	
1957 (1,247,952)	46,532,000	2	2.00	2.00	2.50	3	10.00	3.00
1957D	77,924,160	2	2.00	2.00	2.50	3	10.00	
1958 (875,652)	6,360,000	2	2.00	2.00	2.50	3	9.00	4.00
1958D	78,124,900	2	2.00	2.00	2.50	3	9.00	
1959 (1,149,291)	24,384,000	2	2.00	2.00	2.50	3	9.00	3.00
1959D	62,054,232	2	2.00	2.00	2.50	3	12.00	
1960 (1,691,602)	29,164,000	2	2.00	2.00	2.50	3	6.50	2.00
1960D	63,000,324	2	2.00	2.00	2.50	3	6.50	
1961 (3,028,244)	37,036,000	2	2.00	2.00	2.50	3	6.50	2.00
1961D	83,656,928	2	2.00	2.00	2.50	3	6.50	
1962 (3,218,019)	36,156,000	2	2.00	2.00	2.50	3	6.50	2.00
1962D	127,554,756	2	2.00	2.00	2.50	3	6.50	
1963 (3,075,645)	74,316,000	2	2.00	2.00	2.50	3	6.50	2.00
1963D	135,288,184	2	2.00	2.00	2.50	3	6.50	
1964 (3,950,762)	560,390,585	2	2.00	2.00	2.50	3	6.50	2.00
1964D	704,135,528	2	2.00	2.00	2.50	3	6.50	

* Included in number above.

Clad Coinage and Silver Proofs (1965 to Date)

	Mintage	MS-63	MS-65	PF-65
1965	1,819,717,540	$0.30	$2.00	
1966	821,101,500	0.30	1.00	
1967	1,524,031,848	0.30	1.00	
1968	220,731,500	0.50	1.50	
1968D	101,534,000	0.30	1.00	
1968S	(3,041,506)			$1
1969	176,212,000	0.75	1.50	
1969D	114,372,000	0.50	1.50	
1969S	(2,934,631)			1
1970	136,420,000	0.25	1.75	
1970D	417,341,364	0.25	1.00	
1970S	(2,632,810)			1
1971	109,284,000	$0.30	$1.00	
1971D	258,634,428	0.30	0.50	
1971S	(3,220,733)			$1
1972	215,048,000	0.30	1.00	
1972D	311,067,732	0.30	1.50	
1972S	(3,260,996)			1
1973	346,924,000	0.30	1.50	
1973D	232,977,400	0.30	2.00	
1973S	(2,760,339)			1
1974	801,456,000	0.30	1.00	
1974D	353,160,300	0.30	1.50	
1974S	(2,612,568)			1

Bicentennial (1776–1976)

	Mintage	MS-63	MS-65	PF-65
1776—1976, Copper-Nickel Clad	809,784,016	$0.30	$1	
1776—1976D, Copper-Nickel Clad	860,118,839	0.30	1	
1776—1976S, Copper-Nickel Clad	(7,059,099)			$1
1776—1976S, Silver Clad **(a)**	7,000,000	1.00	2	
1776—1976S, Silver Clad **(a)**	*(4,000,000)*			2

a. Mintage is approximate. Several million were melted in 1982.

Eagle Reverse Resumed (1977–1998)
(Dies Slightly Modified to Lower Relief)

	Mintage	MS-63	MS-65	PF-65
1977	468,556,000	$0.27		
1977D	256,524,978	0.27	$1.00	
1977S	(3,251,152)			$1
1978	521,452,000	0.27	1.50	
1978D	287,373,152	0.27	1.50	
1978S	(3,127,781)			1
1979	515,708,000	0.28	1.50	
1979D	489,789,780	0.27	1.25	
1979S, Proof	(3,677,175)			
Filled S				1
Clear S				1
1980P	635,832,000	0.27	1.50	
1980D	518,327,487	0.27	1.25	
1980S	(3,554,806)			1
1981P	601,716,000	0.27	1.50	
1981D	575,722,833	0.27	1.00	
1981S	(4,063,083)			1
1982P	500,931,000	1.00	8.00	
1982D	480,042,788	0.70	6.00	
1982S	(3,857,479)			1
1983P	673,535,000	2.00	23.00	
1983D	617,806,446	2.00	14.00	
1983S	(3,279,126)			1
1984P	676,545,000	0.30	2.00	
1984D	546,483,064	0.50	2.00	
1984S	(3,065,110)			1
1985P	775,818,962	$0.50	$6.00	
1985D	519,962,888	0.35	2.50	
1985S	(3,362,821)			$1.00
1986P	551,199,333	1.00	4.00	
1986D	504,298,660	1.50	9.00	
1986S	(3,010,497)			1.00
1987P	582,499,481	0.27	2.50	
1987D	655,594,696	0.27	1.00	
1987S	(4,227,728)			1.00
1988P	562,052,000	0.50	5.00	
1988D	596,810,688	0.27	4.00	
1988S	(3,262,948)			1.00
1989P	512,868,000	0.30	4.25	
1989D	896,535,597	0.27	1.00	
1989S	(3,220,194)			1.00
1990P	613,792,000	0.27	4.00	
1990D	927,638,181	0.28	4.00	
1990S	(3,299,559)			1.75
1991P	570,968,000	0.30	4.00	
1991D	630,966,693	0.30	1.50	
1991S	(2,867,787)			1.25
1992P	384,764,000	0.35	4.25	
1992D	389,777,107	0.35	4.25	
1992S	(2,858,981)			1.25
1992S, Silver	(1,317,579)			1.75
1993P	639,276,000	0.30	1.75	

	Mintage	MS-63	MS-65	PF-65
1993D	645,476,128	$0.30	$1.75	
1993S	(2,633,439)			$1.25
1993S, Silver	(761,353)			2.00
1994P	825,600,000	0.30	4.00	
1994D	880,034,110	0.30	4.00	
1994S	(2,484,594)			1.00
1994S, Silver	(785,329)			4.00
1995P	1,004,336,000	0.30	4.00	
1995D	1,103,216,000	0.30	2.50	
1995S	(2,117,496)			4.00
1995S, Silver	(679,985)			4.00
1996P	925,040,000	0.25	2.00	
1996D	906,868,000	$0.25	$2.00	
1996S	(1,750,244)			$1.75
1996S, Silver	(775,021)			4.00
1997P	595,740,000	0.25	1.25	
1997D	599,680,000	0.25	1.25	
1997S	(2,055,000)			3.00
1997S, Silver	(741,678)			3.00
1998P	896,268,000	0.25	1.00	
1998D	821,000,000	0.25	1.00	
1998S	(2,086,507)			2.50
1998S, Silver	(878,792)			2.75

State Quarters (1999–2008)

The United States Mint 50 State Quarters® Program, which began in 1999, is producing a series of 50 quarter dollar coins with special designs honoring each state. Five different designs are being issued each year during the period 1999 to 2008. States are being commemorated in the order of their entrance into statehood.

These are all legal tender coins of standard weight and composition. The obverse side depicting President George Washington has been modified to include some of the wording previously used on the reverse. The modification was authorized by special legislation, and carried out by Mint Sculptor-Engraver William Cousins, whose initials have been added to the truncation of Washington's neck adjacent to those of the original designer, John Flanagan.

Each state theme is proposed and approved by the governor of the state. Final designs are created by Mint personnel.

Circulation coins are made at the Philadelphia and Denver mints. Proof coins are made in San Francisco. Both copper-nickel and silver Proof coins are made each year.

	Mintage	AU-50	MS-63	PF-65
1999P, Delaware	373,400,000	$0.25	$0.50	
1999D, Delaware	401,424,000	0.25	0.50	
1999S, Delaware	(3,713,359)			$1.75
1999S, Delaware, Silver	(804,565)			7.00
1999P, Pennsylvania	349,000,000	0.25	0.50	
1999D, Pennsylvania	358,332,000	0.25	0.50	
1999S, Pennsylvania	(3,713,359)			1.75
1999S, Pennsylvania, Silver	(804,565)			6.00
1999P, New Jersey	363,200,000	0.25	0.30	
1999D, New Jersey	299,028,000	0.25	0.35	
1999S, New Jersey	(3,713,359)			1.75
1999S, New Jersey, Silver	(804,565)			6.00
1999P, Georgia	451,188,000	0.25	0.30	
1999D, Georgia	488,744,000	0.25	0.30	
1999S, Georgia	(3,713,359)			1.75
1999S, Georgia, Silver	(804,565)			6.00
1999P, Connecticut	688,744,000	0.25	0.30	
1999D, Connecticut	657,880,000	0.25	0.30	
1999S, Connecticut	(3,713,359)			1.75
1999S, Connecticut, Silver	(804,565)			7.00

	Mintage	AU-50	MS-63	PF-65
2000P, Massachusetts	628,600,000	$0.25	$0.30	
2000D, Massachusetts	535,184,000	0.25	0.30	
2000S, Massachusetts	(4,020,172)			$1.50
2000S, Massachusetts, Silver	(965,421)			2.50
2000P, Maryland	678,200,000	0.25	0.30	
2000D, Maryland	556,532,000	0.25	0.30	
2000S, Maryland	(4,020,172)			1.50
2000S, Maryland, Silver	(965,421)			2.50
2000P, South Carolina	742,576,000	0.25	0.32	
2000D, South Carolina	566,208,000	0.25	0.32	
2000S, South Carolina	(4,020,172)			1.50
2000S, South Carolina, Silver	(965,421)			2.50
2000P, New Hampshire	673,040,000	0.25	0.30	
2000D, New Hampshire	495,976,000	0.25	0.30	
2000S, New Hampshire	(4,020,172)			1.50
2000S, New Hampshire, Silver	(965,421)			2.50
2000P, Virginia	943,000,000	0.25	0.30	
2000D, Virginia	651,616,000	0.25	0.30	
2000S, Virginia	(4,020,172)			1.50
2000S, Virginia, Silver	(965,421)			2.50

	Mintage	AU-50	MS-63	PF-65
2001P, New York	655,400,000	$0.25	$0.30	
2001D, New York	619,640,000	0.25	0.30	
2001S, New York	(3,094,140)			$1.50
2001S, New York, Silver	(889,697)			3.00
2001P, North Carolina	627,600,000	0.25	0.30	
2001D, North Carolina	427,876,000	0.25	0.30	
2001S, North Carolina	(3,094,140)			1.50
2001S, North Carolina, Silver	(889,697)			3.00
2001P, Rhode Island	423,000,000	0.25	0.30	
2001D, Rhode Island	447,100,000	0.25	0.30	
2001S, Rhode Island	(3,094,140)			1.50
2001S, Rhode Island, Silver	(889,697)			3.00
2001P, Vermont	423,400,000	0.25	0.30	
2001D, Vermont	459,404,000	0.25	0.30	
2001S, Vermont	(3,094,140)			1.50
2001S, Vermont, Silver	(889,697)			3.00
2001P, Kentucky	353,000,000	0.25	0.30	
2001D, Kentucky	370,564,000	0.25	0.30	
2001S, Kentucky	(3,094,140)			1.50
2001S, Kentucky, Silver	(889,697)			3.00

	Mintage	AU-50	MS-63	PF-65
2002P, Tennessee	361,600,000	$0.30	$0.40	
2002D, Tennessee	286,468,000	0.30	0.40	
2002S, Tennessee	(3,084,245)			$1.50
2002S, Tennessee, Silver	(892,229)			2.50
2002P, Ohio	217,200,000	0.25	0.30	
2002D, Ohio	414,832,000	0.25	0.30	
2002S, Ohio	(3,084,245)			1.50
2002S, Ohio, Silver	(892,229)			2.50
2002P, Louisiana	362,000,000	0.25	0.30	
2002D, Louisiana	402,204,000	0.25	0.30	
2002S, Louisiana	(3,084,245)			1.50
2002S, Louisiana, Silver	(892,229)			2.50
2002P, Indiana	362,600,000	0.25	0.30	
2002D, Indiana	327,200,000	0.25	0.30	
2002S, Indiana	(3,084,245)			1.50
2002S, Indiana, Silver	(892,229)			2.50
2002P, Mississippi	290,000,000	0.25	0.30	
2002D, Mississippi	289,600,000	0.25	0.30	
2002S, Mississippi	(3,084,245)			1.50
2002S, Mississippi, Silver	(892,229)			2.50

	Mintage	AU-50	MS-63	PF-65
2003P, Illinois	225,800,000	$0.25	$0.30	
2003D, Illinois	237,400,000	0.25	0.30	
2003S, Illinois	(3,408,516)			$1.50
2003S, Illinois, Silver	(1,125,755)			2.50
2003P, Alabama	225,000,000	0.25	0.30	
2003D, Alabama	232,400,000	0.25	0.30	
2003S, Alabama	(3,408,516)			1.50
2003S, Alabama, Silver	(1,125,755)			2.50
2003P, Maine	217,400,000	0.25	0.30	
2003D, Maine	231,400,000	0.25	0.30	
2003S, Maine	(3,408,516)			1.50
2003S, Maine, Silver	(1,125,755)			2.50
2003P, Missouri	225,000,000	0.25	0.30	
2003D, Missouri	228,200,000	0.25	0.30	
2003S, Missouri	(3,408,516)			1.50
2003S, Missouri, Silver	(1,125,755)			2.50
2003P, Arkansas	228,000,000	0.25	0.30	
2003D, Arkansas	229,800,000	0.25	0.30	
2003S, Arkansas	(3,408,516)			1.50
2003S, Arkansas, Silver	(1,125,755)			2.50

	Mintage	MS-63	MS-65	PF-65
2004P, Michigan	233,800,000	$0.25	$0.30	
2004D, Michigan	225,800,000	0.25	0.30	
2004S, Michigan	(2,740,684)			$1.50
2004S, Michigan, Silver	(1,769,786)			2.50
2004P, Florida	240,200,000	0.25	0.30	
2004D, Florida	241,600,000	0.25	0.30	
2004S, Florida	(2,740,684)			1.50
2004S, Florida, Silver	(1,769,786)			2.50
2004P, Texas	278,800,000	0.25	0.30	
2004D, Texas	263,000,000	0.25	0.30	
2004S, Texas	(2,740,684)			1.50
2004S, Texas, Silver	(1,769,786)			2.50
2004P, Iowa	213,800,000	0.25	0.30	
2004D, Iowa	251,400,000	0.25	0.30	
2004S, Iowa	(2,740,684)			1.50
2004S, Iowa, Silver	(1,769,786)			2.50
2004P, Wisconsin	226,400,000	0.25	0.30	
2004D, Wisconsin	226,800,000	0.25	0.30	
2004S, Wisconsin	(2,740,684)			1.50
2004S, Wisconsin, Silver	(1,769,786)			2.50

	Mintage	MS-63	MS-65	PF-65
2005P, California	*257,200,000*	$0.25	$0.30	
2005D, California	*263,200,000*	0.25	0.30	
2005S, California	*(3,262,960)*			$1.50
2005S, California, Silver	*(1,678,649)*			2.50
2005P, Minnesota	*239,600,000*	0.25	0.30	
2005D, Minnesota	*248,400,000*	0.25	0.30	
2005S, Minnesota	*(3,262,960)*		1.50	
2005S, Minnesota, Silver	*(1,678,649)*			2.50
2005P, Oregon	*316,200,000*	0.25	0.30	
2005D, Oregon	*404,000,000*	0.25	0.30	
2005S, Oregon	*(3,262,960)*		1.50	
2005S, Oregon, Silver	*(1,678,649)*			2.50
2005P, Kansas	*263,400,000*	0.25	0.30	
2005D, Kansas	*300,000,000*	0.25	0.30	
2005S, Kansas	*(3,262,960)*		1.50	
2005S, Kansas, Silver	*(1,678,649)*			2.50
2005P, West Virginia	*365,400,000*	0.25	0.30	
2005D, West Virginia	*356,200,000*	0.25	0.30	
2005S, West Virginia	*(3,262,960)*		1.50	
2005S, West Virginia, Silver	*(1,678,649)*			2.50

		Mintage	MS-63	MS-65	PF-65
2006P, Nevada		*277,000,000*	$0.25	$0.30	
2006D, Nevada		*312,800,000*	0.25	0.30	
2006S, Nevada	*(2,816,965)*				$1.50
2006S, Nevada, Silver	*(1,519,140)*				2.50
2006P, Nebraska		*318,000,000*	0.25	0.30	
2006D, Nebraska		*273,000,000*	0.25	0.30	
2006S, Nebraska	*(2,816,965)*				1.50
2006S, Nebraska, Silver	*(1,519,140)*				2.50
2006P, Colorado		*274,800,000*	0.25	0.30	
2006D, Colorado		*294,200,000*	0.25	0.30	
2006S, Colorado	*(2,816,965)*				1.50
2006S, Colorado, Silver	*(1,519,140)*				2.50
2006P, North Dakota		*305,800,000*	0.25	0.30	
2006D, North Dakota		*359,000,000*	0.25	0.30	
2006S, North Dakota	*(2,816,965)*				1.50
2006S, North Dakota, Silver	*(1,519,140)*				2.50
2006P, South Dakota		*245,000,000*	0.25	0.30	
2006D, South Dakota		*265,800,000*	0.25	0.30	
2006S, South Dakota	*(2,816,965)*				1.50
2006S, South Dakota, Silver	*(1,519,140)*				2.50

	Mintage	MS-63	MS-65	PF-65
2007P, Montana		$0.25	$0.30	
2007D, Montana		0.25	0.30	
2007S, Montana				$1.50
2007S, Montana, Silver				2.50
2007P, Washington		0.25	0.30	
2007D, Washington		0.25	0.30	
2007S, Washington				1.50
2007S, Washington, Silver				2.50
2007P, Idaho		0.25	0.30	
2007D, Idaho		0.25	0.30	
2007S, Idaho				1.50
2007S, Idaho, Silver				2.50
2007P, Wyoming		0.25	0.30	
2007D, Wyoming		0.25	0.30	
2007S, Wyoming				1.50
2007S, Wyoming, Silver				2.50
2007P, Utah		0.25	0.30	
2007D, Utah		0.25	0.30	
2007S, Utah				1.50
2007S, Utah, Silver				2.50

The half dollar, authorized by the Act of April 2, 1792, was not minted until December, 1794. The weight of the half dollar was 208 grains and its fineness .8924 when first issued. This standard was not changed until 1837 when the Act of January 18, 1837 specified 206-1/4 grains, .900 fine. This fineness continued in use until 1965.

Arrows at the date in 1853 indicate the reduction of weight to 192 grains. During that year only, rays were added to the reverse. Arrows remained in 1854 and 1855. In 1873 the weight was raised by .9 grains and arrows were again placed at the date.

FLOWING HAIR (1794–1795)

AG-3 ABOUT GOOD—Clear enough to identify.
G-4 GOOD—Date and letters sufficient to be legible. Main devices outlined, but lacking in detail.
VG-8 VERY GOOD—Major details discernible. Letters well formed but worn.
F-12 FINE—Hair ends distinguishable. Top hair lines visible, but otherwise worn smooth.
VF-20 VERY FINE—Some detail visible in hair in center; other details more bold.
EF-40 EXTREMELY FINE—Hair above head and down neck detailed, with slight wear.
AU-50 ABOUT UNCIRCULATED—All hair visible; slight wear on bust of Liberty and on top edges of eagle's wings, head, and breast.

2 Leaves Under Wings

3 Leaves Under Wings

	Mintage	AG-3	G-4	VG-8	F-12	VF-20	EF-40	AU-50
1794	23,464	$900	$1,300	$2,200	$3,500	$7,500	$15,000	$37,500
1795	299,680	160	335	425	700	1,400	4,000	7,000
1795, Recut Date	*	160	335	425	700	1,400	4,200	7,500
1795, 3 Leaves Under Each Wing	*	400	700	950	1,800	2,750	6,000	11,000

* Included in number above.

DRAPED BUST (1796–1807)

AG-3 ABOUT GOOD—Clear enough to identify.
G-4 GOOD—Date and letters sufficiently clear to be legible. Main devices outlined, but lacking in detail.
VG-8 VERY GOOD—Major details discernible. Letters well formed but worn.
F-12 FINE—Hair ends distinguishable. Top hair lines visible, but otherwise worn smooth.
VF-20 VERY FINE—Right side of drapery slightly worn. Left side to curls smooth.
EF-40 EXTREMELY FINE—All lines in drapery on bust distinctly visible around to hair curls.
AU-50 ABOUT UNCIRCULATED—Slight trace of wear on cheek, hair, and shoulder.

Small Eagle Reverse (1796–1797)

1796, 16 Stars

1797, 15 Stars

	Mintage	AG-3	G-4	VG-8	F-12	VF-20	EF-40	AU-50
1796, All kinds	3,918							
1796, 15 Stars		$7,000	$14,000	$16,000	$23,000	$34,000	$50,000	$70,000
1796, 16 Stars		7,500	15,000	17,000	25,000	36,000	52,500	75,000
1797, 15 Stars		7,000	14,000	16,000	23,000	34,000	50,000	70,000

Heraldic Eagle Reverse (1801–1807)

	Mintage	G-4	VG-8	F-12	VF-20	EF-40	AU-50	MS-60
1801	30,289	$125	$185	$350	$700	$1,500	$5,000	$13,000
1802	29,890	110	160	300	600	1,100	4,500	11,000
1803	188,234	75	90	150	250	475	1,200	4,000

1805, 5 Over 4

1806, 6 Over 5

	Mintage	G-4	VG-8	F-12	VF-20	EF-40	AU-50	MS-60
1805, All kinds	211,722							
1805, 5 Over 4		$100	$150	$275	$375	$1,100	$2,500	$10,000
1805, Normal Date		75	100	120	225	500	1,200	3,300
1806, All kinds	839,576							
1806, Normal Date		75	100	120	200	425	1,100	2,700
1806, 6 Over 5		75	100	120	200	425	1,100	2,700
1806, 6 Over Inv 6		80	120	200	450	900	2,200	4,750
1807	301,076	75	100	120	200	425	1,100	2,700

CAPPED BUST, LETTERED EDGE (1807–1836)

John Reich designed this capped head concept of Liberty. Reich's design of Liberty facing left was used on all U.S. silver denominations for the next 30 years.

G-4 GOOD—Date and letters legible. Bust worn smooth with outline distinct.
VG-8 VERY GOOD—LIBERTY faint. Legends distinguishable. Clasp at shoulder visible; curl above it nearly smooth.
F-12 FINE—Clasp and adjacent curl clearly outlined with slight details.
VF-20 VERY FINE—Clasp at shoulder clear. Wear visible on highest point of curl. Hair over brow distinguishable.
EF-40 EXTREMELY FINE—Clasp and adjacent curl fairly sharp. Brow and hair above distinct. Curls well defined.
AU-50 ABOUT UNCIRCULATED—Trace of wear on hair over eye and over ear.
MS-60 UNCIRCULATED—No trace of wear. Light blemishes. Possible slide marks from storage handling.
MS-63 CHOICE UNCIRCULATED—Some distracting contact marks or blemishes in prime focal areas. Impaired luster possible.

See next page for chart.

First Style (1807–1808)

	Mintage	G-4	VG-8	F-12	VF-20	EF-40	AU-50	MS-60	MS-63
1807	750,500	$25	$40	$60	$125	$220	$800	$1,500	$3,750
1808, 8 Over 7	*	25	30	40	75	160	400	1,000	2,750
1808	1,368,600	23	27	35	50	115	250	800	1,400

* Included in number below.

Remodeled Portrait and Eagle (1809–1836)

	Mintage	G-4	VG-8	F-12	VF-20	EF-40	AU-50	MS-60	MS-63
1809	1,405,810	$22	$26	$35	$50	$100	$250	$700	$1,600
1810	1,276,276	22	26	35	45	100	225	675	1,500
1811	1,203,644	22	26	34	40	85	175	600	1,100

1812, 2 Over 1

1813, 50 C. Over UNI

1814, 4 Over 3

	Mintage	G-4	VG-8	F-12	VF-20	EF-40	AU-50	MS-60	MS-63
1812, All kinds	1,628,059								
1812, 2 Over 1		$22	$28	$38	$65	$150	$250	$1,000	$2,200
1812		20	27	35	55	100	200	500	1,000
1813	1,241,903	22	27	35	55	100	180	500	1,000
1813, 50 C. Over UNI		22	27	40	70	140	300	700	2,100
1814, All kinds	1,039,075								
1814, 4 Over 3		22	28	45	80	150	350	800	2,100
1814		22	27	38	55	100	180	500	1,100

* Included in number above.

1817, 7 Over 3

1817, 7 Over 4

1817, Punctuated Date

	Mintage	G-4	VG-8	F-12	VF-20	EF-40	AU-50	MS-60	MS-63
1815, 5 Over 2	47,150	$475	$700	$800	$1,100	$2,000	$2,750	$5,000	$14,000
1817, All kinds	1,215,567								
1817, 7 Over 3		30	45	100	200	350	650	1,500	4,500
1817, 7 Over 4				90,000	110,000	150,000			
1817, Dated 181.7		22	27	37	45	85	170	475	1,000
1817		22	27	37	42	65	150	450	1,000

1818, 2nd 8 Over 7

1819, 9 Over 8

1820, 20 Over 19

	Mintage	G-4	VG-8	F-12	VF-20	EF-40	AU-50	MS-60	MS-63
1818, 8 Over 7	*	$22	$27	$32	$40	$65	$170	$500	$900
1818	1,960,322	22	27	32	40	65	150	450	825
1819, 9 Over 8	*	22	27	32	40	65	150	450	825
1819	2,208,000	20	27	32	40	65	150	450	825
1820, 20 Over 19	*	22	32	37	55	120	300	600	900
1820	751,122	20	27	32	40	60	140	475	850
1821	1,305,797	20	27	32	40	60	140	450	850
1822	1,559,573	20	27	32	40	60	140	475	900
1823	1,694,200	20	27	32	40	60	140	375	800

* Included in number below.

"Various Dates" *Probably 4 Over 2 Over 0.*

1824, 4 Over 1

1828, Curl Base, Knob 2

1828, Square Base 2

	Mintage	G-4	VG-8	F-12	VF-20	EF-40	AU-50	MS-60	MS-63
1824, All kinds	3,504,954								
1824, 4 Over Various Dates		$20	$25	$32	$40	$60	$140	$350	$750
1824, 4 Over 1		20	27	32	40	60	140	375	750
1824		20	25	32	40	60	140	400	775
1825	2,943,166	20	25	32	40	60	140	325	725
1826	4,004,180	20	25	32	40	60	140	325	725
1827, All kinds	5,493,400								
1827, 7 Over 6		22	32	37	45	75	145	425	800
1827		20	25	32	40	60	140	325	725
1828, All kinds	3,075,200								
1828, Curl Base No Knob 2		20	25	32	40	60	140	325	725
1828, Curl Base Knob 2		25	35	45	55	75	150	485	750
1828, Square Base 2		20	25	32	40	60	140	325	725

Chart continued on next page.

	Mintage	G-4	VG-8	F-12	VF-20	EF-40	AU-50	MS-60	MS-63
1829, 9 Over 7	*	$20	$27	$35	$45	$75	$170	$450	$1,000
1829	3,712,156	20	25	32	40	60	140	400	850
1830	4,764,800	20	25	32	40	60	140	400	850
1831	5,873,660	20	25	32	40	60	140	400	850
1832	4,797,000	20	25	32	40	60	140	400	850
1833	5,206,000	20	25	32	40	60	140	400	850
1834	6,412,004	20	25	32	40	60	140	400	850
1835	5,352,006	20	25	32	40	60	140	400	850
1836	6,545,000	20	25	32	40	60	140	400	850
1836, 50 Over 00	*	25	35	45	65	100	225	675	1,700

* Included in regular mintage.

CAPPED BUST, REEDED EDGE (1836–1839)

G-4 GOOD—LIBERTY barely discernible on headband.
VG-8 VERY GOOD—Some letters in LIBERTY clear.
F-12 FINE—LIBERTY complete but faint.
VF-20 VERY FINE—LIBERTY sharp. Shoulder clasp clear.
EF-40 EXTREMELY FINE—LIBERTY sharp and strong. Hair details visible.
AU-50 ABOUT UNCIRCULATED—Slight trace of wear on cap, cheek, and hair above forehead, and on eagle's claws, wing tops, and head.
MS-60 UNCIRCULATED—No trace of wear. Light blemishes.
MS-63 CHOICE UNCIRCULATED—Some distracting contact marks or blemishes in prime focal areas. Impaired luster possible.

Reverse 50 CENTS (1836–1837)

	Mintage	G-4	VG-8	F-12	VF-20	EF-40	AU-50	MS-60	MS-63
1836	*1,200*	$400	$500	$650	$900	$1,100	$2,000	$4,500	$8,000
1837	3,629,820	20	22	35	50	75	150	425	900

Reverse HALF DOL. (1838–1839)

On half dollars of 1838 and 1839, the mintmark appears on the obverse; on those thereafter, it is on the reverse below the eagle.

	Mintage	G-4	VG-8	F-12	VF-20	EF-40	AU-50	MS-60	MS-63
1838	3,546,000	$20	$25	$35	$50	$75	$150	$425	$900
1838O	20						90,000	150,000	
1839	1,392,976	20	25	35	50	75	150	525	925
1839O	178,976	65	90	125	175	325	550	1,500	2,750

LIBERTY SEATED (1839–1891)

G-4 GOOD—Scant rim. LIBERTY on shield worn off. Date and letters legible.
VG-8 VERY GOOD—Rim fairly defined. Some letters in LIBERTY evident.
F-12 FINE—LIBERTY complete, but weak.
VF-20 VERY FINE—LIBERTY mostly sharp.
EF-40 EXTREMELY FINE—LIBERTY entirely sharp. Scroll edges and clasp distinct.
AU-50 ABOUT UNCIRCULATED—Slight wear on Liberty's breast and knees; eagle's head, claws, and wing tops.
MS-60 UNCIRCULATED—No trace of wear. Light blemishes.
MS-63 CHOICE UNCIRCULATED—Some distracting blemishes in prime focal areas. Impaired luster possible.
PF-63 CHOICE PROOF—Reflective surfaces with only a few blemishes in secondary focal places. No major flaws.

Variety 1 – No Motto Above Eagle (1839–1853)

No Drapery From Elbow

Drapery From Elbow (Starting 1839)

1842, Small Date

Mintage	G-4	VG-8	F-12	VF-20	EF-40	AU-50	MS-60	MS-63
1839, No Drapery From Elbow . . . *	$18	$30	$50	$140	$325	$500	$2,600	$8,500
1839, Drapery. 1,972,400	11	13	19	30	50	65	275	950
1840 1,435,008	11	14	21	35	60	70	275	650
1840O 855,100	11	13	18	30	48	60	300	800
1841. 310,000	13	15	22	65	110	140	500	800
1841O 401,000	10	14	19	30	50	65	375	500
1842, Small Date 2,012,764	10	13	20	35	55	70	450	950
1842, Medium Date . . . . **	10	13	19	30	50	65	300	850
1842O, Small Date 754,000	200	375	600	1,100	1,900	2,750	4,750	—
1842O, Medium Date . . . . **	10	12	18	28	45	65	300	1,500
1843 3,844,000	10	12	18	28	45	65	300	425
1843O. 2,268,000	10	12	18	28	45	65	300	450
1844 1,766,000	10	12	18	28	45	65	300	425
1844O. 2,005,000	10	12	18	28	45	65	300	800
1845. 589,000	11	13	20	32	50	90	380	1,000
1845O. 2,094,000	10	12	17	24	45	65	360	425
1846 2,210,000	10	12	17	24	45	65	300	500
1846, 6 Over Horizontal 6 . . . . . **	40	75	120	175	300	500	1,000	4,000
1846O. 2,304,000	11	13	17	24	45	65	360	540
1847 1,156,000	10	12	17	24	45	65	300	425
1847O. 2,584,000	10	12	17	24	45	65	300	700
1848. 580,000	14	18	28	40	75	180	420	575
1848O. 3,180,000	10	12	17	24	45	65	360	575
1849 1,252,000	10	12	17	24	45	65	340	500
1849O. 2,310,000	10	12	17	24	45	65	300	650
1850. 227,000	90	100	175	190	300	350	725	1,500
1850O. 2,456,000	10	12	17	24	45	65	300	425

* Included in number below. **Included in number above.

Chart continued on next page.

	Mintage	G-4	VG-8	F-12	VF-20	EF-40	AU-50	MS-60	MS-63
1851	200,750	$60	$100	$175	$250	$260	$275	$700	$1,200
1851O	402,000	10	12	18	23	45	65	300	425
1852	77,130	125	180	280	360	400	550	800	1,100
1852O	144,000	20	30	45	70	180	225	1,000	3,000
1853O			100,000	150,000	250,000				

Variety 2 – Arrows at Date, Rays Around Eagle (1853)

	Mintage	G-4	VG-8	F-12	VF-20	EF-40	AU-50	MS-60	MS-63
1853	3,532,708	$11	$14	$20	$60	$120	$300	$950	$1,500
1853O	1,328,000	12	16	22	65	130	340	1,400	2,000

Variety 3 – Arrows at Date, No Rays (1854–1855)

	Mintage	G-4	VG-8	F-12	VF-20	EF-40	AU-50	MS-60	MS-63
1854	2,982,000	$10	$12	$18	$30	$55	$85	$360	$650
1854O	5,240,000	10	12	18	30	55	85	360	650
1855, Over 1854	*	15	35	70	120	220	275	800	1,300
1855	759,500	10	12	18	30	55	85	360	650
1855O	3,688,000	10	12	18	30	55	85	360	650
1855S	129,950	150	185	300	600	1,400	2,600	6,750	—

* Included in number below.

Variety 1 Resumed (1856–1866; Weight Standard of 1853)

	Mintage	G-4	VG-8	F-12	VF-20	EF-40	AU-50	MS-60	MS-63
1856	938,000	$10	$12	$18	$23	$40	$80	$220	$400
1856O	2,658,000	10	12	20	24	40	80	220	400
1856S	211,000	15	20	37	90	200	425	1,700	—
1857	1,988,000	10	12	18	23	40	80	220	400
1857O	818,000	10	12	20	24	40	80	240	650
1857S	158,000	18	30	45	85	180	400	1,400	—

	Mintage	G-4	VG-8	F-12	VF-20	EF-40	AU-50	MS-60	MS-63	PF-63
1858 . . . . *(300+)*	4,225,700	$10	$11	$18	$28	$40	$80	$220	$400	$1,300
1858O	7,294,000	10	11	18	23	40	80	220	400	
1858S	476,000	12	14	22	30	55	120	525	1,500	
1859 . . . . (800)	747,200	10	11	18	23	45	85	225	450	800
1859O	2,834,000	10	11	18	23	45	85	225	450	
1859S	566,000	12	14	22	30	80	85	250	1,000	
1860 . . . . (1,000)	302,700	12	14	20	28	50	85	225	450	600
1860O	1,290,000	10	11	18	23	45	80	225	450	
1860S	472,000	12	14	22	25	45	80	350	1,000	
1861 . . . . (1,000)	2,887,400	10	11	18	23	45	80	225	400	600
1861O	2,532,633	10	11	18	23	45	80	225	400	
1861S	939,500	10	11	18	23	45	80	275	800	
1862 . . . . (550)	253,000	14	20	25	50	80	100	450	650	600
1862S	1,352,000	10	11	18	23	45	80	275	450	
1863 . . . . (460)	503,200	12	16	22	28	55	85	275	675	600
1863S	916,000	10	11	18	23	45	85	275	450	
1864 . . . . (470)	379,100	14	18	24	32	55	100	275	450	600
1864S	658,000	10	11	18	23	45	85	275	900	
1865 . . . . (500)	511,400	12	14	22	28	50	90	300	450	600
1865S	675,000	10	11	18	23	45	85	275	400	
1866S, No Motto	60,000	50	90	150	200	450	800	2,300	4,000	

Variety 4 – Motto Above Eagle (1866–1873, 1875–1891)

	Mintage	G-4	VG-8	F-12	VF-20	EF-40	AU-50	MS-60	MS-63	PF-63
1866 . . . . .(725)	744,900	$9	$11	$17	$23	$45	$80	$220	$450	$400
1866S	994,000	9	11	17	23	45	90	320	800	
1867 . . . . .(625)	449,300	11	15	25	35	65	95	275	500	400
1867S	1,196,000	9	10	17	22	45	80	300	650	
1868 . . . . .(600)	417,600	13	15	23	30	70	120	325	475	400
1868S	1,160,000	9	11	17	23	40	90	325	600	
1869 . . . . .(600)	795,300	9	11	17	23	40	90	275	450	400
1869S	656,000	9	11	17	23	42	90	350	850	
1870. . . .(1,000)	633,900	9	11	17	23	40	80	300	450	400
1870CC	54,617	300	475	900	2,000	5,000	10,000	—	—	
1870S	1,004,000	9	11	17	23	45	95	300	1,000	
1871 . . . . .(960)	1,203,600	9	11	17	23	45	95	275	450	400
1871CC	153,950	65	100	170	300	900	1,500	6,500	22,000	
1871S	2,178,000	9	11	17	23	42	90	300	500	
1872 . . . . .(950)	880,600	9	11	17	23	40	90	275	550	400
1872CC	257,000	30	45	90	180	450	900	2,700	17,000	
1872S	580,000	10	15	22	35	75	140	425	1,000	
1873 . . . . .(600)	801,200	9	11	17	23	40	95	250	450	400
1873CC	122,500	60	100	150	275	650	1,900	4,500	27,000	

Variety 5 – Arrows at Date (1873–1874)

	Mintage	G-4	VG-8	F-12	VF-20	EF-40	AU-50	MS-60	MS-63	PF-63
1873 . . . . .(550)	1,815,150	$13	$19	$25	$48	$130	$160	$500	$900	$1,100
1873CC	214,560	60	95	150	400	800	1,100	2,750	8,500	
1873S	228,000	20	30	45	95	180	300	950	2,750	
1874 . . . . .(700)	2,359,600	13	19	22	48	130	160	500	900	1,100
1874CC	59,000	125	200	400	700	1,100	2,000	4,500	9,500	
1874S	394,000	16	25	40	90	150	250	875	1,600	

Variety 4 Resumed (1875–1891)

	Mintage	G-4	VG-8	F-12	VF-20	EF-40	AU-50	MS-60	MS-63	PF-63
1875 . . . . .(700)	6,026,800	$9	$10	$16	$22	$35	$75	$220	$300	$400
1875CC	1,008,000	9	12	25	35	60	100	275	500	
1875S	3,200,000	9	10	16	22	35	75	220	300	
1876. . . .(1,150)	8,418,000	9	10	16	22	35	75	220	300	400
1876CC	1,956,000	9	10	16	22	40	80	275	575	

Chart continued on next page.

	Mintage	G-4	VG-8	F-12	VF-20	EF-40	AU-50	MS-60	MS-63	PF-63
1876S	4,528,000	$9	$10	$16	$22	$35	$75	$220	$300	
1877 (510)	8,304,000	9	10	16	22	35	75	220	300	$400
1877CC	1,420,000	9	10	16	22	40	85	260	500	
1877S	5,356,000	9	10	16	22	35	75	220	300	
1878 (800)	1,377,600	9	10	16	22	35	75	220	300	400
1878CC	62,000	125	200	300	600	1,200	1,800	3,000	10,500	
1878S	12,000	6,000	10,000	13,000	17,000	19,000	23,000	26,000	50,000	
1879 (1,100)	4,800	90	110	130	170	200	280	425	500	400
1880 (1,355)	8,400	90	110	130	170	190	250	375	500	400
1881 (975)	10,000	90	110	130	170	190	250	375	500	400
1882 (1,100)	4,400	100	120	180	200	210	280	425	500	400
1883 (1,039)	8,000	90	110	130	170	190	245	375	500	400
1884 (875)	4,400	100	120	180	200	210	280	450	525	400
1885 (930)	5,200	100	120	180	200	210	260	475	550	400
1886 (886)	5,000	100	120	180	200	210	260	475	550	400
1887 (710)	5,000	100	120	180	200	210	260	475	550	400
1888 (832)	12,001	90	120	130	170	190	250	425	500	400
1889 (711)	12,000	90	110	130	170	190	250	425	500	400
1890 (590)	12,000	90	110	130	170	190	250	425	500	400
1891 (600)	200,000	20	25	40	50	65	95	275	370	400

BARBER OR LIBERTY HEAD (1892–1915)

Like the dime and quarter dollar, this type was designed by Charles E. Barber, whose initial B is on the truncation of the neck.

G-4 GOOD—Date and legends legible. LIBERTY worn off headband.
VG-8 VERY GOOD—Some letters legible in LIBERTY.
F-12 FINE—LIBERTY nearly completely legible, but worn.
VF-20 VERY FINE—All letters in LIBERTY evenly plain.
EF-40 EXTREMELY FINE—LIBERTY bold, and its ribbon distinct.
AU-50 ABOUT UNCIRCULATED—Slight trace of wear above forehead, leaf tips, and cheek, and on eagle's head, tail, and wing tips.
MS-60 UNCIRCULATED—No trace of wear. Light blemishes.
MS-63 CHOICE UNCIRCULATED—Some distracting contact marks or blemishes in prime focal areas. Impaired luster possible.
PF-63 CHOICE PROOF—Reflective surfaces with only a few blemishes in secondary focal places. No major flaws.

Mintmark location on reverse, below eagle.

	Mintage	G-4	VG-8	F-12	VF-20	EF-40	AU-50	MS-60	MS-63	PF-63
1892 (1,245)	934,000	$10	$12	$28	$35	$140	$160	$220	$400	$400
1892O	390,000	110	150	190	210	250	275	460	850	
1892S	1,029,028	100	120	175	200	250	300	475	1,200	
1893 (792)	1,826,000	8	12	28	40	100	150	300	700	400
1893O	1,389,000	10	20	32	65	160	200	310	750	
1893S	740,000	60	80	100	160	240	325	620	1,500	
1894 (972)	1,148,000	10	20	32	60	130	170	270	500	400
1894O	2,138,000	7	10	30	50	130	160	260	500	
1894S	4,048,690	8	12	28	45	120	150	255	675	
1895 (880)	1,834,338	7	12	28	40	110	150	260	500	400
1895O	1,766,000	8	12	28	50	110	165	275	675	
1895S	1,108,086	10	14	35	60	125	175	275	650	
1896 (762)	950,000	8	10	28	50	110	150	275	425	425
1896O	924,000	14	17	60	85	175	300	650	2,500	
1896S	1,140,948	35	45	70	110	180	240	600	1,600	

	Mintage	G-4	VG-8	F-12	VF-20	EF-40	AU-50	MS-60	MS-63	PF-63
1897 . . . . .(731)	2,480,000	$5	$6	$15	$35	$65	$140	$220	$400	$425
1897O	632,000	50	100	200	325	400	550	800	1,600	
1897S	933,900	50	75	125	210	350	450	675	1,600	
1898 . . . . .(735)	2,956,000	5	6	13	30	75	150	200	400	425
1898O	874,000	10	25	100	125	185	250	450	1,600	
1898S	2,358,550	8	12	22	50	100	150	400	1,700	
1899 . . . . .(846)	5,538,000	5	6	14	30	65	140	200	400	425
1899O	1,724,000	8	10	22	50	100	160	325	700	
1899S	1,686,411	8	10	22	45	100	150	300	1,000	
1900 . . . . .(912)	4,762,000	5	6	14	35	65	140	200	400	400
1900O	2,744,000	6	8	20	40	125	160	325	1,450	
1900S	2,560,322	5	7	18	40	100	140	275	1,100	
1901 . . . . .(813)	4,268,000	5	6	14	30	60	150	200	400	400
1901O	1,124,000	6	9	25	60	140	200	700	2,600	
1901S	847,044	13	21	70	150	285	450	900	2,700	
1902 . . . . .(777)	4,922,000	5	6	14	30	60	150	200	450	400
1902O	2,526,000	5	7	18	35	90	150	350	1,750	
1902S	1,460,670	6	8	20	45	110	165	350	1,000	
1903 . . . . .(755)	2,278,000	5	6	14	35	70	150	210	750	400
1903O	2,100,000	5	7	16	40	90	160	300	1,000	
1903S	1,920,772	5	7	16	40	95	170	300	950	
1904 . . . . .(670)	2,992,000	5	6	14	30	65	140	200	550	400
1904O	1,117,600	8	11	28	90	150	225	550	1,500	
1904S	553,038	14	25	110	225	450	650	2,300	5,000	
1905 . . . . .(727)	662,000	8	9	30	50	110	140	230	700	400
1905O	505,000	10	15	40	75	135	175	350	850	
1905S	2,494,000	5	7	18	40	90	150	300	900	
1906 . . . . .(675)	2,638,000	5	6	14	36	75	120	200	375	400
1906D	4,028,000	5	6	15	36	75	120	200	375	
1906O	2,446,000	5	6	16	38	80	120	275	700	
1906S	1,740,154	5	6	18	40	90	120	275	525	
1907 . . . . .(575)	2,598,000	5	6	14	32	70	120	200	400	400
1907D	3,856,000	5	6	14	32	70	120	200	400	
1907O	3,946,600	5	6	14	32	70	140	220	400	
1907S	1,250,000	6	8	23	60	120	275	500	2,500	
1908 . . . . .(545)	1,354,000	5	6	14	30	70	120	200	400	400
1908D	3,280,000	5	6	14	30	65	120	200	400	
1908O	5,360,000	5	6	14	30	70	120	210	425	
1908S	1,644,828	5	6	20	42	100	170	350	1,200	
1909 . . . . .(650)	2,368,000	5	6	14	30	65	120	200	400	400
1909O	925,400	7	9	18	45	120	200	350	850	
1909S	1,764,000	5	6	14	32	90	140	260	550	
1910 . . . . .(551)	418,000	8	11	28	50	130	150	290	500	400
1910S	1,948,000	5	6	14	35	85	130	250	850	
1911 . . . . .(543)	1,406,000	5	6	14	28	65	120	180	400	400
1911D	695,080	5	6	15	30	75	125	240	425	
1911S	1,272,000	5	6	14	30	75	130	250	600	
1912 . . . . .(700)	1,550,000	5	6	14	28	70	120	200	400	400
1912D	2,300,800	5	6	14	28	70	120	200	400	
1912S	1,370,000	5	6	14	30	75	130	240	475	
1913 . . . . .(627)	188,000	25	30	85	150	220	350	500	800	500
1913D	534,000	5	6	16	35	90	120	225	425	
1913S	604,000	5	6	18	40	90	140	275	550	
1914 . . . . .(380)	124,230	55	65	120	220	290	425	550	900	700
1914S	992,000	5	6	14	30	80	140	275	500	
1915 . . . . .(450)	138,000	40	65	100	140	210	370	600	1,100	600
1915D	1,170,400	5	6	12	28	60	130	200	400	
1915S	1,604,000	5	6	12	28	60	130	200	400	

LIBERTY WALKING (1916–1947)

This type was designed by Adolph A. Weinman. The designer's monogram AAW appears under the tip of the wing feathers. On the 1916 coins and some of the 1917 coins, the mintmark is located on the obverse below the motto.

G-4 GOOD—Rims defined. Motto IN GOD WE TRUST legible.
VG-8 VERY GOOD—Motto distinct. About half of skirt lines at left clear.
F-12 FINE—All skirt lines evident, but worn in spots. Clear details in sandal below motto.
VF-20 VERY FINE—Skirt lines sharp, including leg area. Little wear on breast and right arm.
EF-40 EXTREMELY FINE—All skirt lines bold.
AU-50 ABOUT UNCIRCULATED—Slight trace of wear on Liberty's head, knee, and breast tips and on eagle's claws and head.
MS-60 UNCIRCULATED—No trace of wear. Light blemishes.
MS-63 CHOICE UNCIRCULATED—Some distracting contact marks or blemishes in prime focal areas. Impaired luster possible.
PF-63 CHOICE PROOF—Reflective surfaces with only a few blemishes in secondary focal places. No major flaws.
PF-65 GEM PROOF—Brilliant surfaces with no noticeable blemishes or flaws. A few scattered, barely noticeable marks or hairlines possible.

Mintmark Locations

Choice Uncirculated well-struck specimens are worth more than values listed.

	Mintage	G-4	VG-8	F-12	VF-20	EF-40	AU-50	MS-60	MS-63
1916	608,000	$16	$25	$40	$80	$120	$145	$180	$250
1916D, Obverse	1,014,400	15	22	35	70	115	145	180	300
1916S, Obverse	508,000	50	60	90	220	325	400	650	1,200
1917	12,292,000	5	6	7	12	20	35	75	120
1917D, Obverse	765,400	10	15	30	65	100	150	275	650
1917D, Reverse	1,940,000	6	8	25	60	140	250	450	950
1917S, Obverse	952,000	12	20	50	165	375	700	1,300	2,500
1917S, Reverse	5,554,000	5	6	8	20	38	85	175	1,000
1918	6,634,000	5	6	8	35	90	150	300	650
1918D	3,853,040	5	6	8	45	120	250	650	1,350
1918S	10,282,000	5	6	8	20	40	100	250	1,300
1919	962,000	10	15	35	150	275	400	650	1,800
1919D	1,165,000	8	12	40	140	350	850	190	8,500
1919S	1,552,000	8	12	35	140	400	900	1,600	5,500
1920	6,372,000	5	6	8	22	45	85	150	350
1920D	1,551,000	6	7	30	120	240	450	750	2,200
1920S	4,624,000	5	6	10	40	110	220	400	1,500
1921	246,000	90	120	175	500	1,000	1,600	2,500	5,000
1921D	208,000	175	200	300	600	1,200	2,000	3,000	6,500
1921S	548,000	25	35	110	450	2,600	4,500	7,000	16,000
1923S	2,178,000	6	7	12	50	250	650	1,000	1,800
1927S	2,392,000	4	5	8	25	70	200	600	1,200
1928S	1,940,000	4	5	9	35	75	220	600	1,300
1929D	1,001,200	4	5	8	15	45	140	225	400
1929S	1,902,000	4	5	8	15	50	140	225	500

	Mintage	G-4	VG-8	F-12	VF-20	EF-40	AU-50	MS-60	MS-63	PF-63	PF-65
1933S	1,786,000	$5	$6	$7	$9.00	$30	$140	$320	$650		
1934	6,964,000	4	4	4	4.00	6	14	40	50		
1934D	2,361,000	4	4	4	4.50	18	45	75	125		
1934S	3,652,000	4	4	4	4.00	15	60	175	450		
1935	9,162,000	4	4	4	4.00	5	12	25	40		
1935D	3,003,800	4	4	4	4.00	18	30	75	125		
1935S	3,854,000	4	4	4	4.00	18	60	125	235		
1936 (3,901)	12,614,000	4	4	4	4.00	5	12	27	40	$950	$3,500
1936D	4,252,400	4	4	4	4.00	12	20	45	60		
1936S	3,884,000	4	4	4	4.00	12	22	75	90		
1937 (5,728)	9,522,000	4	4	4	4.00	5	12	22	35	300	800
1937D	1,676,000	4	4	4	4.50	18	50	120	150		
1937S	2,090,000	4	4	4	4.25	12	32	85	120		
1938 (8,152)	4,110,000	4	4	4	4.00	6	25	35	65	275	650
1938D	491,600	50	60	70	80.00	90	140	275	350		
1939 (8,808)	6,812,000	3	3	3	4.00	6	12	22	35	250	600
1939D	4,267,800	3	3	3	4.00	6	12	22	40		
1939S	2,552,000	3	3	3	4.00	10	35	70	90		

	Mintage	VG-8	F-12	VF-20	EF-40	AU-50	MS-60	MS-63	PF-63	PF-65
1940 (11,279)	9,156,000	$4	$4	$4	$4.25	$5	$15	$22	$225	$575
1940S	4,550,000	4	4	4	4.25	6	30	40		
1941 (15,412)	24,192,000	4	4	4	4.25	5	15	30	235	550
1941D	11,248,400	4	4	4	4.25	5	18	35		
1941S	8,098,000	4	4	4	4.25	20	32	55		
1942 (21,120)	47,818,000	4	4	4	4.25	5	15	25	235	550
1942D	10,973,800	4	4	4	4.25	5	18	35		
1942S	12,708,000	4	4	4	4.25	5	20	28		
1943	53,190,000	4	4	4	4.25	5	15	21		
1943D	11,346,000	4	4	4	4.25	5	22	32		
1943S	13,450,000	4	4	4	4.25	5	20	25		
1944	28,206,000	4	4	4	4.25	5	15	21		
1944D	9,769,000	4	4	4	4.25	5	18	25		
1944S	8,904,000	4	4	4	4.25	5	22	28		
1945	31,502,000	4	4	4	4.25	5	15	21		
1945D	9,966,800	4	4	4	4.25	5	15	22		
1945S	10,156,000	4	4	4	4.25	5	15	25		
1946	12,118,000	4	4	4	4.25	5	15	21		
1946D	2,151,000	4	4	4	4.25	5	15	21		
1946S	3,724,000	4	4	4	4.25	5	15	21		
1947	4,094,000	4	4	4	4.25	5	15	21		
1947D	3,900,600	4	4	4	4.25	5	15	21		

FRANKLIN (1948–1963)

The Benjamin Franklin half dollar and the Roosevelt dime were both designed by John R. Sinnock. His initials appear below the shoulder.

VF-20 VERY FINE—At least half of the lower and upper incused lines on rim of Liberty Bell on reverse visible.
EF-40 EXTREMELY FINE—Wear spots at top of end of Franklin's curls and hair at back of ears. Wear evident at top and on lettering of Liberty Bell.
MS-60 UNCIRCULATED—No trace of wear. Light blemishes.
MS-63 CHOICE UNCIRCULATED—Some distracting contact marks or blemishes in prime focal areas. Impaired luster possible.
MS-65 GEM UNCIRCULATED—Only light, scattered contact marks that are not distracting. Strong luster, good eye appeal.
PF-63 CHOICE PROOF—Reflective surfaces with only a few blemishes in secondary focal places. No major flaws.
PF-65 GEM PROOF—Brilliant surfaces with no noticeable blemishes or flaws. A few scattered, barely noticeable marks or hairlines possible.

Mintmark Location

Choice, well-struck Uncirculated halves with full bell lines command higher prices.

	Mintage	VF-20	EF-40	MS-60	MS-63	MS-65	PF-63	PF-65
1948	3,006,814	$4.00	$4.00	$6.00	$9.00	$38		
1948D	4,028,600	4.00	4.00	4.50	7.50	65		
1949	5,614,000	4.00	4.50	15.00	20.00	70		
1949D	4,120,600	4.00	5.00	15.00	23.00	385		
1949S	3,744,000	4.50	8.00	25.00	35.00	60		
1950 (51,386)	7,742,123	4.00	4.00	10.00	16.00	50	$115	$200
1950D	8,031,600	4.00	4.00	9.00	15.00	225		
1951 (57,500)	16,802,102	4.00	4.00	4.50	8.00	30	65	150
1951D	9,475,200	4.00	4.50	11.00	17.00	120		
1951S	13,696,000	4.00	4.00	9.00	15.00	50		
1952 (81,980)	21,192,093	4.00	4.00	4.50	8.00	27	35	100
1952D	25,395,600	4.00	4.00	4.50	6.00	100		
1952S	5,526,000	4.00	4.50	15.00	20.00	55		
1953 (128,800)	2,668,120	4.00	4.50	6.00	10.00	100	26	60
1953D	20,900,400	4.00	4.00	4.50	6.00	50		
1953S	4,148,000	4.00	4.00	8.00	12.00	30		
1954 (233,300)	13,188,202	4.00	4.00	4.50	5.00	27	18	45
1954D	25,445,580	4.00	4.00	4.50	5.50	65		
1954S	4,993,400	4.00	4.00	4.50	5.50	25		
1955 (378,200)	2,498,181	4.50	5.00	6.00	7.50	25	14	40
1956 (669,384)	4,032,000	4.00	4.00	4.50	6.00	20	7	20
1957 (1,247,952)	5,114,000	4.00	4.00	4.50	5.50	20	7	12
1957D	19,966,850	4.00	4.00	4.50	5.50	20		
1958 (875,652)	4,042,000	4.00	4.00	4.50	6.00	25	7	15
1958D	23,962,412	4.00	4.00	4.50	5.50	20		
1959 (1,149,291)	6,200,000	4.00	4.00	4.50	5.50	50	5	13
1959D	13,053,750	4.00	4.00	4.50	5.50	65		
1960 (1,691,602)	6,024,000	4.00	4.00	4.50	5.50	65	5	13
1960D	18,215,812	4.00	4.00	4.50	6.00	225		
1961 (3,028,244)	8,290,000	4.00	4.00	4.50	5.00	70	5	17
1961D	20,276,442	4.00	4.00	4.50	5.00	110		
1962 (3,218,019)	9,714,000	4.00	4.00	4.50	5.00	90	5	12
1962D	35,473,281	4.00	4.00	4.50	5.00	120		
1963 (3,075,645)	22,164,000	4.00	4.00	4.50	5.00	30	5	13
1963D	67,069,292	4.00	4.00	4.50	5.00	30		

KENNEDY (1964 TO DATE)

Gilroy Roberts, then chief engraver of the Mint, designed the obverse of this coin. His stylized initials are on the truncation of the forceful bust of President John F. Kennedy. The reverse, which uses the eagle from the Great Seal for the motif, is the work of assistant engraver Frank Gasparro.

Mintmark Location (1964)

Mintmark Location (1968 to Date)

Silver Coinage (1964)

	Mintage	MS-63	PF-63	PF-65
1964	(3,950,762) . . . 273,304,004	$4.50	$5	$6
1964D	156,205,446	4.50		

Silver Clad Coinage (1965–1970)

	Mintage	MS-63	PF-63	PF-65
1965	65,879,366	$1.25		
1966	108,984,932	1.25		
1967	295,046,978	1.25		
1968D	246,951,930	1.25		
1968S	(3,041,506)		$1.50	$3
1969D	129,881,800	$1.25		
1969S	(2,934,631)		$1.50	$3
1970D	2,150,000	7.00		
1970S	(2,632,810)		4.00	8

Clad Coinage and Silver Proofs (1971 to Date)

	Mintage	MS-63	PF-63	PF-65
1971	155,164,000	$0.55		
1971D	302,097,424	0.55		
1971S	(3,220,733)		$1.50	$3
1972	153,180,000	0.60		
1972D	141,890,000	0.60		
1972S	(3,260,996)		1.50	3
1973	64,964,000	$0.55		
1973D	83,171,400	0.55		
1973S	(2,760,339)		$1.50	$3
1974	201,596,000	0.55		
1974D	79,066,300	0.55		
1974S	(2,612,568)		1.50	3

Bicentennial (1976)

	Mintage	MS-63	PF-63	PF-65
1976, Clad	234,308,000	$0.55		
1976D, Clad	287,565,248	0.55		
1976S, Clad	(7,059,099)		$0.75	$1.25
1976S, Silver	*11,000,000*	$1.50		
1976S, Silver	*(4,000,000)*		$2.00	$3.50

Eagle Reverse Resumed (1977)

	Mintage	MS-63	PF-63	PF-65
1977	43,598,000	$0.60		
1977D	31,449,106	0.60		
1977S	(3,251,152)		$1.00	$1.25
1978	14,350,000	0.60		
1978D	13,765,799	1.00		
1978S	(3,127,781)		1.00	1.50
1979	68,312,000	0.55		
1979D	15,815,422	0.55		
1979S	(3,677,175)			
Filled S			1.00	1.25
Clear S			6.00	9.00
1980P	44,134,000	0.55		
1980D	33,456,449	0.55		
1980S	(3,554,806)		1.00	1.50
1981P	29,544,000	0.75		
1981D	27,839,533	0.55		
1981S	(4,063,083)		1.00	6.00
1982P	10,819,000	1.50		
1982D	13,140,102	1.50		
1982S	(3,857,479)		1.00	1.50
1983P	34,139,000	1.75		
1983D	32,472,244	1.75		
1983S	(3,279,126)		1.00	1.75
1984P	26,029,000	0.75		
1984D	26,262,158	0.75		
1984S	(3,065,110)		1.00	2.00
1985P	18,706,962	1.50		
1985D	19,814,034	1.25		
1985S	(3,362,821)		1.00	1.75
1986P	13,107,633	2.50		
1986D	15,336,145	2.00		
1986S	(3,010,497)		4.00	4.50
1987P **(a)**	2,890,758	2.00		
1987D **(a)**	2,890,758	2.00		
1987S	(4,227,728)		1.00	1.75
1988P	13,626,000	1.50		
1988D	12,000,096	1.00		
1988S	(3,262,948)		2.00	2.50
1989P	24,542,000	1.00		
1989D	23,000,216	0.90		
1989S	(3,220,194)		1.50	3.00
1990P	22,278,000	1.00		
1990D	20,096,242	1.10		
1990S	(3,299,559)		1.50	2.00
1991P	14,874,000	0.75		
1991D	15,054,678	1.25		
1991S	(2,867,787)		4.00	5.00
1992P	17,628,000	0.50		
1992D	17,000,106	1.00		
1992S	(2,858,981)		3.00	3.50
1992S, Silver	(1,317,579)		5.00	6.00
1993P	15,510,000	0.50		
1993D	15,000,006	0.50		
1993S	(2,633,439)		5.00	6.00
1993S, Silver	(761,353)		10.00	15.00
1994P	23,718,000	0.50		
1994D	23,828,110	$0.50		
1994S	(2,484,594)		$3.00	$4
1994S, Silver	(785,329)		12.00	16
1995P	26,496,000	0.50		
1995D	26,288,000	0.50		
1995S	(2,117,496)		10.00	14
1995S, Silver	(679,985)		40.00	60
1996P	24,442,000	0.50		
1996D	24,744,000	0.50		
1996S	(1,750,244)		3.00	5
1996S, Silver	(775,021)		20.00	25
1997P	20,882,000	0.50		
1997D	19,876,000	0.50		
1997S	(2,055,000)		9.00	14
1997S, Silver	(741,678)		40.00	60
1998P	15,646,000	0.50		
1998D	15,064,000	0.50		
1998S	(2,086,507)		5.00	7
1998S, Silver	878,792		10.00	13
1998S, Silver, Matte Finish			125.00	150
1999P	8,900,000	0.55		
1999D	10,682,000	0.55		
1999S	(2,543,401)		3.00	5
1999S, Silver	(804,565)		8.00	13
2000P	22,600,000	0.60		
2000D	19,466,000	0.60		
2000S	(3,082,483)		2.00	3
2000S, Silver	(965,421)		5.00	7
2001P **(a)**	21,200,000	4.00		
2001D	19,504,000	0.55		
2001S	(2,294,909)		3.25	4
2001S, Silver	(889,697)		6.00	7
2002P **(a)**	3,100,000	0.65		
2002D **(a)**	2,500,000	0.65		
2002S	(2,319,766)		2.00	3
2002S, Silver	(892,229)		6.00	7
2003P **(a)**	2,500,000	0.65		
2003D **(a)**	2,500,000	0.65		
2003S	(2,172,684)		2.00	3
2003S, Silver	(1,125,755)		3.25	5
2004P **(a)**	2,900,000	0.65		
2004D **(a)**	2,900,000	0.65		
2004S	(1,789,488)		2.00	3
2004S, Silver	(1,175,934)		3.25	5
2005P **(a)**	*3,800,000*	0.65		
2005D **(a)**	*3,500,000*	0.65		
2005S	*(2,275,000)*		2.00	
2005S, Silver	*(1,069,679)*		3.25	5
2006P(**a)**	*2,400,000*	0.65		
2006D **(a)**	*2,000,000*	0.65		
2006S	*(1,934,965)*		2.00	
2006S, Silver	*(988,140)*		3.25	5
2007P **(a)**		0.65		
2007D **(a)**		0.65		
2007S			2.00	
2007S, Silver			3.25	5

a. Not issued for circulation.

The silver dollar was authorized by Congress April 2, 1792. Its weight was specified at 416 grains and its fineness at .8924. The first issues appeared in 1794, and until 1804 all silver dollars had the value stamped on the edge: HUNDRED CENTS, ONE DOLLAR OR UNIT. After a lapse in coinage of the silver dollar during the period 1804 to 1835, coins were made with either plain (1836 only) or reeded edges and the value was placed on the reverse side.

The weight was changed by the law of January 18, 1837 to 412-1/2 grains, fineness .900. The coinage was discontinued by the Act of February 12, 1873 and reauthorized by the Act of February 28, 1878. The dollar was again discontinued after 1935, and since then copper-nickel and other base metal pieces have been coined for circulation.

FLOWING HAIR (1794–1795)

AG-3 ABOUT GOOD—Clear enough to identify.
G-4 GOOD—Date and letters legible. Main devices outlined, but lacking in detail.
VG-8 VERY GOOD—Major details discernible. Letters well formed but worn.
F-12 FINE—Hair ends distinguishable. Top hair lines visible, but otherwise worn smooth.
VF-20 VERY FINE—Some detail visible in hair in center. Other details more bold.
EF-40 EXTREMELY FINE—Hair well defined but with some wear.
AU-50 ABOUT UNCIRCULATED—Slight trace of wear on tips of highest curls; breast feathers usually weak.
MS-60 UNCIRCULATED—No trace of wear. Light blemishes.

	Mintage	AG-3	G-4	VG-8	F-12	VF-20	EF-40	AU-50	MS-60
1794	1,758	$14,000	$23,000	$38,000	$46,000	$80,000	$140,000	$200,000	—
1795	160,295	425	800	1,000	2,000	3,000	8,000	11,000	$26,000

DRAPED BUST (1795–1804)
Small Eagle Reverse (1795–1798)

AG-3 ABOUT GOOD—Clear enough to identify.
G-4 GOOD—Bust outlined, no detail. Date legible, some leaves evident.
VG-8 VERY GOOD—Drapery worn except deepest folds. Hair lines smooth.
F-12 FINE—All drapery lines distinguishable. Some detail visible in hair lines near cheek and neck.
VF-20 VERY FINE—Left side of drapery worn smooth.
EF-40 EXTREMELY FINE—Drapery distinctly visible. Hair well outlined and detailed.
AU-50 ABOUT UNCIRCULATED—Slight trace of wear on the bust shoulder and hair to left of forehead, as well as on eagle's breast and top edges of wings.
MS-60 UNCIRCULATED—No trace of wear. Light blemishes.

	Mintage	AG-3	G-4	VG-8	F-12	VF-20	EF-40	AU-50	MS-60
1795, Bust Type	*42,738*	$375	$650	$900	$1,500	$2,500	$5,500	$8,500	$21,000
1796	79,920	375	650	900	1,500	2,500	5,500	8,500	21,000
1797	7,776	375	650	900	1,500	2,500	5,500	8,500	21,000
1798	327,536	375	650	900	1,500	2,500	5,500	9,000	21,000

Heraldic Eagle Reverse (1798–1804)

G-4 GOOD—Letters and date legible. E PLURIBUS UNUM illegible.
VG-8 VERY GOOD—Motto partially legible. Only deepest drapery details visible. All other lines smooth.
F-12 FINE—All drapery lines distinguishable. Some detail visible in hair lines near cheek and neck.
VF-20 VERY FINE—Left side of drapery worn smooth.
EF-40 EXTREMELY FINE—Drapery distinct. Hair well detailed.
AU-50 ABOUT UNCIRCULATED—Slight trace of wear on the bust shoulder and hair to left of forehead, as well as on eagle's breast and top edges of wings.
MS-60 UNCIRCULATED—No trace of wear. Light blemishes.

	Mintage	G-4	VG-8	F-12	VF-20	EF-40	AU-50	MS-60
1798, Heraldic Eagle	*	$450	$550	$750	$1,300	$2,500	$5,000	$11,000
1799	423,515	450	550	750	1,300	2,500	5,000	11,000
1800	220,920	450	550	750	1,300	2,500	5,000	11,000
1801	54,454	450	550	750	1,300	2,500	5,000	11,000
1802	41,650	450	550	750	1,300	2,500	5,000	11,000
1803	85,634	450	550	750	1,300	2,500	5,000	12,000
1804, Variety 1, O Above Cloud						Proof: $3,000,000		
1804, Variety 2, O Above Space Between Cloud						Proof: $2,000,000		

* Included in number above.

GOBRECHT DOLLARS (1836–1839)

Silver dollars of 1836, 1838, and 1839 were mostly made as patterns and restrikes, but some were made in quantities for general circulation.

	VF-20	EF-40	AU-50	PF-60
1836, C GOBRECHT F. on base. Reverse eagle flying upward amid stars. Plain edge. Although scarce, this is the most common variety and was issued for circulation as regular coinage	$5,000	$8,000	$10,000	$13,500

	VF-20	EF-40	AU-50	PF-60
1838, Similar obverse, designer's name omitted, stars added around border. Reverse eagle flying left in plain field. Reeded edge.	$8,000	$12,000	$15,000	$19,000
1839, Obverse as above. Reverse eagle in plain field. Reeded edge. Issued for circulation as regular coinage	8,000	11,000	13,000	15,000

LIBERTY SEATED (1840–1873)

In 1840, silver dollars were again issued for general circulation. The seated figure of Liberty device was adopted for the obverse, and a heraldic eagle for the reverse.

VG-8 VERY GOOD—Any three letters of LIBERTY at least two-thirds complete.
F-12 FINE—All seven letters of LIBERTY visible, though weak.
VF-20 VERY FINE—LIBERTY strong, but slight wear visible on its ribbon.
EF-40 EXTREMELY FINE—Horizontal lines of shield complete. Eagle's eye plain.
AU-50 ABOUT UNCIRCULATED—Traces of light wear on only the high points of the design. Half of mint luster present.
MS-60 UNCIRCULATED—No trace of wear. Light marks or blemishes.
PF-60 PROOF—Several contact marks, hairlines, or light rubs possible on surface. Luster possibly dull and eye appeal lacking.
PF-63 CHOICE PROOF—Reflective surfaces with only a few blemishes in secondary focal places. No major flaws.

No Motto (1840–1865)

Mintmark location is on reverse, below eagle.

	Mintage	VG-8	F-12	VF-20	EF-40	AU-50	MS-60	PF-60	PF-63
1840	61,005	$120	$130	$180	$275	$425	$1,500	$8,000	$18,000
1841	173,000	100	120	160	250	350	1,000	8,000	20,000
1842	184,618	100	120	160	250	300	800	8,000	18,000
1843	165,100	100	120	160	250	300	850	8,000	18,000
1844	20,000	110	150	200	275	500	1,500	6,000	18,000
1845	24,500	115	150	200	300	600	3,750	8,000	18,000
1846	110,600	100	120	170	250	350	900	6,000	16,000
1846O	59,000	120	150	200	275	500	2,200		
1847	140,750	100	120	160	250	300	800	8,000	15,000
1848	15,000	175	250	350	450	800	1,800	8,000	18,000
1849	62,600	100	120	160	250	300	1,000	9,000	24,000
1850	7,500	275	325	500	800	1,200	2,800	8,000	16,000
1850O	40,000	135	210	370	800	1,650	7,000		
1851	1,300	2,700	4,500	6,000	8,000	12,000	15,000	15,000	19,000
1852	1,100	2,500	4,500	6,000	8,000	12,000	15,000	17,500	22,000
1853	46,110	120	170	225	325	700	1,400	12,000	22,000
1854	33,140	750	1,200	1,500	2,200	3,500	4,600	7,000	12,000
1855	26,000	500	800	1,200	1,800	2,800	4,500	7,000	13,000
1856	63,500	175	260	350	700	1,200	2,500	3,500	9,000
1857	94,000	175	250	350	750	900	1,600	3,000	4,750
1858 *(300+)*		1,800	2,200	2,700	3,500	4,000		5,000	7,500
1859 (800)	255,700	130	180	250	315	450	1,200	1,200	2,750
1859O	360,000	100	120	170	250	350	650		
1859S	20,000	170	250	350	1,000	2,000	8,000		
1860 (1,330)	217,600	110	150	230	300	400	700	1,000	2,200
1860O	515,000	100	120	170	250	350	625		
1861 (1,000)	77,500	300	400	500	650	1,200	1,700	1,000	2,200

	Mintage	VG-8	F-12	VF-20	EF-40	AU-50	MS-60	PF-60	PF-63
1862 . . . . (550)	11,540	$280	$375	$475	$650	$1,200	$1,700	$1,100	$2,300
1863 . . . . (460)	27,200	200	230	250	350	750	1,600	1,000	2,300
1864 . . . . (470)	30,700	110	160	270	350	750	1,900	1,000	2,300
1865 . . . . (500)	46,500	110	150	250	325	700	1,500	1,000	2,300

With Motto (1866–1873)

Motto IN GOD WE TRUST on Reverse (1866–1873)

	Mintage	VG-8	F-12	VF-20	EF-40	AU-50	MS-60	PF-60	PF-63
1866 . . . . (725)	48,900	$120	$160	$230	$325	$550	$1,000	$850	$2,000
1867 . . . . (625)	46,900	120	150	225	275	500	1,000	850	2,000
1868 . . . . (600)	162,100	110	140	210	250	500	900	850	2,000
1869 . . . . (600)	423,700	110	140	175	230	400	900	850	2,000
1870 . . . . (1,000)	415,000	110	140	175	230	350	800	850	2,000
1870CC	11,758	250	375	600	850	2,000	6,500		
1870S			65,000	80,000	150,000	275,000	400,000		
1871 . . . . (960)	1,073,800	110	150	175	250	375	700	850	2,000
1871CC	1,376	1,300	2,100	3,000	5,500	13,000	35,000		
1872 . . . . (950)	1,105,500	110	140	175	250	375	700	850	2,000
1872CC	3,150	700	1,100	1,700	2,700	6,500	14,000		
1872S	9,000	150	250	350	800	1,600	4,700		
1873 . . . . (600)	293,000	110	150	175	250	400	800	850	2,000
1873CC	2,300	2,600	3,500	5,500	10,000	17,000	45,000		

TRADE DOLLARS (1873–1885)

This trade dollar was issued for circulation in the Orient to compete with dollar-size coins of other countries. It weighed 420 grains compared to 412-1/2 grains, the weight of the regular silver dollar.

VG-8 VERY GOOD—About half of mottoes IN GOD WE TRUST (on Liberty's pedestal) and E PLURIBUS UNUM (on obverse ribbon) visible. Rim on both sides well defined.

F-12 FINE—Mottoes and liberty legible but worn.

EF-40 EXTREMELY FINE—Mottoes and liberty sharp. Only slight wear on rims.

AU-50 ABOUT UNCIRCULATED—Slight trace of wear on Liberty's left breast and left knee and on hair above ear, as well as on eagle's head, knee, and wing tips.

MS-60 UNCIRCULATED—No trace of wear. Light blemishes.

MS-63 CHOICE UNCIRCULATED—Some distracting contact marks or blemishes in prime focal areas. Impaired luster possible.

PF-63 CHOICE PROOF—Reflective surfaces with only a few blemishes in secondary focal places. No major flaws.

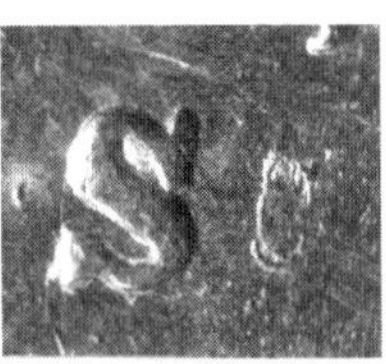

1875-S, S Over CC

	Mintage	VG-8	F-12	EF-40	AU-50	MS-60	MS-63	PF-63
1873 . . . .(865)	396,635	$55	$65	$85	$150	$400	$1,850	$1,500
1873CC	124,500	100	150	320	800	2,500	13,000	
1873S	703,000	55	65	90	175	500	1,100	
1874 . . . .(700)	987,100	55	65	85	150	275	850	1,500
1874CC	1,373,200	100	150	250	300	700	3,800	
1874S	2,549,000	55	65	85	150	275	850	
1875 . . . .(700)	218,200	80	180	295	500	1,000	1,700	1,500
1875CC	1,573,700	80	180	285	450	900	1,500	
1875S	4,487,000	55	65	85	150	275	850	
1875S, S Over CC	*	125	200	450	700	1,500	6,000	
1876 . . . .(1,150)	455,000	55	65	85	150	275	850	1,500
1876CC	509,000	80	125	225	600	1,700	13,000	
1876S	5,227,000	55	65	85	150	275	850	
1877 . . . .(510)	3,039,200	55	65	85	150	275	850	1,500
1877CC	534,000	100	150	300	375	700	3,500	
1877S	9,519,000	55	65	85	150	275	850	
1878 . . . .(900)				600				1,500
1878CC **(a)**	97,000	250	375	1,100	2,000	6,000	13,000	
1878S	4,162,000	55	65	85	150	275	850	
1879 . . . .(1,541)				600				1,500
1880 . . . .(1,987)				600				1,500
1881 . . . .(960)				600				1,500
1882 . . . .(1,097)				600				1,500
1883 . . . .(979)				600				1,500
1884 **(b)** . . . .(10)				600				300,000
1885 **(b)** . . . .(5)				600				900,000

* Included in number above. **a.** 44,148 trade dollars were melted on July 19, 1878. Many of these may have been 1878-CC. **b.** The trade dollars of 1884 and 1885 were unknown to collectors until 1908. None are listed in the Mint director's report, and numismatists believe that they are not a part of the regular Mint issue.

MORGAN (1878–1921)

George T. Morgan, formerly a pupil of William Wyon's at the Royal Mint in London, designed the new dollar. His initial M is found at the truncation of the neck, at the last tress. It also appears on the reverse on the left-hand loop of the ribbon.

Sharply struck prooflike coins have a highly reflective surface and usually command substantial premiums.

VF-20 VERY FINE—Two thirds of hair lines from top of forehead to ear visible. Ear well defined. Feathers on eagle's breast worn.

EF-40 EXTREMELY FINE—All hair lines strong and ear bold. Eagle's feathers all plain but with slight wear on breast and wing tips.

AU-50 ABOUT UNCIRCULATED—Slight trace of wear on the bust shoulder and hair left of forehead, and on eagle's breast and top edges of wings.

MS-60 UNCIRCULATED—No trace of wear. Full mint luster present, but may be noticeably marred by scuff marks or bag abrasions.

MS-63 CHOICE UNCIRCULATED—No trace of wear; full mint luster; few noticeable surface marks.

MS-64 UNCIRCULATED—A few scattered contact marks. Good eye appeal and attractive luster.

MS-65 GEM UNCIRCULATED—Only light, scattered contact marks that are not distracting. Strong luster, good eye appeal.

8 Tail Feathers, 1878, Philadelphia Only

Mintmark location on reverse, below wreath.

See next page for chart.

Most Proof Morgan dollars, where indicated in mintage records (quantity shown in parentheses), are valued approximately as follows:

Proof-60 – $600.; Proof-63 – $1,200.; Proof-65 – $3,000.

Most Uncirculated silver dollars have scratches or nicks because of handling of mint bags. Choice sharply struck coins with full brilliance and without blemishes are worth more than listed values.

	Mintage	VF-20	EF-40	AU-50	MS-60	MS-63	MS-65
1878, 8 Feathers (500)	*749,500*	$12	$16	$19	$60	$85	$700
1878, 7 Feathers (250)	*9,759,300*	10	14	15	28	45	700
1878, 7 Over 8 Clear Double Feathers	*	15	17	26	55	120	1,400
1878CC	2,212,000	47	60	65	110	175	1,000
1878S	9,774,000	10	11	13	22	35	150
1879 (1,100)	14,806,000	10	11	13	20	28	500
1879CC, CC Over CC	756,000	70	240	400	1,450	3,000	12,000
1879O	2,887,000	10	11	13	33	90	1,500
1879S	9,110,000	10	11	13	20	25	90
1880 (1,355)	12,600,000	10	11	13	20	25	375
1880CC	591,000	75	95	120	260	320	625
1880O	5,305,000	10	11	13	30	175	9,000
1880S	8,900,000	10	11	13	20	25	90
1881 (984)	9,163,000	10	11	13	20	25	425
1881CC	296,000	130	160	180	220	260	450
1881O	5,708,000	10	11	13	20	25	700
1881S	12,760,000	10	11	13	20	25	90
1882 (1,100)	11,100,000	10	11	13	20	25	170
1882CC	1,133,000	50	60	65	90	120	235
1882O	6,090,000	10	11	13	20	25	400
1882S	9,250,000	10	11	13	20	25	90
1883 (1,039)	12,290,000	10	11	13	20	25	90
1883CC	1,204,000	55	60	65	90	120	225
1883O	8,725,000	10	11	13	20	25	90
1883S	6,250,000	11	15	65	300	1,250	9,250
1884 (875)	14,070,000	10	11	13	20	25	125
1884CC	1,136,000	50	60	70	100	125	215
1884O	9,730,000	10	11	13	20	25	90
1884S	3,200,000	11	20	240	2,500	14,000	96,000
1885 (930)	17,787,000	10	11	13	20	25	90
1885CC	228,000	120	165	200	250	320	700
1885O	9,185,000	10	11	13	20	25	90
1885S	1,497,000	10	18	48	80	120	750
1886 (886)	19,963,000	10	11	13	20	25	90
1886O	10,710,000	10	13	45	260	2,000	96,000
1886S	750,000	22	35	55	125	200	1,500
1887 (710)	20,290,000	10	11	13	20	25	90
1887O	11,550,000	10	11	13	22	60	1,500
1887S	1,771,000	10	11	18	50	115	1,500
1888 (832)	19,183,100	10	11	13	20	25	95
1888O	12,150,000	10	11	13	20	25	200
1888S	657,000	30	42	60	125	180	1,500
1889 (811)	21,726,000	10	11	13	20	25	90
1889CC	350,000	725	1,750	3,250	10,000	16,500	150,000
1889O	11,875,000	10	11	20	65	200	2,200
1889S	700,000	22	25	50	120	200	850

* Included in number above.

	Mintage	VF-20	EF-40	AU-50	MS-60	MS-63	MS-65
1890	(590) . . . 16,802,000	$10	$11	$13	$20	$25	$950
1890CC	2,309,041	55	65	90	175	450	3,000
1890O	10,701,000	10	11	14	28	50	700
1890S	8,230,373	10	11	14	24	50	450
1891	(650) . . . 8,693,556	10	11	15	25	90	2,600
1891CC	1,618,000	55	60	100	200	450	2,300
1891O	7,954,529	11	14	30	70	190	3,500
1891S	5,296,000	10	11	14	20	65	600
1892	(1,245) . . . 1,036,000	11	15	40	80	200	1,700
1892CC	1,352,000	85	175	260	450	1,200	4,500
1892O	2,744,000	12	14	35	80	165	2,200
1892S	1,200,000	28	100	950	15,500	31,000	90,000
1893	(792) . . . 378,000	85	120	150	300	700	3,500
1893CC	677,000	200	800	950	1,800	3,600	26,000
1893O	300,000	125	250	450	1,100	3,600	100,000
1893S	100,000	3,500	4,800	12,000	42,000	75,000	250,000
1894	(972) . . . 110,000	800	1,000	1,250	2,500	3,500	16,000
1894O	1,723,000	25	45	125	310	2,000	22,000
1894S	1,260,000	40	65	175	300	500	2,900
1895	(880) . . . 12,880		**(a)** 15,000	**(a)** 17,000	**(a)** 22,000	**(a)** 30,000	**(a)** 42,000
1895O	450,000	175	250	650	8,200	21,000	110,000
1895S	400,000	150	350	750	1,600	2,500	10,000
1896	(762) . . . 9,976,000	10	11	13	20	25	90
1896O	4,900,000	10	11	75	500	4,000	85,000
1896S	5,000,000	25	85	225	650	1,400	8,000
1897	(731) . . . 2,822,000	10	11	13	20	25	120
1897O	4,004,000	10	11	60	350	2,700	24,000
1897S	5,825,000	10	11	14	30	55	300
1898	(735) . . . 5,884,000	10	11	13	20	25	125
1898O	4,440,000	10	11	13	20	25	90
1898S	4,102,000	10	18	42	125	210	950
1899	(846) . . . 330,000	40	60	80	150	160	390
1899O	12,290,000	10	11	13	20	25	90
1899S	2,562,000	14	22	50	160	250	800
1900	(912) . . . 8,830,000	10	11	13	20	25	90
1900O	12,590,000	10	11	13	20	25	100
1900S	3,540,000	12	20	35	135	210	700
1901	(813) . . . 6,962,000	26	35	250	1,000	8,000	100,000
1901O	13,320,000	10	11	13	20	25	100
1901S	2,284,000	15	25	75	180	350	1,700
1902	(777) . . . 7,994,000	10	11	13	22	55	220
1902O	8,636,000	10	11	13	20	25	90
1902S	1,530,000	50	70	125	175	300	1,300
1903	(755) . . . 4,652,000	20	30	35	40	50	125
1903O	4,450,000	125	140	160	180	225	350
1903S	1,241,000	50	140	750	1,800	2,900	4,500
1904	(650) . . . 2,788,000	10	11	17	40	130	1,900
1904O	3,720,000	10	11	13	20	25	90
1904S	2,304,000	30	100	300	650	1,500	3,800
1921	44,690,000	10	10	10	11	15	80
1921D	20,345,000	10	10	11	16	30	150
1921S	21,695,000	10	10	11	14	32	600

a. Values are for Proofs.

PEACE (1921–1935)

Anthony De Francisci, a medalist, designed this dollar. His monogram is located in the field of the coin under the neck of Liberty.

VF-20 VERY FINE—Hair over eye well worn. Some strands over ear well defined. Some eagle feathers on top and outside edge of right wing visible.
EF-40 EXTREMELY FINE—Hair lines over brow and ear are strong, though slightly worn. Outside wing feathers at right and those at top visible but faint.
AU-50 ABOUT UNCIRCULATED—Slight trace of wear. Most luster present, although marred by contact marks.
MS-60 UNCIRCULATED—No trace of wear. Full mint luster, but possibly noticeably marred by stains, surface marks, or bag abrasions.
MS-63 CHOICE UNCIRCULATED—Some distracting contact marks or blemishes in prime focal areas. Impaired luster possible.
MS-64 UNCIRCULATED—A few scattered contact marks. Good eye appeal and attractive luster.
MS-65 GEM UNCIRCULATED—Only light, scattered, non-distracting contact marks. Strong luster, good eye appeal.
PF-65 CHOICE PROOF—Satin surfaces, no noticeable blemishes or flaws.

Mintmark location on reverse, below ONE.

Most Uncirculated silver dollars have scratches or nicks because of handling of mint bags. Choice sharply struck coins with full brilliance and without blemishes are worth more than listed values.

	Mintage	VF-20	EF-40	AU-50	MS-60	MS-63	MS-65	PF-65
1921	1,006,473	$50	$60	$75	$125	$200	$1,400	$22,000
1922	51,737,000	10	10	11	12	18	80	30,000
1922D	15,063,000	10	10	11	13	24	175	
1922S	17,475,000	10	10	11	13	30	1,000	
1923	30,800,000	10	10	11	12	18	80	
1923D	6,811,000	10	10	12	25	60	525	
1923S	19,020,000	10	10	11	13	40	3,000	
1924	11,811,000	10	10	11	12	18	80	
1924S	1,728,000	11	12	30	90	225	4,500	
1925	10,198,000	10	10	11	12	18	80	
1925S	1,610,000	10	10	15	32	85	12,000	
1926	1,939,000	10	10	11	18	40	175	
1926D	2,348,700	10	10	15	30	90	260	
1926S	6,980,000	10	10	11	18	42	400	
1927	848,000	11	14	22	35	80	1,000	
1927D	1,268,900	11	14	45	75	140	2,750	
1927S	866,000	11	13	40	75	170	5,000	
1928	360,649	225	250	275	300	350	2,100	
1928S	1,632,000	13	14	25	75	300	11,000	
1934	954,057	10	11	18	50	100	450	
1934D	1,569,500	10	11	18	60	170	875	
1934S	1,011,000	38	85	275	950	2,000	4,750	
1935	1,576,000	10	10	15	40	60	300	
1935S	1,964,000	10	12	45	120	200	650	

EISENHOWER (1971–1978)
Eagle Reverse (1971–1974)

Honoring both President Dwight D. Eisenhower and the first landing of man on the moon, this design is the work of Chief Engraver Frank Gasparro, whose initials are on the truncation and below the eagle. The reverse is an adaptation of the official Apollo 11 insignia.

Mintmark location is above date.

	Mintage	EF-40	MS-63	PF-63	PF-65
1971, Copper-Nickel Clad	47,799,000	$1.05	$1.75		
1971D, Copper-Nickel Clad	68,587,424	1.05	1.25		
1971S, Silver Clad (4,265,234)	6,868,530		3.50	$3.50	$4.50
1972, Copper-Nickel Clad	75,890,000	1.05	1.25		
1972D, Copper-Nickel Clad	92,548,511	1.05	1.25		
1972S, Silver Clad (1,811,631)	2,193,056		2.50	3.50	6.00
1973, Copper-Nickel Clad	**(a)** 2,000,056	1.05	5.50		
1973D, Copper-Nickel Clad	**(a)** 2,000,000	1.05	5.50		
1973S, Copper-Nickel Clad (2,760,339)				3.00	7.00
1973S, Silver Clad (1,013,646)	1,883,140		4.50	10.00	18.00
1974, Copper-Nickel Clad	27,366,000	1.05	2.00		
1974D, Copper-Nickel Clad	45,517,000	1.05	2.00		
1974S, Copper-Nickel Clad (2,612,568)				2.50	3.50
1974S, Silver Clad (1,306,579)	1,900,156		3.50	5.00	7.00

a. 1,769,258 of each sold only in sets and not released for circulation. Unissued coins destroyed at mint.

Bicentennial Coinage Dated 1776–1976

Obverse

Reverse Variety 2 **Reverse Variety 1**

Variety 1: Design in low relief, bold lettering on reverse.
Variety 2: Sharp design, delicate lettering on reverse.

See next page for chart.

	Mintage	EF-40	MS-63	PF-63	PF-65
1776–1976, Copper-Nickel Clad, Variety 1	4,019,000	$1.10	$3.00		
1776–1976, Copper-Nickel Clad, Variety 2	113,318,000	1.10	1.50		
1776–1976D, Copper-Nickel Clad, Variety 1	21,048,710	1.10	1.50		
1776–1976D,Copper-Nickel Clad, Variety 2	82,179,564	1.10	1.50		
1776–1976S, Copper-Nickel Clad, Variety 1	(2,845,450)			$2.50	$5.50
1776–1976S, Copper-Nickel Clad, Variety 2	(4,149,730)			2.50	3.50
1776–1976S, Silver Clad, Variety 1	*11,000,000*		5.00		
1776–1976S, Silver Clad, Variety 1	*(4,000,000)*			5.00	10.00

Eagle Reverse Resumed (1977–1978)

	Mintage	EF-40	MS-63	PF-63	PF-65
1977, Copper-Nickel Clad	12,596,000	$1.05	$2.00		
1977D, Copper-Nickel Clad	32,983,006	1.05	1.50		
1977S, Copper-Nickel Clad	(3,251,152)			$2.50	$4.00
1978, Copper-Nickel Clad	25,702,000	1.05	1.25		
1978D, Copper-Nickel Clad	33,012,890	1.05	1.50		
1978S, Copper-Nickel Clad	(3,127,781)			2.50	4.75

SUSAN B. ANTHONY (1979–1999)

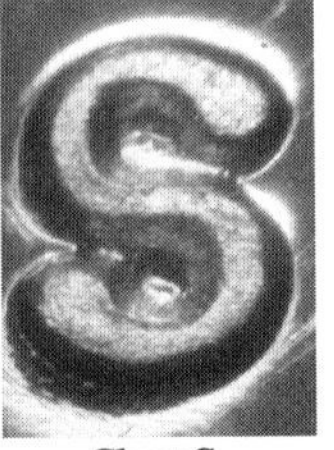
Clear S

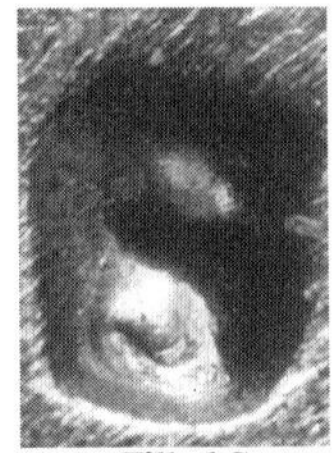
Filled S

	Mintage	MS-63	PF-63	PF-65
1979P, Narrow Rim	360,222,000	$1		
1979P, Wide Rim	*	8		
1979D	288,015,744	1		
1979S	109,576,000	1		
Proof, Filled S			$2.50	$5
Proof, Clear S			35.00	60
1980P	27,610,000	1		
1980D	41,628,708	1		
1980S	20,422,000	1		

	Mintage	MS-63	PF-63	PF-65
1980S, Proof	(3,554,806)		$2.50	$5
1981P	3,000,000	$2.00		
1981D	3,250,000	2.00		
1981S	3,492,000	2.00		
1981S, Proof	(4,063,083)		2.50	4
1981S, Proof, Clear S			90.00	125
1999P	29,592,000	1.25		
1999P, Proof			10.00	15
1999D	11,776,000	1.25		

* Included in number above.

SACAGAWEA (2000 TO DATE)

The design of this coin was selected in national competition from among 120 submissions that were considered by a panel appointed by Treasury Secretary Robert Rubin. The adopted motif depicts Sacagawea, a young Native American Shoshone, as rendered by artist Glenna Goodacre. On her back she carries Jean Baptiste, her infant son. The reverse shows an eagle in flight, designed by Mint engraver Thomas D. Rogers Sr.

The composition exemplifies the spirit of Liberty, Peace, and Freedom shown by Sacagawea in her conduct as interpreter and guide to explorers Meriwether Lewis and William Clark during their famed journey westward from the great northern plains to the Pacific.

These coins have a distinctive golden color and a plain edge to distinguish them from other denominations or coins of a similar size. The change in composition and appearance was mandated under the United States Dollar Coin Act of 1997.

Several distinctive finishes can be identified on the Sacagawea dollars as a result of the mint attempting to adjust the dies, blanks, strikes, or finishing to produce coins with minimal spotting and a better surface color. One group of 5,000 pieces dated 2000, with a special finish were presented to sculptor Glenna Goodacre in payment for the obverse design. Unexplained error coins made from mismatched dies (a state quarter obverse combined with a Sacagawea dollar reverse) are extremely rare.

	Mintage	MS-63	PF-63	PF-65
2000P	767,140,000	$1.00		
2000D	518,916,000	1.00		
2000S	(4,047,904)		$3	$6
2001P	62,468,000	1.00		
2001D	70,939,500	1.00		
2001S	(3,183,740)		20	40
2002P	3,865,610	1.10		
2002D	3,732,000	1.10		
2002S	(3,211,995)		8	15
2003P	3,080,000	1.10		
2003D	3,080,000	1.10		
2003S	(3,298,439)		4	8
2004P	2,660,000	$1.10		
2004D	2,660,000	1.10		
2004S	(2,965,422)		$4	$8
2005P	*2,520,000*	1.10		
2005D	*2,520,000*	1.10		
2005S	*(3,344,679)*		3	5
2006P	*4,900,000*	1.10		
2006D	*2,800,000*	1.10		
2006S	*(2,923,105)*		3	5
2007P		1.10		
2007D		1.10		
2007S			3	5

PRESIDENTIAL DOLLARS (2006–2016)

Four different coins, each bearing the image of a former U.S. president, are issued each year in the order that the presidents served. The size and composition of these coins is the same as that of the Sacagawea dollars that are also made each year. A companion series of $10 gold bullion coins (listed in the Bullion section) honors the spouses of each president.

	MS-65	PF-65
2007P, George Washington		
2007D, George Washington		
2007S, George Washington		
2007P, John Adams		
2007D, John Adams		
2007S, John Adams		
2007P, Thomas Jefferson		
2007D, Thomas Jefferson		
2007S, Thomas Jefferson		
2007P, James Madison		
2007D, James Madison		
2007S, James Madison		

Note: Errors have been reported in the Presidential dollar series, including coins minted without edge lettering. Depending on their rarity, such errors can be worth a premium to collectors.

GOLD DOLLARS

Coinage of the gold dollar was authorized by the Act of March 3, 1849. The weight was 25.8 grains, fineness .900. The first type, struck until 1854, is known as the Liberty Head type.

In 1854, the piece was made larger in diameter and thinner. The design was changed to a feather headdress on a female, generally referred to as the Indian Princess Head type. In 1856 the type was changed slightly by enlarging the size of the head.

LIBERTY HEAD (1849–1854)

VF-20 VERY FINE—LIBERTY on headband complete and legible. Knobs on coronet defined.
EF-40 EXTREMELY FINE—Slight wear on Liberty's hair. Knobs on coronet sharp.
AU-50 ABOUT UNCIRCULATED—Trace of wear on headband. Nearly full luster.
AU-55 CHOICE ABOUT UNCIRCULATED—Evidence of friction on design high points.
MS-60 UNCIRCULATED—No trace of wear. Light marks and blemishes.
MS-63 CHOICE UNCIRCULATED—Some distracting contact marks or blemishes in prime focal areas. Impaired luster possible.

	Mintage	VF-20	EF-40	AU-50	AU-55	MS-60	MS-63
1849	688,567	$100	$145	$170	$190	$280	$1,200
1849, Small Head, No L	*	100	145	175	200	300	1,400
1849C	11,634	650	950	1,400	2,500	6,000	13,000
1849D	21,588	850	1,150	1,450	2,250	3,750	8,500
1849O	21,500	110	175	230	375	500	2,250
1850	481,953	100	140	150	165	260	750
1850C	6,966	700	975	1,600	3,250	5,800	18,000
1850D	8,382	850	1,100	2,000	3,500	7,000	19,000
1850O	14,000	185	250	525	1,100	2,000	4,250
1851	3,317,671	100	145	155	165	200	750
1851C	41,267	750	900	1,200	1,500	2,000	4,500
1851D	9,882	800	1,100	1,550	2,400	4,000	10,000
1851O	290,000	120	155	175	225	525	1,800
1852	2,045,351	100	145	155	165	200	750
1852C	9,434	725	950	1,200	1,700	3,000	8,000
1852D	6,360	900	1,200	1,600	3,200	6,000	22,000
1852O	140,000	105	175	240	450	800	4,200
1853	4,076,051	100	145	155	165	200	750
1853C	11,515	750	900	1,500	2,200	3,800	8,000
1853D	6,583	850	1,100	1,800	3,000	6,000	20,000
1853O	290,000	115	155	170	225	425	1,500
1854	855,502	100	145	155	165	200	750
1854D	2,935	900	1,350	4,000	5,000	8,000	27,000
1854S	14,632	200	300	450	800	1,650	3,200

* Included in number above.

INDIAN PRINCESS HEAD, SMALL HEAD (1854–1856)

VF-20 VERY FINE—Feather-curl tips on headdress outlined but details worn.
EF-40 EXTREMELY FINE—Slight wear on tips of feather curls on headdress.
AU-50 ABOUT UNCIRCULATED—Trace of wear on feathers, nearly full luster.
AU-55 CHOICE ABOUT UNCIRCULATED—Evidence of friction on design high points. Most of original mint luster present.
MS-60 UNCIRCULATED—No trace of wear. Light marks and blemishes.
MS-63 CHOICE UNCIRCULATED—Some distracting contact marks or blemishes in prime focal areas. Impaired luster possible.
PF-63 CHOICE PROOF—Reflective surfaces with only a few blemishes in secondary focal areas. No major flaws.

	Mintage	VF-20	EF-40	AU-50	AU-55	MS-60	MS-63	PF-63
1854	783,943	$210	$325	$400	$800	$1,700	$7,200	—
1855	758,269	210	325	400	800	1,700	7,200	—
1855C	9,803	850	2,200	3,500	6,500	17,000		
1855D	1,811	3,000	6,500	16,000	20,000	35,000	65,000	
1855O	55,000	300	400	975	1,800	4,500	15,000	
1856S	24,600	550	900	1,300	2,000	5,000	24,000	

INDIAN PRINCESS HEAD, LARGE HEAD (1856–1889)

VF-20 VERY FINE—Slight detail in curled feathers in headdress. Details worn smooth at eyebrow, hair below headdress, and behind ear and bottom curl.
EF-40 EXTREMELY FINE—Slight wear above and to right of eye and on top of curled feathers.
AU-50 ABOUT UNCIRCULATED—Trace of wear on feathers, nearly full luster.
AU-55 CHOICE ABOUT UNCIRCULATED—Evidence of friction on design high points. Most of original mint luster present.
MS-60 UNCIRCULATED—No trace of wear. Light marks and blemishes.
MS-63 CHOICE UNCIRCULATED—Some distracting contact marks or blemishes in prime focal areas. Impaired luster possible.
PF-63 CHOICE PROOF—Reflective surfaces with only a few blemishes in secondary focal places. No major flaws.

	Mintage	VF-20	EF-40	AU-50	AU-55	MS-60	MS-63	PF-63
1856	1,762,936	$105	$150	$160	$185	$200	$700	$15,000
1856D	1,460	2,500	4,000	5,000	8,600	20,000	36,000	
1857	774,789	100	145	160	185	200	700	8,000
1857C	13,280	700	900	2,000	3,000	8,000	20,000	
1857D	3,533	750	1,100	2,700	3,500	7,500	24,000	
1857S	10,000	350	400	800	1,100	4,000	14,000	
1858	117,995	100	145	165	175	200	700	4,750
1858D	3,477	900	1,200	2,000	3,000	7,250	18,000	
1858S	10,000	250	325	850	1,000	3,800	11,500	
1859 (80)	168,244	100	145	165	175	200	700	3,500

Chart continued on next page.

	Mintage	VF-20	EF-40	AU-50	AU-55	MS-60	MS-63	PF-63
1859C	5,235	$700	$900	$2,000	$3,750	$7,500	$20,000	
1859D	4,952	700	800	1,800	3,000	7,000	15,000	
1859S	15,000	160	350	775	1,250	3,500	10,000	
1860	(154) 36,514	100	145	165	175	260	750	$3,350
1860D	1,566	1,750	3,600	4,500	6,000	11,500	38,000	
1860S	13,000	200	325	450	700	1,700	3,700	
1861	(349) 527,150	100	145	165	175	210	700	3,500
1861D		4,750	7,000	13,000	15,000	22,500	43,000	
1862	(35) 1,361,355	100	145	165	175	200	700	4,100
1863	(50) 6,200	325	625	1,200	1,450	2,850	5,000	3,800
1864	(50) 5,900	250	300	550	610	725	1,800	5,500
1865	(25) 3,725	260	325	575	625	1,050	2,000	3,800
1866	(30) 7,100	250	325	500	550	725	1,300	4,000
1867	(50) 5,200	300	350	475	550	850	1,300	4,000
1868	(25) 10,500	150	250	325	350	725	1,300	4,500
1869	(25) 5,900	200	275	475	525	800	1,300	4,750
1870	(35) 6,300	200	275	360	400	725	1,300	4,750
1870S	3,000	350	550	850	1,100	1,700	5,000	
1871	(30) 3,900	200	275	300	400	575	1,300	3,600
1872	(30) 3,500	200	260	300	400	575	1,300	5,250
1873, Close 3	(25) 1,800	250	500	675	725	1,100	2,750	10,000
1873, Open 3	123,300	100	145	160	170	200	700	
1874	(20) 198,800	100	145	160	170	200	700	5,750
1875	(20) 400	1,400	2,800	3,500	3,750	5,250	8,000	10,500
1876	(45) 3,200	175	200	300	360	475	710	3,800
1877	(20) 3,900	150	200	300	360	475	710	4,600
1878	(20) 3,000	150	200	300	360	475	710	3,800
1879	(30) 3,000	120	175	200	250	360	710	4,100
1880	(36) 1,600	115	150	170	190	300	710	3,650
1881	(87) 7,620	115	150	170	190	300	710	3,600
1882	(125) 5,000	120	150	170	190	300	700	3,250
1883	(207) 10,800	120	150	170	190	300	700	3,250
1884	(1,006) 5,230	120	150	170	190	300	700	3,250
1885	(1,105) 11,156	120	150	170	190	300	700	3,250
1886	(1,016) 5,000	120	150	170	190	300	700	3,250
1887	(1,043) 7,500	120	150	170	190	300	700	3,250
1888	(1,079) 15,501	120	150	170	190	300	700	3,250
1889	(1,779) 28,950	120	150	170	190	300	700	3,250

Although authorized by the Act of April 2, 1792, coinage of quarter eagles ($2.50 gold coins) was not begun until 1796.

CAPPED BUST TO RIGHT (1796–1807)

F-12 FINE—Hair worn smooth on high spots. E PLURIBUS UNUM on ribbon weak but legible.
VF-20 VERY FINE—Some wear on high spots.
EF-40 EXTREMELY FINE—Only slight wear on Liberty's hair and cheek.
AU-50 ABOUT UNCIRCULATED—Trace of wear on cap, hair, cheek, and drapery.
AU-55 CHOICE ABOUT UNCIRCULATED—Evidence of friction on design high points. Some original mint luster.
MS-60 UNCIRCULATED—No trace of wear. Light blemishes.

No Stars on Obverse (1796)

Stars on Obverse (1796–1807)

	Mintage	F-12	VF-20	EF-40	AU-50	AU-55	MS-60
1796, No Stars on Obverse	963	$19,000	$27,500	$50,000	$60,000	$70,000	$120,000
1796, Stars on Obverse	432	16,000	25,000	45,000	55,000	65,000	110,000
1797	427	10,000	12,500	20,000	35,000	40,000	80,000
1798	1,094	3,250	5,250	7,000	15,000	20,000	40,000
1802, 2 Over 1	3,035	3,250	5,250	6,000	8,000	10,000	16,000
1804, 13-Star Reverse	*	18,000	23,000	50,000	85,000	100,000	150,000
1804, 14-Star Reverse	3,327	3,250	5,000	6,500	8,000	10,000	16,000
1805	1,781	3,250	5,000	6,500	8,000	10,500	17,000
1806, 6/4, 8 Stars Left, 5 Right	1,136	3,500	5,250	6,750	8,500	12,000	18,000
1806, 6/5, 7 Stars Left, 6 Right	480	4,500	6,500	9,000	15,000	22,000	50,000
1807	6,812	3,250	4,800	5,750	8,500	10,000	15,000

* Included in number below.

CAPPED BUST TO LEFT, LARGE SIZE (1808)

F-12 FINE—E PLURIBUS UNUM on reverse, and LIBERTY on headband, legible but weak.
VF-20 VERY FINE—Motto and LIBERTY clear.
EF-40 EXTREMELY FINE—All details of hair plain.
AU-50 ABOUT UNCIRCULATED—Trace of wear above eye, on top of cap, and on cheek and hair.
AU-55 CHOICE ABOUT UNCIRCULATED—Evidence of friction on design high points. Some original mint luster present.
MS-60 UNCIRCULATED—No trace of wear. Light blemishes.

	Mintage	F-12	VF-20	EF-40	AU-50	AU-55	MS-60
1808	2,710	$16,500	$23,000	$29,000	$56,000	$66,000	$95,000

CAPPED HEAD TO LEFT (1821–1834)

Those dated 1829 to 1834 are smaller in diameter than the 1821 to 1827 pieces.

	Mintage	F-12	VF-20	EF-40	AU-50	AU-55	MS-60
1821	6,448	$3,500	$4,750	$6,000	$7,500	$8,500	$17,500
1824, 4 Over 1	2,600	3,500	4,750	6,000	7,500	8,500	15,000
1825	4,434	3,500	4,750	6,000	7,500	8,500	13,000
1826, 6 Over 6	760	4,000	5,500	6,250	8,000	12,000	25,000
1827	2,800	4,000	5,250	6,000	8,000	10,000	15,000
1829	3,403	3,500	4,250	5,000	6,500	8,000	10,000
1830	4,540	3,500	4,250	5,000	6,500	8,000	10,000
1831	4,520	3,500	4,250	5,000	6,500	8,000	10,000
1832	4,400	3,500	4,250	5,000	6,500	8,000	11,000
1833	4,160	3,500	4,250	5,250	6,750	8,000	12,000
1834, With Motto	4,000	5,000	7,500	11,000	15,000	19,000	27,000

CLASSIC HEAD, NO MOTTO ON REVERSE (1834–1839)

In 1834, the quarter eagle was redesigned. A ribbon binding the hair, bearing the word LIBERTY, replaces the Liberty cap. The motto was omitted from the reverse.

F-12 FINE—LIBERTY on headband legible and complete. Curl under ear outlined but no detail.
VF-20 VERY FINE—LIBERTY plain; detail in hair curl.
EF-40 EXTREMELY FINE—Small amount of wear on top of hair and below L in LIBERTY. Wear evident on wing.
AU-50 ABOUT UNCIRCULATED—Trace of wear on coronet and hair above ear.
AU-55 CHOICE ABOUT UNCIRCULATED—Evidence of friction on design high points. Some of original mint luster present.
MS-60 UNCIRCULATED—No trace of wear. Light blemishes.
MS-63 CHOICE UNCIRCULATED—Some distracting contact marks or blemishes in prime focal areas. Impaired luster possible.

Mintmark location.

	Mintage	F-12	VF-20	EF-40	AU-50	AU-55	MS-60	MS-63
1834, No Motto	112,234	$185	$275	$400	$650	$850	$2,000	$4,250
1835	131,402	185	275	400	650	850	2,000	5,000
1836	547,986	185	275	400	650	850	2,000	4,500
1837	45,080	200	275	400	750	850	2,400	8,000
1838	47,030	200	275	400	700	850	2,000	5,000
1838C	7,880	750	1,000	1,750	4,500	6,000	17,500	27,500
1839	27,021	200	300	550	1,200	1,700	3,250	12,500
1839C	18,140	700	1,000	1,600	2,500	4,500	14,000	32,000
1839D	13,674	700	1,000	2,000	4,000	6,000	15,000	35,000
1839O	17,781	300	400	725	1,300	1,800	4,200	16,000

LIBERTY HEAD (1840–1907)

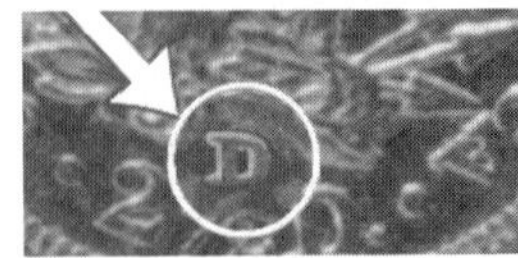

Mintmark location.

4 Plain 4

4 Crosslet 4

	Mintage	VF-20	EF-40	AU-50	AU-55	MS-60	MS-63
1840	18,859	$135	$650	$2,000	$2,350	$4,750	$9,000
1840C	12,822	850	1,200	3,100	4,300	9,000	25,000
1840D	3,532	2,100	6,000	8,500	15,000	27,000	
1840O	33,580	185	600	1,400	2,500	8,000	19,500
1841		36,000	70,000	80,000	85,000	110,000	
1841C	10,281	850	1,200	2,500	5,500	13,000	32,500
1841D	4,164	1,250	3,100	7,750	10,000	20,000	42,500

	Mintage	VF-20	EF-40	AU-50	AU-55	MS-60	MS-63
1842	2,823	$700	$1,850	$4,750	$7,000	$15,000	$37,500
1842C	6,729	1,000	2,300	5,250	7,500	18,000	36,000
1842D	4,643	1,250	2,750	8,250	12,500	25,000	40,000
1842O	19,800	260	800	1,650	3,250	8,250	22,500
1843	100,546	125	200	300	600	1,500	3,500
1843C	26,064	850	1,200	2,100	3,250	6,250	15,000
1843D	36,209	1,000	1,450	2,100	5,500	7,250	21,500
1843O	364,002	135	180	265	550	1,500	6,000
1844	6,784	275	650	1,450	3,250	5,500	16,500
1844C	11,622	900	1,550	5,000	7,250	14,000	34,000
1844D	17,332	1,000	1,400	2,000	3,500	5,100	20,000
1845	91,051	190	230	275	375	875	3,500
1845D	19,460	1,000	1,400	2,600	5,000	10,000	26,000
1845O	4,000	725	1,650	4,500	5,250	14,000	37,500
1846	21,598	200	375	650	1,500	4,000	17,500
1846C	4,808	975	1,850	6,500	8,500	13,000	27,000
1846D	19,303	1,000	1,400	2,000	3,500	8,000	20,000
1846O	62,000	220	300	800	1,500	4,750	14,500
1847	29,814	170	275	625	850	2,650	6,500
1847C	23,226	850	1,200	1,800	2,500	4,800	11,000
1847D	15,784	975	1,425	2,000	3,500	7,500	18,500
1847O	124,000	165	275	750	1,250	3,000	13,500
1848	6,500	375	650	1,350	2,250	4,500	12,000

CAL. Gold Quarter Eagle (1848)

In 1848, about 230 ounces of gold were sent to Secretary of War Marcy by Colonel R.B. Mason, military governor of California. The gold was turned over to the Mint and made into quarter eagles. The distinguishing mark “CAL.” was punched above the eagle on the reverse side, while the coins were in the die.

CAL. Above Eagle on Reverse (1848)

	Mintage	VF-20	EF-40	AU-50	AU-55	MS-60	MS-63
1848, CAL. Above Eagle	1,389	$10,000	$20,000	$25,000	$30,000	$40,000	$57,000
1848C	16,788	850	1,250	2,350	3,000	8,500	23,000
1848D	13,771	1,000	1,450	2,250	3,000	7,000	22,000
1849	23,294	215	360	650	975	1,800	5,500
1849C	10,220	850	1,300	3,750	6,000	16,000	40,000
1849D	10,945	1,000	1,400	2,750	4,250	10,000	25,000
1850	252,923	130	165	275	375	800	2,900
1850C	9,148	850	1,200	2,650	5,000	10,000	27,000
1850D	12,148	975	1,200	2,450	4,750	10,000	34,000
1850O	84,000	160	350	900	1,350	3,500	10,000
1851	1,372,748	130	155	175	190	240	900
1851C	14,923	850	1,200	3,500	4,500	9,250	27,500
1851D	11,264	1,000	1,500	3,000	4,750	9,000	23,500
1851O	148,000	140	160	650	1,250	3,000	9,500
1852	1,159,681	130	155	175	190	250	900
1852C	9,772	850	1,300	3,350	5,000	11,000	25,000
1852D	4,078	1,000	1,950	5,500	6,250	12,500	30,000
1852O	140,000	140	230	700	1,200	3,750	9,000
1853	1,404,668	130	155	175	195	275	900
1853D	3,178	1,200	2,250	3,700	5,000	12,000	35,000

Chart continued on next page.

	Mintage	VF-20	EF-40	AU-50	AU-55	MS-60	MS-63	PF-63
1854	596,258	$130	$155	$175	$195	$275	$1,175	
1854C	7,295	850	1,550	3,900	5,250	10,000	30,000	
1854D	1,760	2,100	4,000	8,500	12,500	20,000	55,000	
1854O	153,000	130	165	325	550	1,200	6,000	
1854S	246	65,000	100,000	210,000				
1855	235,480	130	155	175	195	280	1,250	
1855C	3,677	1,050	2,350	4,650	6,500	19,000	35,000	
1855D	1,123	2,500	5,750	13,500	20,000	38,000	62,500	
1856	384,240	130	155	175	200	300	1,100	$35,000
1856C	7,913	900	1,750	3,000	5,000	11,500	24,500	
1856D	874	5,000	9,000	19,000	25,000	55,000	95,000	
1856O	21,100	155	525	925	2,400	4,000	23,500	
1856S	72,120	150	275	675	1,200	3,350	8,000	
1857	214,130	130	155	175	210	300	1,300	30,000
1857D	2,364	1,000	1,950	2,950	4,750	9,750	22,000	
1857O	34,000	150	275	750	1,250	3,250	9,500	
1857S	69,200	150	260	650	1,500	4,000	9,500	
1858	47,377	130	185	265	350	800	2,500	21,000
1858C	9,056	850	1,200	2,250	2,600	7,000	25,000	
1859 (80)	39,364	130	190	300	400	925	2,400	14,000
1859D	2,244	1,250	2,250	3,600	5,000	14,500	50,000	
1859S	15,200	235	700	1,900	2,600	5,000	13,000	
1860 (112)	22,563	130	190	350	400	850	1,800	13,500
1860C	7,469	850	1,400	2,800	6,000	16,500	28,000	
1860S	35,600	165	500	850	1,200	3,000	8,000	
1861 (90)	1,283,788	135	155	180	195	250	800	14,500
1861S	24,000	260	675	2,250	3,100	5,800	13,000	
1862, 2 Over 1	*	650	1,300	2,600	3,200	6,250		
1862 (35)	98,508	150	235	375	450	925	2,850	12,500
1862S	8,000	650	1,600	3,300	4,750	13,500	28,500	
1863, Proof only (30)								35,000
1863S	10,800	360	1,100	2,400	4,000	10,500	20,000	
1864 (50)	2,824	4,250	8,500	17,500	20,000	30,000		9,000
1865 (25)	1,520	3,600	5,500	14,500	16,000	28,000	34,000	11,500
1865S	23,376	160	475	1,100	1,500	3,350	7,500	
1866 (30)	3,080	950	2,650	4,250	5,500	9,000	19,000	8,000
1866S	38,960	210	475	1,100	1,650	4,750	15,500	
1867 (50)	3,200	275	600	875	1,250	3,000	6,000	8,000
1867S	28,000	180	475	900	1,500	3,100	9,000	
1868 (25)	3,600	170	300	500	650	1,175	5,500	9,000
1868S	34,000	140	225	825	1,000	3,000	9,000	
1869 (25)	4,320	180	250	550	900	2,400	5,500	6,500
1869S	29,500	165	360	625	1,250	3,200	6,750	
1870 (35)	4,520	175	325	575	950	2,850	6,000	6,750
1870S	16,000	140	325	600	1,250	3,200	10,500	
1871 (30)	5,320	180	250	450	625	1,750	3,000	6,750
1871S	22,000	140	210	415	575	1,725	3,600	
1872 (30)	3,000	280	600	825	1,750	3,600	9,000	5,750
1872S	18,000	140	280	700	1,200	3,450	8,500	
1873 (25)	178,000	125	155	185	200	300	800	5,500
1873S	27,000	160	280	675	800	2,100	6,250	
1874 (20)	3,920	185	280	550	725	1,650	4,500	7,500
1875 (20)	400	2,750	4,000	7,000	8,500	15,000	23,000	10,000
1875S	11,600	125	225	600	900	3,350	6,750	
1876 (45)	4,176	215	500	700	1,250	2,600	4,600	5,500
1876S	5,000	175	400	725	1,500	2,600	7,000	
1877 (20)	1,632	280	600	825	1,150	2,350	7,000	6,000
1877S	35,400	125	150	180	210	475	1,800	
1878 (20)	286,240	125	150	180	200	300	800	8,750
1878S	178,000	125	150	180	200	260	1,500	
1879 (30)	88,960	125	150	175	190	260	800	6,250
1879S	43,500	150	210	375	725	1,600	3,800	
1880 (36)	2,960	135	260	475	625	1,000	2,800	6,250

* Included in number below.

	Mintage	VF-20	EF-40	AU-50	AU-55	MS-60	MS-63	PF-63
1881	(51) 640	$1,500	$2,400	$3,500	$4,200	$7,000	$14,000	$5,500
1882	(67) 4,000	150	225	310	390	525	2,000	4,500
1883	(82) 1,920	150	300	750	975	1,500	4,000	4,500
1884	(73) 1,950	150	300	450	600	1,200	2,250	4,500
1885	(87) 800	475	1,300	1,800	2,000	3,500	6,000	4,750
1886	(88) 4,000	140	200	325	375	850	1,800	4,750
1887	(122) 6,160	135	190	260	300	525	1,800	4,350
1888	(97) 16,001	125	170	210	220	240	800	4,350
1889	(48) 17,600	125	160	200	210	250	800	5,250
1890	(93) 8,720	135	175	220	240	375	850	4,500
1891	(80) 10,960	125	155	180	200	310	850	4,250
1892	(105) 2,440	130	180	250	290	575	1,950	4,250
1893	(106) 30,000	125	150	170	190	220	800	4,250
1894	(122) 4,000	130	170	240	260	600	1,250	4,250
1895	(119) 6,000	125	160	210	225	300	850	4,250
1896	(132) 19,070	125	150	175	190	220	800	4,250
1897	(136) 29,768	125	150	175	190	220	800	4,100
1898	(165) 24,000	125	150	175	190	220	800	4,250
1899	(150) 27,200	125	150	175	190	220	800	4,100
1900	(205) 67,000	125	160	200	210	220	800	4,100
1901	(223) 91,100	125	150	175	190	220	800	4,100
1902	(193) 133,540	125	150	175	190	220	800	4,100
1903	(197) 201,060	125	150	175	190	220	800	4,100
1904	(170) 160,790	125	150	175	190	220	800	4,100
1905	(144) 217,800	125	150	175	190	220	800	4,100
1906	(160) 176,330	125	150	175	190	220	800	4,100
1907	(154) 336,294	125	150	175	190	220	800	4,100

INDIAN HEAD (1908–1929)

Bela Lyon Pratt designed this coin and the similar $5 gold piece. The design is incuse.

VF-20 VERY FINE—Hair-cord knot distinct. Feathers at top of head clear. Cheekbone worn.
EF-40 EXTREMELY FINE—Cheekbone, war bonnet, and headband feathers slightly worn.
AU-50 ABOUT UNCIRCULATED—Trace of wear on cheekbone and headdress.
MS-60 UNCIRCULATED—No trace of wear. Light blemishes.
MS-63 CHOICE UNCIRCULATED—Some distracting contact marks or blemishes in prime focal areas. Impaired luster possible.
MS-64 UNCIRCULATED—A few scattered contact marks visible. Good eye appeal and attractive luster.
MATTE PF-63 CHOICE PROOF—Few blemishes in secondary focal areas. No major flaws. Matte surfaces.

Mintmark location is on reverse, to left of arrows.

	Mintage	VF-20	EF-40	AU-50	MS-60	MS-63	MS-64	MATTE PF-63
1908	(236) 564,821	$125	$135	$140	$210	$1,200	$1,600	$5,500
1909	(139) 441,760	125	135	140	200	1,600	2,100	5,500
1910	(682) 492,000	125	135	140	200	1,500	2,500	5,500
1911	(191) 704,000	125	135	140	200	1,200	1,800	5,500
1911D		55,680	1,500	2,600	3,500	6,500	18,500	25,000
1912	(197) 616,000	125	135	140	210	1,700	2,700	5,500
1913	(165) 722,000	125	135	140	210	1,100	1,900	5,750
1914	(117) 240,000	135	150	160	300	5,000	7,500	5,750
1914D	448,000	125	135	140	210	1,700	4,000	
1915	(100) 606,000	125	135	140	190	1,000	1,750	6,000
1925D	578,000	125	130	140	185	800	1,200	
1926	446,000	125	130	140	185	800	1,200	
1927	388,000	125	130	140	185	800	1,200	
1928	416,000	125	130	140	185	800	1,200	
1929	532,000	125	130	140	185	800	1,200	

THREE-DOLLAR GOLD PIECES

The three-dollar gold piece was authorized by the Act of February 21, 1853. Coinage was struck beginning in 1854. It was never popular and saw very little circulation.

VF-20 VERY FINE—Eyebrow, hair about forehead and ear, and bottom curl all worn smooth. Faint details visible on curled feather-ends of headdress.
EF-40 EXTREMELY FINE—Light wear above and to right of eye, and on top of curled feathers.
AU-50 ABOUT UNCIRCULATED—Trace of wear on top of curled feathers and in hair above and to right of eye.
AU-55 CHOICE ABOUT UNCIRCULATED—Evidence of friction on design high points. Much of original mint luster present.
MS-60 UNCIRCULATED—No trace of wear. Light blemishes.
MS-63 CHOICE UNCIRCULATED—Some distracting contact marks or blemishes in prime focal areas. Impaired luster possible.
PF-63 CHOICE PROOF—Reflective surfaces with only a few blemishes in secondary focal places. No major flaws.

Mintmark location is on reverse, below wreath.

	Mintage	VF-20	EF-40	AU-50	AU-55	MS-60	MS-63	PF-63
1854	138,618	$575	$800	$1,100	$1,300	$2,000	$5,000	$47,500
1854D	1,120	6,750	12,000	22,000	32,500	53,000		
1854O	24,000	750	1,500	2,500	5,700	13,500	22,000	
1855	50,555	575	800	1,100	1,300	2,000	5,250	27,500
1855S	6,600	800	1,700	4,500	6,250	19,000	65,000	
1856	26,010	575	850	1,100	1,300	2,100	5,750	15,000
1856S	34,500	600	1,000	1,800	3,700	7,500	17,000	
1857	20,891	575	850	1,100	1,350	2,250	7,500	13,000
1857S	14,000	650	1,500	3,750	5,000	13,000		
1858	2,133	700	1,200	1,800	3,000	5,800	13,000	15,000
1859 (80)	15,558	600	800	1,100	1,350	2,000	5,300	11,000
1860 (119)	7,036	600	850	1,100	1,500	2,200	5,250	7,500
1860S	7,000	650	1,350	4,000	6,500	12,000	30,000	
1861 (113)	5,959	600	850	1,300	1,500	2,700	6,500	11,000
1862 (35)	5,750	600	850	1,300	1,500	2,700	6,500	8,000
1863 (39)	5,000	650	950	1,300	1,600	2,900	6,000	9,000
1864 (50)	2,630	650	950	1,300	1,600	2,900	6,250	9,500
1865 (25)	1,140	850	1,800	3,750	4,500	6,750	12,000	14,000
1866 (30)	4,000	650	800	1,100	1,500	2,700	7,000	9,500
1867 (50)	2,600	650	825	1,100	1,600	2,700	7,000	9,500
1868 (25)	4,850	600	800	1,200	1,450	2,250	5,500	10,000
1869 (25)	2,500	625	825	1,300	1,600	3,000	7,500	10,000
1870 (35)	3,500	600	900	1,400	1,700	3,100	7,750	8,000
1870S *(unique)*			—					
1871 (30)	1,300	650	875	1,250	1,500	3,000	6,750	8,750
1872 (30)	2,000	600	825	1,200	1,400	2,700	7,000	10,500
1873, Open 3 (Original) (25)		2,350	3,500	6,500	9,500			16,000
1873, Close 3		2,200	3,500	6,600	10,000	20,000	30,000	
1874 (20)	41,800	600	800	1,000	1,300	2,000	5,000	12,750
1875, Proof only (20)		15,500	22,000	36,000	40,000			65,000
1876, Proof only (45)		4,500	8,000	10,500	15,000			22,000
1877 (20)	1,468	1,000	2,500	5,000	7,000	12,000	25,000	14,000
1878 (20)	82,304	575	800	1,000	1,300	2,000	5,000	12,500
1879 (30)	3,000	575	800	1,000	1,400	2,100	5,000	10,500
1880 (36)	1,000	600	1,400	1,700	1,825	2,500	5,000	10,000
1881 (54)	500	1,000	2,000	3,400	4,000	5,200	11,000	8,000
1882 (76)	1,500	675	850	1,300	1,500	2,500	5,250	8,000
1883 (89)	900	650	1,100	1,675	2,000	2,700	5,250	8,000
1884 (106)	1,000	650	1,300	1,750	2,000	2,700	5,250	8,000
1885 (109)	801	650	1,300	1,700	2,100	2,800	6,250	8,000
1886 (142)	1,000	625	1,100	1,750	2,000	3,200	6,250	8,000
1887 (160)	6,000	575	625	1,300	1,450	2,500	5,000	8,000
1888 (291)	5,000	575	625	1,100	1,400	2,200	5,000	8,000
1889 (129)	2,300	575	625	1,100	1,400	2,200	5,000	8,000

STELLA (1879–1880)

These pattern coins were first suggested by the Hon. John A. Kasson, then U.S. envoy extraordinary and minister plenipotentiary to Austria-Hungary. It was through the efforts of Dr. W.W. Hubbell, who patented the alloy goloid (used in making another pattern piece, the goloid metric dollar) that we have these beautiful and interesting coins.

The $4 Stella—so called because of the five-pointed star on the reverse—was envisioned by Kasson as America's answer to various foreign gold coins popular in the international market. The British sovereign, Italy's 20 lire, and the 20 pesetas of Spain were three such coins: each smaller than a U.S. $5 gold piece, they were used widely in international trade.

The Stella was one of many proposals made to Congress for an international trade coin, and one of only several that made it to pattern coin form (others include the 1868 $5 and 1874 Bickford $10).

Odds were stacked against the Stella from the start. The denomination of four U.S. dollars didn't match any of the coin's European counterparts, and at any rate the U.S. double eagle ($20 coin)—already used in international commerce—was a more convenient medium of exchange. The Stella was never minted in quantities for circulation.

There are two distinct types in both years of issue. Charles E. Barber designed the Flowing Hair type, and George T. Morgan the Coiled Hair. They were struck as patterns in gold, aluminum, copper, and white metal. Only those struck in gold are listed.

Flowing Hair

Coiled Hair

	Mintage	EF-40	AU-50	PF-60	PF-63	PF-65
1879, Flowing Hair	(425+)	$35,000	$45,000	$65,000	$100,000	$140,000
1879, Coiled Hair *(12 known)*		75,000	95,000	125,000	200,000	365,000
1880, Flowing Hair *(17 known)*		60,000	65,000	80,000	125,000	240,000
1880, Coiled Hair *(8 known)*		115,000	150,000	220,000	350,000	600,000

The half eagle ($5 gold coin) was the first gold coin struck for the United States. It was authorized to be coined by the Act of April 2, 1792. The first type weighed 135 grains, of .91667 fineness. The weight was changed by the Act of June 28, 1834, to 129 grains, of .899225 fineness. Fineness became .900 by the Act of January 18, 1837.

CAPPED BUST TO RIGHT (1795–1807)

F-12 FINE—Liberty's hair worn smooth but with distinct outline. For heraldic type, E PLURIBUS UNUM faint but legible.
VF-20 VERY FINE—Slight to noticeable wear on high spots such as hair, turban, and eagle's head and wings.
EF-40 EXTREMELY FINE—Slight wear on hair and highest part of cheek.
AU-50 ABOUT UNCIRCULATED—Trace of wear on cap, hair, cheek, and drapery.
MS-60 UNCIRCULATED—No trace of wear. Light blemishes.
MS-63 CHOICE UNCIRCULATED—Some distracting contact marks or blemishes in prime focal areas. Impaired luster possible.

Small Eagle (1795–1798)

	Mintage	F-12	VF-20	EF-40	AU-50	AU-55	MS-60	MS-63
1795, Small Eagle	8,707	$8,000	$11,000	$14,000	$19,000	$22,000	$30,000	$100,000

1796, 6 Over 5

1797, 15 Stars

1797, 16 Stars

	Mintage	F-12	VF-20	EF-40	AU-50	AU-55	MS-60	MS-63
1796, 6 Over 5	6,196	$8,500	$12,000	$17,000	$22,000	$24,000	$45,000	$110,000
1797, 15 Stars	3,609	9,500	13,000	23,000	45,000	60,000	90,000	
1797, 16 Stars	3,609	9,500	13,000	21,000	40,000	50,000	85,000	
1798, Small Eagle *(7 known)*			70,000	110,000	190,000	300,000	—	

Heraldic Eagle (1795–1807)

	Mintage	F-12	VF-20	EF-40	AU-50	AU-55	MS-60	MS-63
1795, Heraldic Eagle		$6,000	$9,000	$15,000	$27,500	$35,000	$55,000	$115,000
1797, 7 Over 5		6,000	9,000	16,500	35,000	42,500	100,000	
1798, Large 8, 13-Star Reverse	24,867	1,700	2,300	3,200	6,500	8,000	12,500	
1798, Large 8, 14-Star Reverse	*	2,000	2,700	4,500	10,000	16,000	24,000	
1799	7,451	1,800	2,400	3,000	5,500	6,000	13,000	37,000

* Included in number above.

	Mintage	F-12	VF-20	EF-40	AU-50	AU-55	MS-60	MS-63
1800	37,628	$1,750	$2,200	$2,600	$4,700	$5,200	$7,000	$15,000
1802, 2 Over 1	53,176	1,750	2,200	2,600	4,500	4,700	6,750	13,000
1803, 3 Over 2	33,506	1,750	2,200	2,600	4,500	4,700	6,750	13,000
1804	30,475	1,750	2,200	2,600	4,500	4,700	6,750	13,000
1805	33,183	1,750	2,200	2,600	4,500	4,700	6,750	13,000
1806	64,093	1,750	2,200	2,600	4,500	4,700	6,750	13,000
1807	32,488	1,750	2,200	2,600	4,500	4,700	6,750	13,000

CAPPED BUST TO LEFT (1807–1812)

F-12 FINE—LIBERTY on cap legible but partly weak.
VF-20 VERY FINE—Headband edges slightly worn. LIBERTY bold.
EF-40 EXTREMELY FINE—Slight wear on highest portions of hair; 80% of major curls plain.
AU-50 ABOUT UNCIRCULATED—Trace of wear above eye and on top of cap, cheek, and hair.
AU-55 CHOICE ABOUT UNCIRCULATED—Evidence of friction on design high points. Some mint luster present.
MS-60 UNCIRCULATED—No trace of wear. Light blemishes.
MS-63 CHOICE UNCIRCULATED—Some distracting contact marks or blemishes in prime focal areas. Impaired luster possible.

	Mintage	F-12	VF-20	EF-40	AU-50	AU-55	MS-60	MS-63
1807	51,605	$1,300	$1,600	$2,200	$3,300	$4,000	$5,000	$9,500
1808, All kinds	55,578							
1808, 8 Over 7		1,500	2,200	2,500	4,000	5,250	7,500	17,500
1808		1,300	1,600	2,200	3,300	4,000	5,000	10,000
1809, 9 Over 8	33,875	1,300	1,600	2,200	3,300	4,000	5,000	10,000
1810	100,287	1,300	1,600	2,200	3,300	4,000	5,000	10,000
1811	99,581	1,300	1,600	2,200	3,300	4,000	5,000	10,000
1812	58,087	1,300	1,600	2,200	3,300	4,000	5,000	10,000

CAPPED HEAD TO LEFT (1813–1834)
Large Diameter (1813–1829)

	Mintage	F-12	VF-20	EF-40	AU-50	AU-55	MS-60	MS-63
1813	95,428	$1,500	$1,900	$2,500	$3,500	$4,000	$5,500	$10,000
1814, 4 Over 3	15,454	1,750	2,000	2,750	4,000	4,750	6,500	17,000
1815	635	25,000	35,000	50,000	75,000	85,000	110,000	175,000
1818	48,588	1,800	2,000	2,500	4,000	4,750	6,500	14,500
1819	51,723	7,500	12,500	17,500	25,000	30,000	40,000	65,000
1820	263,806	1,800	2,000	2,500	4,000	4,750	7,500	17,000
1821	34,641	4,000	8,500	13,500	20,000	25,000	45,000	100,000
1822 *(3 known)*	17,796			3,000,000				
1823	14,485	1,800	2,500	3,500	5,000	6,500	13,000	22,500
1824	17,340	3,500	7,500	10,500	15,000	17,500	25,000	42,500
1825, 5 Over Partial 4	29,060	3,500	5,500	8,000	12,500	15,000	25,000	45,000
1825, 5 Over 4 *(2 known)*	*			225,000				
1826	18,069	2,700	5,000	6,500	10,000	12,500	17,500	35,000
1827	24,913	4,000	6,500	8,500	12,500	15,000	25,000	45,000
1828, 8 Over 7 *(5 known)*	*	10,000	15,000	27,500	40,000	45,000	80,000	125,000
1828	28,029	4,000	8,000	12,500	20,000	25,000	45,000	65,000
1829, Large Date	57,442	10,000	18,000	25,000	40,000	45,000	75,000	125,000

* Included in number above.

Reduced Diameter (1829–1834)

	Mintage	F-12	VF-20	EF-40	AU-50	AU-55	MS-60	MS-63
1829, Small Date	*	$25,000	$35,000	$60,000	$80,000	$95,000	$125,000	$175,000
1830	126,351	9,000	12,500	13,500	15,500	17,500	25,000	45,000
1831	140,594	9,000	12,500	13,500	15,500	17,500	25,000	45,000
1832, Curved-Base 2, 12 Stars *(5 known)*	157,487	25,000	35,000	75,000	100,000			
1832, Sq-Base 2, 13 Stars	*	9,000	12,500	13,500	15,500	17,500	25,000	45,000
1833	193,630	9,000	12,500	13,500	15,500	17,500	25,000	45,000
1834	50,141	9,000	12,500	13,500	15,500	17,500	27,500	47,500

* Included in number above.

CLASSIC HEAD (1834–1838)

	Mintage	F-12	VF-20	EF-40	AU-50	AU-55	MS-60	MS-63
1834	657,460	$200	$300	$450	$900	$1,100	$2,500	$6,000
1835	371,534	200	300	450	900	1,100	2,500	6,000
1836	553,147	200	300	450	900	1,100	2,500	6,000
1837	207,121	200	300	475	900	1,100	2,600	9,000
1838	286,588	200	300	475	900	1,100	2,500	8,000
1838C	17,179	800	1,500	3,200	7,500	9,500	21,000	55,000
1838D	20,583	750	1,400	3,000	6,000	8,500	17,000	27,000

LIBERTY HEAD (1839–1908)
Variety 1 – No Motto Above Eagle (1839–1866)

VF-20 VERY FINE—LIBERTY on coronet bold. Major lines show in curls on neck.
EF-40 EXTREMELY FINE—Details clear in curls on neck. Slight wear on top and lower part of coronet and on hair.
AU-50 ABOUT UNCIRCULATED—Trace of wear on coronet and hair above eye.
AU-55 CHOICE ABOUT UNCIRCULATED—Evidence of friction on design high points. Some original mint luster.
MS-60 UNCIRCULATED—No trace of wear. Light blemishes.
MS-63 CHOICE UNCIRCULATED—Some distracting contact marks or blemishes in prime focal areas. Impaired luster possible.
PF-63 CHOICE PROOF—Attractive reflective surfaces with only a few blemishes in secondary focal places. No major flaws.

Mintmark: 1839, above date; 1840–1908, below eagle.

	Mintage	VF-20	EF-40	AU-50	AU-55	MS-60	MS-63
1839	118,143	$185	$325	$750	$1,250	$2,500	$14,000
1839C	17,205	1,200	1,600	4,000	6,000	12,500	32,000

	Mintage	VF-20	EF-40	AU-50	AU-55	MS-60	MS-63	PF-63
1839D	18,939	$1,000	$1,500	$3,650	$5,500	$13,000		
1840	137,382	160	250	875	1,375	2,600	$7,500	
1840C	18,992	1,000	1,750	4,750	8,000	17,500	47,500	
1840D	22,896	1,000	1,450	4,750	5,250	10,500	33,500	
1840O	40,120	220	575	1,275	2,250	7,000	17,500	
1841	15,833	260	625	1,250	1,550	3,550	7,750	$47,500
1841C	21,467	950	1,300	2,150	4,000	11,500	32,500	
1841D	29,392	1,000	1,300	2,250	4,000	10,000	19,000	

1842, Large Date

Large Letters

Small Letters

	Mintage	VF-20	EF-40	AU-50	AU-55	MS-60	MS-63	PF-63
1842, Small Letters	27,578	$230	$750	$2,200	$3,750	$9,500	$16,750	$57,500
1842, Large Letters	*	475	1,400	2,000	3,250	7,750	17,500	
1842C, Small Date	27,432	7,250	16,500	30,000	40,000	77,500		
1842C, Large Date	*	950	1,400	2,350	4,750	12,000	27,500	
1842D, Small Date	59,608	1,000	1,350	2,200	3,750	10,500	25,000	
1842D, Large Date	*	1,675	4,250	10,000	14,000	34,000		
1842O	16,400	700	2,100	6,750	8,000	16,000	30,000	
1843	611,205	150	180	250	375	1,200	7,250	
1843C	44,277	950	1,300	2,650	3,750	8,000	24,000	
1843D	98,452	1,000	1,300	2,250	3,750	8,000	18,000	
1843O, Small Letters	19,075	375	1,000	1,650	3,250	13,500	28,000	
1843O, Large Letters	82,000	200	775	1,375	3,000	8,500	20,000	
1844	340,330	150	165	260	350	1,400	6,500	
1844C	23,631	950	2,100	4,500	6,000	15,500	30,000	
1844D	88,982	1,000	1,550	2,450	3,500	7,500	18,000	
1844O	364,600	180	265	410	1,000	3,000	10,000	
1845	417,099	150	165	250	425	1,450	6,500	
1845D	90,629	1,000	1,300	2,250	3,250	8,250	19,000	
1845O	41,000	275	475	1,900	3,000	7,000	19,500	
1846, Large Date	395,942	150	165	275	700	1,900	11,000	
1846, Small Date	*	150	165	250	425	1,750	9,500	
1846C	12,995	1,000	2,000	4,500	5,500	16,000	50,000	
1846D	80,294	1,000	1,450	2,500	3,250	9,000	16,500	
1846O	58,000	265	675	2,200	3,250	8,250	20,000	
1847	915,981	150	170	230	325	1,000	5,250	
1847C	84,151	950	1,350	2,400	3,000	9,250	19,500	
1847D	64,405	1,000	1,350	2,200	3,250	7,250	13,500	
1847O	12,000	1,300	5,000	6,750	9,000	18,000	26,500	
1848	260,775	155	190	290	400	1,000	8,000	
1848C	64,472	950	1,350	2,500	4,750	14,000	36,000	
1848D	47,465	1,000	1,350	2,200	3,750	10,000	21,000	
1849	133,070	150	185	500	800	1,900	9,500	
1849C	64,823	950	1,350	2,100	4,000	9,500	20,000	
1849D	39,036	1,000	1,350	2,300	3,500	9,500	22,000	
1850	64,491	190	425	750	850	2,600	13,500	
1850C	63,591	950	1,350	2,100	2,500	8,500	17,000	
1850D	43,984	1,000	1,300	2,800	5,500	22,000		

* Included in number above.

Chart continues on next page.

	Mintage	VF-20	EF-40	AU-50	AU-55	MS-60	MS-63	PF-63
1851	377,505	$150	$165	$250	$500	$2,000	$7,250	
1851C	49,176	950	1,300	2,250	4,750	11,000	37,500	
1851D	62,710	1,000	1,300	2,200	4,250	10,000	19,500	
1851O	41,000	400	1,000	2,750	4,250	9,500	14,000	
1852	573,901	150	170	230	300	850	5,000	
1852C	72,574	950	1,350	2,100	2,400	5,000	17,000	
1852D	91,584	1,000	1,350	2,200	3,750	8,000	20,000	
1853	305,770	150	170	250	375	1,000	6,500	
1853C	65,571	950	1,350	2,200	3,100	6,000	20,000	
1853D	89,678	1,000	1,350	2,200	3,200	7,250	18,000	
1854	160,675	150	170	360	800	1,450	6,000	
1854C	39,283	950	1,350	2,700	3,500	8,500	30,000	
1854D	56,413	1,000	1,350	2,200	3,500	7,500	21,000	
1854O	46,000	210	370	975	1,650	5,750	14,500	
1854S	268	—	—	250,000	—			
1855	117,098	150	165	250	400	1,250	6,200	—
1855C	39,788	950	1,400	2,300	3,500	11,000	28,000	
1855D	22,432	1,000	1,350	2,250	3,500	12,000	31,000	
1855O	11,100	425	1,500	3,250	4,500	14,500		
1855S	61,000	275	650	1,550	3,750	10,000		
1856	197,990	150	170	230	400	1,500	8,000	—
1856C	28,457	950	1,300	2,300	4,100	14,500		
1856D	19,786	1,000	1,300	2,600	3,750	7,750	28,500	
1856O	10,000	450	850	3,250	4,500	8,750		
1856S	105,100	215	425	875	1,750	4,750	21,500	
1857	98,188	150	170	275	400	1,100	5,500	—
1857C	31,360	950	1,300	2,250	3,500	6,250	24,000	
1857D	17,046	1,000	1,300	2,500	3,500	9,250	30,000	
1857O	13,000	450	975	3,250	4,250	10,000	39,000	
1857S	87,000	215	375	800	2,000	6,750	13,500	
1858	15,136	170	375	500	950	2,750	6,500	—
1858C	38,856	950	1,350	2,200	3,250	7,250	27,500	
1858D	15,362	1,000	1,350	2,200	3,750	8,750	30,000	
1858S	18,600	475	1,600	3,850	8,000	21,500		
1859 (80)	16,734	225	425	575	1,200	5,000	8,000	$28,000
1859C	31,847	950	1,350	2,650	3,750	10,500	35,000	
1859D	10,366	1,000	1,350	2,250	4,250	10,000	29,000	
1859S	13,220	875	2,500	3,750	5,750	20,000		
1860 (62)	19,763	190	400	775	950	2,800	11,500	22,000
1860C	14,813	950	1,500	2,300	4,000	9,250	20,000	
1860D	14,635	1,000	1,450	2,500	5,000	12,000	36,000	
1860S	21,200	750	1,500	4,000	7,250	18,000		
1861 (66)	688,084	150	175	255	375	850	2,150	21,000
1861C	6,879	1,400	2,800	5,500	8,000	17,000	70,000	
1861D	1,597	3,500	6,000	13,000	19,000	38,000	95,000	
1861S	18,000	600	3,000	4,000	5,500	22,500		
1862 (35)	4,430	350	1,000	2,000	2,750	10,000	25,000	21,000
1862S	9,500	2,000	4,500	10,000	16,000	40,000		
1863 (30)	2,442	750	2,500	4,000	5,500	15,000		21,000
1863S	17,000	850	2,500	6,500	8,000	18,000		
1864 (50)	4,170	400	1,250	2,750	3,500	8,000		21,000
1864S	3,888	3,500	9,000	20,000	25,000	40,000		
1865 (25)	1,270	750	1,500	5,500	6,750	10,000		18,000
1865S	27,612	650	1,500	2,500	3,500	10,000	15,000	
1866S	9,000	1,000	2,200	6,500	9,000	22,500		

Variety 2 – Motto Above Eagle (1866–1908)

VF-20 VERY FINE—Half of hair lines above coronet missing. Hair curls under ear evident, but worn. Motto and its ribbon sharp.
EF-40 EXTREMELY FINE—Small amount of wear on top of hair and below L in LIBERTY. Wear evident on wing tips and neck of eagle.
AU-50 ABOUT UNCIRCULATED—Trace of wear on tip of coronet and hair above eye.
AU-55 CHOICE ABOUT UNCIRCULATED—Evidence of friction on design high points. Some original mint luster present.
MS-60 UNCIRCULATED—No trace of wear. Light blemishes.
MS-63 CHOICE UNCIRCULATED—Some distracting contact marks or blemishes in prime focal areas. Impaired luster possible.
PF-63 CHOICE PROOF—Reflective surfaces with only a few blemishes in secondary focal places. No major flaws.

	Mintage	VF-20	EF-40	AU-50	AU-55	MS-60	MS-63	PF-63
1866 (30)	6,700	$400	$900	$2,000	$2,500	$8,000		$13,000
1866S	34,920	500	1,500	4,500	5,500	14,000		
1867 (50)	6,870	250	900	2,000	2,500	6,500		11,000
1867S	29,000	750	1,550	4,500	6,000	16,000		
1868 (25)	5,700	400	650	1,500	2,000	6,000		13,000
1868S	52,000	250	1,000	1,900	2,500	10,000		
1869 (25)	1,760	500	1,250	1,700	2,200	9,000		13,000
1869S	31,000	300	1,000	1,700	2,500	15,000		
1870 (35)	4,000	400	1,200	1,200	1,800	8,500		13,000
1870CC	7,675	3,000	9,000	17,500	22,000	60,000		
1870S	17,000	450	1,500	4,500	6,000	18,000		
1871 (30)	3,200	500	850	1,850	2,500	8,000		12,000
1871CC	20,770	750	2,250	8,000	12,000	30,000	$60,000	
1871S	25,000	250	500	1,500	2,000	8,000		
1872 (30)	1,660	450	1,000	1,500	2,000	7,500	11,000	12,000
1872CC	16,980	850	3,200	13,000	18,000	40,000		
1872S	36,400	250	350	1,500	1,850	7,500		
1873 (25)	112,505	125	150	200	225	450	2,200	12,000
1873CC	7,416	1,500	8,000	16,000	23,000	40,000		
1873S	31,000	250	750	1,850	2,150	11,000		
1874 (20)	3,488	300	850	1,250	1,500	6,500	12,500	12,000
1874CC	21,198	500	1,200	6,000	7,500	25,000		
1874S	16,000	300	1,200	2,500	3,000	12,000		
1875 (20)	200	22,000	30,000	40,000	55,000			45,000
1875CC	11,828	900	2,500	7,500	11,000	35,000		
1875S	9,000	300	1,100	2,800	4,200	12,000		
1876 (45)	1,432	675	1,300	2,000	3,000	6,500	13,000	10,000
1876CC	6,887	800	3,500	8,500	10,500	27,500		
1876S	4,000	850	1,800	5,000	6,000	14,000		
1877 (20)	1,132	500	1,500	2,000	2,750	7,000	15,000	14,000
1877CC	8,680	600	2,000	6,500	8,500	30,000		
1877S	26,700	200	250	700	800	4,000	10,000	
1878 (20)	131,720	125	135	150	160	225	1,000	15,000
1878CC	9,054	1,700	5,200	13,000	17,000	40,000		
1878S	144,700	125	140	160	175	300	2,000	
1879 (30)	301,920	125	135	150	165	225	1,000	12,000
1879CC	17,281	300	950	2,250	3,500	14,000		
1879S	426,200	125	135	150	170	400	1,500	
1880 (36)	3,166,400	125	135	140	145	160	650	10,000
1880CC	51,017	300	500	1,000	2,000	6,500		
1880S	1,348,900	125	135	140	145	160	600	
1881 (42)	5,708,760	125	135	140	145	160	600	9,500
1881CC	13,886	350	850	4,000	5,500	16,000	40,000	

Chart continues on next page.

	Mintage	VF-20	EF-40	AU-50	AU-55	MS-60	MS-63	PF-63
1881S	969,000	$125	$135	$140	$145	$160	$600	
1882 (48)	2,514,520	125	135	140	145	160	600	$9,500
1882CC	82,817	250	400	500	650	5,000	25,000	
1882S	969,000	125	135	140	145	160	600	
1883 (61)	233,400	125	135	140	145	160	800	9,500
1883CC	12,598	300	750	2,000	3,200	13,000		
1883S	83,200	125	135	170	190	450	1,500	
1884 (48)	191,030	125	135	140	170	400	1,480	9,500
1884CC	16,402	350	700	1,800	3,200	12,500		
1884S	177,000	125	135	140	145	200	1,260	
1885 (66)	601,440	125	135	140	145	160	600	9,500
1885S	1,211,500	125	135	140	145	160	600	
1886 (72)	388,360	125	135	140	145	160	650	9,200
1886S	3,268,000	125	135	140	145	160	600	
1887, Proof Only (87)								32,500
1887S	1,912,000	125	135	140	145	160	600	
1888 (95)	18,201	125	135	140	145	200	900	7,500
1888S	293,900	125	135	185	250	750	2,500	
1889 (45)	7,520	160	220	285	320	750	1,300	8,500
1890 (88)	4,240	240	265	340	500	1,250	4,000	8,500
1890CC	53,800	180	210	320	350	800	4,000	
1891 (53)	61,360	125	135	150	185	280	1,000	8,500
1891CC	208,000	175	210	325	340	425	2,100	
1892 (92)	753,480	125	135	140	145	160	600	8,500
1892CC	82,968	175	210	360	420	1,000	3,500	
1892O	10,000	280	580	800	1,000	2,200	7,000	
1892S	298,400	125	135	160	180	300	2,300	
1893 (77)	1,528,120	125	135	140	145	160	600	8,500
1893CC	60,000	160	250	400	500	900	4,000	
1893O	110,000	135	180	285	350	600	3,800	
1893S	224,000	125	135	140	145	160	650	
1894 (75)	957,880	125	135	140	145	160	600	8,500
1894O	16,600	125	200	310	375	820	3,250	
1894S	55,900	150	215	315	380	1,800	6,400	
1895 (81)	1,345,855	125	135	140	145	160	600	7,200
1895S	112,000	130	150	235	310	2,000	3,750	
1896 (103)	58,960	125	135	140	145	160	650	7,200
1896S	155,400	130	150	190	300	685	3,600	
1897 (83)	867,800	125	135	140	145	160	600	7,200
1897S	354,000	125	135	150	200	550	3,300	
1898 (75)	633,420	125	135	140	145	160	600	7,200
1898S	1,397,400	125	135	140	150	170	650	
1899 (99)	1,710,630	125	135	140	145	160	600	7,200
1899S	1,545,000	125	135	140	145	170	500	
1900 (230)	1,405,500	125	135	140	145	160	600	7,200
1900S	329,000	125	135	140	145	160	600	
1901 (140)	615,900	125	135	140	145	160	600	7,200
1901S, 1 Over 0	3,648,000	125	135	140	145	200	600	
1901S	*	125	135	140	145	160	600	
1902 (162)	172,400	125	135	140	145	160	600	7,200
1902S	939,000	125	135	140	145	160	600	
1903 (154)	226,870	125	135	140	145	160	600	7,200
1903S	1,855,000	125	135	140	145	160	600	
1904 (136)	392,000	125	135	140	145	160	600	7,200
1904S	97,000	125	135	140	200	650	2,500	
1905 (108)	302,200	125	135	140	145	160	600	7,200
1905S	880,700	125	135	140	175	350	950	
1906 (85)	348,735	125	135	140	145	160	600	7,200
1906D	320,000	125	135	140	145	160	600	
1906S	598,000	125	135	140	145	160	700	
1907 (92)	626,100	125	135	140	145	160	600	7,200
1907D	888,000	125	135	140	145	160	600	
1908	421,874	125	135	140	145	160	600	

* Included in number above.

INDIAN HEAD (1908–1929)

This type conforms in design to the quarter eagle of the same date. The incuse designs and lettering make the Indian Head a unique series, along with the quarter eagle, in United States coinage.

VF-20 VERY FINE—Noticeable wear on large middle feathers and tip of eagle's wing.
EF-40 EXTREMELY FINE—Cheekbone, war bonnet, and headband feathers slightly worn. Feathers on eagle's upper wing show considerable wear.
AU-50 ABOUT UNCIRCULATED—Trace of wear on cheekbone and headdress.
AU-55 CHOICE ABOUT UNCIRCULATED—Evidence of friction on design high points. Much of original mint luster present.
MS-60 UNCIRCULATED—No trace of wear. Light blemishes.
MS-63 CHOICE UNCIRCULATED—Some distracting contact marks or blemishes in prime focal areas. Impaired luster possible.
MATTE PF-63—Matte surfaces with only a few blemishes in secondary focal places. No major flaws.

Mintmark Location

Scarcer coins with well struck mintmarks command higher prices.

	Mintage	VF-20	EF-40	AU-50	AU-55	MS-60	MS-63	MATTE PF-63
1908 . . . . . . (167)	577,845	$200	$210	$225	$240	$300	$1,600	$7,000
1908D	148,000	200	210	225	240	300	1,600	
1908S	82,000	225	275	300	340	800	2,000	
1909 . . . . . . (78)	627,060	200	225	225	240	300	1,600	7,500
1909D	3,423,560	200	225	225	240	300	1,600	
1909O	34,200	1,500	1,800	3,000	4,500	14,000	40,000	
1909S	297,200	225	250	270	300	850	7,500	
1910 . . . . . . (250)	604,000	200	225	225	240	300	1,600	7,500
1910D	193,600	210	220	225	240	300	1,850	
1910S	770,200	225	250	270	290	650	3,800	
1911 . . . . . . (139)	915,000	200	210	225	240	300	1,600	7,200
1911D	72,500	300	300	375	500	2,500	24,000	
1911S	1,416,000	225	250	270	285	400	2,700	
1912 . . . . . . (144)	790,000	200	210	225	240	300	1,600	7,200
1912S	392,000	225	235	290	350	1,000	8,500	
1913 . . . . . . (99)	915,901	200	210	225	240	300	1,600	7,200
1913S	408,000	225	225	275	325	900	7,500	
1914 . . . . . . (125)	247,000	200	210	225	240	300	1,600	7,200
1914D	247,000	200	210	225	240	300	2,000	
1914S	263,000	225	235	290	310	800	9,000	
1915 . . . . . . (75)	588,000	200	210	225	240	300	1,600	10,000
1915S	164,000	225	250	320	415	1,350	12,000	
1916S	240,000	225	250	300	290	420	2,000	
1929	662,000	4,200	5,000	5,500	6,500	7,000	12,500	

Coinage authority including specified weights and fineness of the eagle conforms to that of the half eagle. The small eagle reverse was used until 1797, when the large, heraldic eagle replaced it.

CAPPED BUST TO RIGHT (1795–1804)

F-12 FINE—Details on turban and head obliterated.
VF-20 VERY FINE—Hair lines in curls on neck and details under turban and over forehead worn but distinguishable.
EF-40 EXTREMELY FINE—Definite wear on hair to left of eye and strand of hair across and around turban, as well as on eagle's wing tips.
AU-50 ABOUT UNCIRCULATED—Trace of wear on cap, hair, cheek, and drapery
AU-55 CHOICE ABOUT UNCIRCULATED—Evidence of friction on design high points. Most of original mint luster present.
MS-60 UNCIRCULATED—No trace of wear. Light blemishes.
MS-63 CHOICE UNCIRCULATED—Some distracting contact marks or blemishes in prime focal areas. Impaired luster possible.

Small Eagle (1795–1797)

	Mintage	F-12	VF-20	EF-40	AU-50	AU-55	MS-60	MS-63
1795	5,583	$11,000	$14,000	$16,000	$25,000	$32,000	$55,000	$140,000
1796	4,146	12,000	16,000	22,000	30,000	32,000	60,000	160,000
1797, Small Eagle	3,615	17,000	22,000	27,000	55,000	65,000	135,000	

Heraldic Eagle (1797–1804)

	Mintage	F-12	VF-20	EF-40	AU-50	AU-55	MS-60	MS-63
1797, Large Eagle	10,940	$6,000	$7,000	$10,000	$16,500	$20,000	$25,000	$50,000
1798, 8/7, 9 Stars Left, 4 Rt	900	8,000	10,000	19,000	26,000	36,000	65,000	170,000
1798, 8/7, 7 Stars Left, 6 Rt	842	17,000	25,000	45,000	90,000	100,000	150,000	
1799	37,449	4,500	6,000	6,500	9,000	12,000	17,000	27,000
1800	5,999	4,500	6,000	6,500	9,500	13,000	20,000	43,000

	Mintage	F-12	VF-20	EF-40	AU-50	AU-55	MS-60	MS-63
1801	44,344	$4,500	$6,000	$6,500	$9,000	$12,000	$15,000	$22,000
1803	15,017	4,500	6,000	6,500	10,000	12,500	16,000	35,000
1804	3,757	7,000	9,000	13,000	17,000	20,000	27,000	90,000

LIBERTY HEAD, NO MOTTO ABOVE EAGLE (1838–1866)

In 1838 the weight and diameter of the eagle were reduced and the obverse and reverse were redesigned. Liberty now faced left and the word LIBERTY was placed on the coronet.

VF-20 VERY FINE—Hair lines above coronet partly worn. Curls under ear worn but defined.
EF-40 EXTREMELY FINE—Small amount of wear on top of hair and below L in LIBERTY. Wear evident on wing tips and neck of eagle.
AU-50 ABOUT UNCIRCULATED—Trace of wear on tip of coronet and hair above eye.
AU-55 CHOICE ABOUT UNCIRCULATED—Evidence of friction on design high points. Some of original mint luster present.
MS-60 UNCIRCULATED—No trace of wear. Light blemishes.
MS-63 CHOICE UNCIRCULATED—Some distracting contact marks or blemishes in prime focal areas. Impaired luster possible.
PF-63 CHOICE PROOF—Attractive reflective surfaces with only a few blemishes in secondary focal places. No major flaws.

Mintmark is on reverse, below eagle.

	Mintage	VF-20	EF-40	AU-50	AU-55	MS-60	MS-63	PF-63
1838	7,200	$560	$1,575	$3,400	$4,800	$22,000	$55,000	
1839, Large Letters	25,801	560	1,075	3,000	4,000	20,000	36,000	
1839, Small Letters	12,447	775	1,950	4,000	5,200	22,000	64,000	
1840	47,338	330	360	800	1,000	6,800		
1841	63,131	330	360	640	800	5,000	18,000	
1841O	2,500	1,120	2,700	7,200	9,600	21,000		
1842	81,507	325	360	700	1,000	6,800	13,000	
1842O	27,400	330	390	1,400	2,000	11,700	23,000	
1843	75,462	330	365	800	1,200	8,000		
1843O	175,162	330	360	620	1,000	7,200		
1844	6,361	580	1,640	3,200	4,000	11,000	20,000	
1844O	118,700	330	360	1,040	1,240	9,800		
1845	26,153	370	450	1,260	1,500	9,000		
1845O	47,500	330	430	1,120	1,700	10,000	30,000	
1846	20,095	400	600	3,200	4,200	15,000		
1846O	81,780	330	450	2,000	2,520	9,000	27,000	
1847	862,258	320	330	365	420	2,100	16,500	
1847O	571,500	320	330	365	425	3,750	14,000	
1848	145,484	300	340	500	600	3,420	18,000	$135,000
1848O	35,850	400	750	2,000	2,480	9,400	20,000	
1849	653,618	320	340	360	420	2,400	9,200	
1849O	23,900	375	1,200	3,000	3,980	15,800		
1850	291,451	320	330	360	425	2,650	12,600	
1850O	57,500	350	500	1,960	2,420	11,300		
1851	176,328	320	330	365	460	3,000	18,000	
1851O	263,000	320	350	560	680	4,160	16,000	
1852	263,106	320	330	365	460	3,000	18,000	
1852O	18,000	400	620	2,280	4,000	13,000		
1853, 3 Over 2	201,253	350	460	1,100	1,400	10,400		
1853	*	320	330	360	420	2,600	12,000	
1853O	51,000	320	350	600	985	9,100		
1854	54,250	320	330	440	560	4,000	13,000	
1854O	52,500	320	425	960	1,160	6,260	25,000	
1854S	123,826	320	375	495	680	7,160	28,000	

* Included in number above.

Chart continued on next page.

	Mintage	VF-20	EF-40	AU-50	AU-55	MS-60	MS-63	PF-63
1855	121,701	$320	$330	$360	$425	$2,660	$12,300	—
1855O	18,000	400	800	3,000	4,100	15,000		
1855S	9,000	900	1,360	4,000	5,500	22,400		
1856	60,490	320	330	360	600	2,650	8,000	—
1856O	14,500	450	800	2,300	3,000	11,000		
1856S	68,000	325	450	640	1,300	6,500	14,000	
1857	16,606	350	600	1,160	1,800	9,000		—
1857O	5,500	500	1,140	1,975	2,380	13,800		
1857S	26,000	340	500	1,260	1,340	7,725	10,800	
1858	2,521	3,000	4,500	7,000	9,000	23,000		—
1858O	20,000	325	460	1,000	1,500	6,500	15,000	
1858S	11,800	900	1,875	2,700	6,000	19,800		
1859 (80)	16,013	320	400	700	1,300	5,000	8,000	$39,000
1859O	2,300	3,000	4,500	9,000	12,000	33,000		
1859S	7,000	1,200	3,000	7,500	9,000	30,000		
1860 (50)	15,055	320	425	900	1,400	4,750	11,300	28,000
1860O	11,100	350	800	1,400	1,800	8,800		
1860S	5,000	1,500	3,200	9,200	12,000	28,000		
1861 (69)	113,164	320	330	360	400	2,100	8,000	26,000
1861S	15,500	900	2,000	3,480	6,000	22,000		
1862 (35)	10,960	350	650	1,325	1,500	7,600		26,000
1862S	12,500	1,000	2,000	3,000	5,000	24,000		
1863 (30)	1,218	2,500	5,000	10,000	12,000	33,000	60,000	28,000
1863S	10,000	900	2,060	5,000	7,000	15,600		
1864 (50)	3,530	1,200	2,200	4,420	5,280	10,000		28,000
1864S	2,500	3,000	6,590	15,800	17,800	36,000		
1865 (25)	3,980	1,100	1,900	4,500	5,000	25,000	35,000	28,000
1865S	16,700	2,000	5,125	9,600	11,400	31,000		
1866S	8,500	1,100	2,300	7,500	9,000	30,000		

LIBERTY HEAD, MOTTO ABOVE EAGLE (1866–1907)

VF-20 VERY FINE—Half of hair lines over coronet visible. Curls under ear worn but defined. IN GOD WE TRUST and its ribbon sharp.
EF-40 EXTREMELY FINE—Small amount of wear on top of hair and below L in LIBERTY. Wear evident on wing tips and neck of eagle.
AU-50 ABOUT UNCIRCULATED—Trace of wear on hair above eye and on coronet.
AU-55 CHOICE ABOUT UNCIRCULATED—Evidence of friction on design high points. Some of original mint luster present.
MS-60 UNCIRCULATED—No trace of wear. Light blemishes.
MS-63 CHOICE UNCIRCULATED—Some distracting contact marks or blemishes in prime focal areas. Impaired luster possible.
PF-63 CHOICE PROOF—Reflective surfaces with only a few blemishes in secondary focal areas. No major flaws.

Mintmark is on reverse, below eagle.

	Mintage	VF-20	EF-40	AU-50	AU-55	MS-60	MS-63	PF-63
1866 (30)	3,750	$500	$1,020	$2,720	$3,260	$14,500		$21,500
1866S	11,500	900	2,000	4,000	5,000	20,000		
1867 (50)	3,090	1,000	1,475	2,920	3,600	18,000		22,500
1867S	9,000	1,500	3,490	5,100	6,200	29,750		
1868 (25)	10,630	350	500	1,000	1,500	10,000		23,800
1868S	13,500	900	1,275	2,200	3,450	17,000		
1869 (25)	1,830	1,000	1,600	3,000	7,000	20,000		21,500
1869S	6,430	900	1,500	3,500	7,000	16,000		
1870 (35)	3,990	600	700	1,250	1,600	10,000		21,500
1870CC	5,908	6,000	16,000	30,000	50,000	70,000	$112,000	
1870S	8,000	600	1,500	3,800	7,500	18,000		

	Mintage	VF-20	EF-40	AU-50	AU-55	MS-60	MS-63	PF-63
1871	(30) 1,790	$900	$1,700	$2,485	$5,000	$12,750		$22,800
1871CC	8,085	1,300	3,200	9,500	11,260	42,900	$54,000	
1871S	16,500	625	1,000	3,425	4,040	18,800		
1872	(30) 1,620	1,500	2,100	6,000	7,250	10,200	23,000	21,500
1872CC	4,600	1,400	5,000	14,000	16,900	43,000	54,000	
1872S	17,300	400	550	1,060	2,000	12,000		
1873	(25) 800	3,000	6,500	10,000	12,000	35,000		25,000
1873CC	4,543	2,200	6,400	14,500	18,000	45,000	54,000	
1873S	12,000	600	1,000	2,700	3,500	20,000		
1874	(20) 53,140	330	340	350	370	1,200	5,000	23,800
1874CC	16,767	575	1,500	4,800	5,800	32,000	53,000	
1874S	10,000	750	2,100	4,000	5,600	30,000		
1875	(20) 100	27,000	32,000	42,000				80,000
1875CC	7,715	2,200	5,500	14,000	16,750	47,000	63,000	
1876	(45) 687	1,900	4,000	7,600	8,900	38,000		19,000
1876CC	4,696	2,000	4,200	11,200	13,000	38,000	50,000	
1876S	5,000	850	1,000	3,225	3,800	27,600		
1877	(20) 797	1,500	3,000	4,500	5,300	18,000		19,000
1877CC	3,332	1,500	3,000	8,000	9,860	34,000		
1877S	17,000	340	550	1,200	1,380	16,600		
1878	(20) 73,780	320	330	340	360	575	3,400	19,000
1878CC	3,244	2,000	5,500	11,200	14,500	34,000		
1878S	26,100	330	400	965	1,125	8,500	20,000	
1879	(30) 384,740	320	330	340	350	375	2,680	16,600
1879CC	1,762	3,500	7,500	14,000	16,600	47,000		
1879O	1,500	1,200	2,750	5,125	6,200	21,750		
1879S	224,000	320	330	340	345	675	3,960	
1880	(36) 1,644,840	320	330	340	345	350	2,000	15,200
1880CC	11,190	330	500	925	1,085	8,920		
1880O	9,200	325	450	820	975	5,100		
1880S	506,250	320	330	340	345	350		
1881	(40) 3,877,220	320	330	340	345	350	800	15,200
1881CC	24,015	350	400	580	685	3,900	14,400	
1881O	8,350	325	430	675	800	4,700		
1881S	970,000	320	330	340	345	350	2,400	
1882	(40) 2,324,440	320	330	340	345	350	700	13,300
1882CC	6,764	400	640	1,800	2,500	9,900	18,000	
1882O	10,820	325	400	725	1,200	3,900	11,000	
1882S	132,000	320	330	340	345	360	1,800	
1883	(40) 208,700	320	330	340	345	350	1,650	13,300
1883CC	12,000	350	550	1,320	1,460	8,900	27,000	
1883O	800	1,600	4,750	6,500	7,500	22,500		
1883S	38,000	320	330	340	345	650	7,200	
1884	(45) 76,860	320	330	340	345	360	2,500	13,300
1884CC	9,925	400	600	1,350	2,000	7,860	25,000	
1884S	124,250	320	330	340	345	370	3,000	
1885	(65) 253,462	320	330	340	345	350	2,650	11,400
1885S	228,000	320	330	340	345	350	2,000	
1886	(60) 236,100	320	330	340	345	350	2,200	10,900
1886S	826,000	320	330	340	345	350	900	
1887	(80) 53,600	320	330	340	345	425	2,600	10,900
1887S	817,000	320	330	340	345	350	1,800	
1888	(75) 132,921	320	330	340	345	400	2,600	10,500
1888O	21,335	320	330	340	345	360	3,000	
1888S	648,700	320	330	340	345	350	2,000	
1889	(45) 4,440	330	360	500	800	1,600	3,800	10,500
1889S	425,400	320	330	340	345	350	900	
1890	(63) 57,980	320	330	340	345	475	3,200	8,500
1890CC	17,500	375	340	350	600	1,250	9,000	
1891	(48) 91,820	320	330	340	345	350	2,650	8,500
1891CC	103,732	320	340	360	450	550	3,160	
1892	(72) 797,480	320	330	340	345	350	900	8,500
1892CC	40,000	375	380	425	500	2,200	5,860	
1892O	28,688	320	330	340	345	350	3,600	
1892S	115,500	320	330	340	345	350	2,600	
1893	(55) 1,840,840	320	330	340	345	350	720	8,500

Chart continues on next page.

	Mintage	VF-20	EF-40	AU-50	AU-55	MS-60	MS-63	PF-63
1893CC	14,000	$375	$550	$950	$1,600	$4,000	$12,500	
1893O	17,000	320	330	340	345	420	3,750	
1893S	141,350	320	330	340	345	350	3,000	
1894	(43) 2,470,735	320	330	340	345	350	700	$8,500
1894O	107,500	320	330	340	345	600	3,400	
1894S	25,000	320	330	500	675	2,200	8,000	
1895	(56) 567,770	320	330	340	345	350	750	8,500
1895O	98,000	320	330	340	345	350	2,750	
1895S	49,000	320	330	360	380	1,450	6,200	
1896	(78) 76,270	320	330	340	345	350	1,400	8,500
1896S	123,750	320	330	350	400	1,425	7,750	
1897	(69) 1,000,090	320	330	340	345	350	700	8,500
1897O	42,500	320	330	340	345	560	2,675	
1897S	234,750	320	330	340	345	565	2,500	
1898	(67) 812,130	320	330	340	345	350	1,120	8,300
1898S	473,600	320	330	340	345	350	2,700	
1899	(86) 1,262,219	320	330	340	345	350	740	8,300
1899O	37,047	320	330	340	345	420	3,000	
1899S	841,000	320	330	340	345	350	1,650	
1900	(120) 293,840	320	330	340	345	350	740	8,300
1900S	81,000	320	330	340	345	575	3,000	
1901	(85) 1,718,740	320	330	340	345	350	700	8,300
1901O	72,041	320	330	340	345	350	1,950	
1901S	2,812,750	320	330	340	345	350	700	
1902	(113) 82,400	320	330	340	345	350	950	8,300
1902S	469,500	320	330	340	345	350	700	
1903	(96) 125,830	320	330	340	345	350	700	8,300
1903O	112,771	320	330	340	345	360	2,400	
1903S	538,000	320	330	340	345	350	775	
1904	(108) 161,930	320	330	340	345	350	700	8,300
1904O	108,950	320	330	340	345	350	2,000	
1905	(86) 200,992	320	330	340	345	350	860	8,300
1905S	369,250	320	330	340	345	675	3,000	
1906	(77) 165,420	320	330	340	345	350	1,000	8,300
1906D	981,000	320	330	340	345	350	750	
1906O	86,895	320	330	340	345	350	2,200	
1906S	457,000	320	330	340	345	360	2,500	
1907	(74) 1,203,899	320	330	340	345	350	700	8,300
1907D	1,030,000	320	330	340	345	350	1,000	
1907S	210,500	320	330	340	345	380	2,400	

INDIAN HEAD (1907–1933)

VF-20 VERY FINE—Bonnet feathers worn near band. Wear visible on high points of hair.
EF-40 EXTREMELY FINE—Slight wear on cheekbone and headdress feathers. Slight wear visible on eagle's eye and left wing.
AU-50 ABOUT UNCIRCULATED—Trace of wear on hair above eye and on forehead.
AU-55 CHOICE ABOUT UNCIRCULATED—Evidence of friction on design high points. Much of original mint luster present.
MS-60 UNCIRCULATED—No trace of wear. Light blemishes.
MS-63 CHOICE UNCIRCULATED—Some distracting contact marks or blemishes in prime focal areas. Impaired luster possible.
MATTE PF-63—Matte surfaces with only a few blemishes in secondary focal places. No major flaws.

No Motto
Mintmark is above left tip of branch on 1908-D No Motto.

With Motto IN GOD WE TRUST
Mintmark is at left of arrow points.

Gem Uncirculated (MS-65) coins are rare and worth substantial premiums.

	Mintage	VF-20	EF-40	AU-50	AU-55	MS-60	MS-63
1907, Wire Rim, Periods	500	$8,500	$9,500	$11,000	$12,000	$12,500	$18,000
1907, Rounded Rim, Periods Before and After E PLURIBUS UNUM	42	16,000	18,000	20,000	25,000	30,000	50,000
1907, No Periods	239,406	350	360	400	420	475	1,800
1908, No Motto	33,500	390	390	410	425	580	2,800
1908D, No Motto	210,000	350	360	400	420	600	4,200

Variety 2 – Motto on Reverse (1908–1933)

		Mintage	VF-20	EF-40	AU-50	AU-55	MS-60	MS-63	MATTE PF-63
1908	(116)	341,370	$375	$390	$400	$410	$440	$1,250	$11,000
1908D		836,500	375	390	400	410	525	4,500	
1908S		59,850	375	400	425	490	1,500	5,700	
1909	(74)	184,789	375	390	400	410	440	1,600	11,000
1909D		121,540	375	390	400	410	470	2,600	
1909S		292,350	375	390	400	410	500	2,600	
1910	(204)	318,500	375	390	400	410	440	1,100	11,000
1910D		2,356,640	375	390	400	410	440	950	
1910S		811,000	375	390	400	410	500	3,800	
1911	(95)	505,500	375	390	400	410	440	1,000	11,000
1911D		30,100	440	500	600	800	2,800	11,500	
1911S		51,000	375	450	475	550	750	4,750	
1912	(83)	405,000	375	390	400	410	440	950	11,000
1912S		300,000	375	390	400	410	600	3,600	
1913	(71)	442,000	375	390	400	410	440	850	11,000
1913S		66,000	425	450	600	800	2,500	18,000	
1914	(50)	151,000	375	390	400	420	440	1,350	11,000
1914D		343,500	375	390	400	420	440	1,350	
1914S		208,000	375	390	400	420	475	3,500	
1915	(75)	351,000	375	390	400	410	440	1,100	11,000
1915S		59,000	475	500	600	800	2,000	8,000	
1916S		138,500	375	390	400	420	500	3,000	
1920S		126,500	5,000	5,500	6,000	7,500	12,500	42,000	
1926		1,014,000	375	390	400	410	440	850	
1930S		96,000	4,200	5,000	6,000	7,000	8,500	17,000	
1932		4,463,000	375	390	400	410	440	850	
1933		312,500	40,000	50,000	60,000	75,000	120,000	160,000	

This largest denomination of all regular United States issues was authorized to be coined by the Act of March 3, 1849. The coin's weight was set at 516 grains, and its fineness at .900. A single pattern of 1849 resides in the Smithsonian.

LIBERTY HEAD (1849–1907)

VF-20 VERY FINE—LIBERTY on crown bold; prongs on crown defined; lower half worn flat. Hair worn about ear.
EF-40 EXTREMELY FINE—Trace of wear on rounded prongs of crown and down hair curls. Minor bagmarks.
AU-50 ABOUT UNCIRCULATED—Trace of wear on hair over eye and on coronet.
AU-55 CHOICE ABOUT UNCIRCULATED—Evidence of friction on design high points. Some of original mint luster present.
MS-60 UNCIRCULATED—No trace of wear. Light blemishes.
MS-63 CHOICE UNCIRCULATED—Some distracting contact marks or blemishes in prime focal areas. Impaired luster possible.
PF-63 CHOICE PROOF—Reflective surfaces with only a few blemishes in secondary focal areas. No major flaws.

Without Motto on Reverse (1849–1866)

Mintmark is below eagle.

	Mintage	VF-20	EF-40	AU-50	AU-55	MS-60	MS-63	PF-63
1850	1,170,261	$650	$660	$1,525	$2,000	$5,500	$30,000	
1850O	141,000	650	1,500	5,000	10,000	22,000		
1851	2,087,155	650	660	675	800	2,100	12,500	
1851O	315,000	650	660	1,500	5,000	15,000	40,000	
1852	2,053,026	650	660	675	700	2,100	8,600	
1852O	190,000	650	700	2,100	4,000	14,000	32,000	
1853	1,261,326	650	660	675	700	2,700	14,000	
1853O	71,000	680	800	1,800	4,000	17,000		
1854	757,899	650	660	675	700	3,600	16,000	
1854O	3,250	45,000	100,000	190,000	250,000	400,000		
1854S	141,468	650	660	950	1,500	3,200	9,000	
1855	364,666	650	660	800	1,400	6,000		
1855O	8,000	1,800	4,500	13,000	20,000	50,000		
1855S	879,675	650	660	750	1,300	4,250	11,000	
1856	329,878	650	660	750	1,500	5,200	14,000	
1856O	2,250	50,000	90,000	200,000	230,000	350,000	450,000	
1856S	1,189,750	650	660	800	1,000	3,000	7,400	
1857	439,375	650	660	600	800	2,000	16,100	
1857O	30,000	700	1,200	3,000	7,000	17,000	80,000	
1857S	970,500	650	660	675	1,000	2,600	4,500	
1858	211,714	650	660	700	1,500	2,900	22,000	
1858O	35,250	850	1,300	4,000	9,000	18,000		
1858S	846,710	650	660	800	1,500	5,600	18,000	
1859 (80)	43,597	675	1,160	2,300	3,500	18,000		$55,000
1859O	9,100	2,500	4,750	15,000	20,000	60,000		
1859S	636,445	650	675	900	1,500	3,000		
1860 (59)	577,670	650	660	675	700	2,260	12,000	45,000
1860O	6,600	1,750	3,600	13,000	22,000	70,000		
1860S	544,950	650	750	1,000	2,000	4,000	12,300	
1861 (66)	2,976,453	650	660	675	750	1,600	6,000	45,000
1861O	17,741	1,400	2,600	14,000	20,000	52,000		
1861S	768,000	650	660	1,100	2,000	6,500	35,000	
1862 (35)	92,133	650	1,000	2,500	4,000	10,000	20,600	38,000

Chart continued on next page.

	Mintage	VF-20	EF-40	AU-50	AU-55	MS-60	MS-63	PF-63
1862S	854,173	$650	$700	$1,000	$2,000	$6,200		
1863 (30)	142,790	650	700	1,500	4,000	11,000	$22,000	
1863S	966,570	650	700	1,000	1,500	4,500	19,000	
1864 (50)	204,235	650	700	1,200	2,500	8,000	16,000	$38,000
1864S	793,660	650	700	1,000	1,600	3,800	20,000	
1865 (25)	351,175	650	675	700	1,000	3,600	10,000	38,000
1865S	1,042,500	650	660	700	1,000	2,000	4,000	
1866S	12,000	1,900	6,000	20,000	40,000	110,000		

Motto Above Eagle

Value TWENTY D. (1866–1876)

	Mintage	VF-20	EF-40	AU-50	AU-55	MS-60	MS-63	PF-63
1866 (30)	698,745	$640	$650	$800	$1,200	$3,500	$18,000	$38,000
1866S	842,250	640	650	900	2,100	9,500		
1867 (50)	251,015	640	650	675	900	1,600	12,400	38,000
1867S	920,750	640	650	880	1,500	9,000		
1868 (25)	98,575	640	650	1,000	1,600	6,500	20,000	30,000
1868S	837,500	640	650	700	1,200	6,000		
1869 (25)	175,130	640	650	700	1,100	3,750	12,750	30,000
1869S	686,750	640	650	675	1,000	4,000	20,000	
1870 (35)	155,150	640	650	925	1,100	5,750		30,000
1870CC	3,789	60,000	90,000	190,000	250,000	350,000		
1870S	982,000	640	650	660	850	3,000	16,500	
1871 (30)	80,120	640	650	860	1,000	3,100	14,000	28,000
1871CC	17,387	3,100	6,000	13,000	19,000	27,500		
1871S	928,000	640	650	665	675	2,600	13,600	
1872 (30)	251,850	640	650	665	675	1,700	16,000	28,000
1872CC	26,900	1,000	1,400	3,500	6,500	16,000		
1872S	780,000	640	650	665	675	1,800	15,200	
1873 (25)	1,709,800	640	650	665	675	700	7,250	28,000
1873CC	22,410	1,250	2,200	3,600	7,000	20,000	66,000	
1873S	1,040,600	640	650	665	665	1,000	12,000	
1874 (20)	366,780	640	650	665	675	1,000	12,300	30,000
1874CC	115,085	600	825	1,300	1,700	4,800		
1874S	1,214,000	640	650	660	675	900	15,000	
1875 (20)	295,720	640	650	660	665	675	6,800	55,000
1875CC	111,151	650	700	860	1,000	1,500	11,000	
1875S	1,230,000	640	650	660	665	675	10,000	
1876 (45)	583,860	640	650	660	665	675	7,300	29,000
1876CC	138,441	600	700	900	1,200	2,700	19,000	
1876S	1,597,000	640	650	660	665	675	7,500	

Value TWENTY DOLLARS (1877–1907)

	Mintage	VF-20	EF-40	AU-50	AU-55	MS-60	MS-63	PF-63
1877 (20)	397,650	$640	$650	$660	$665	$675	$6,000	$20,000
1877CC	42,565	850	900	1,500	2,500	11,000		
1877S	1,735,000	640	650	660	665	675	7,750	
1878 (20)	543,625	640	650	660	665	675	4,500	23,500
1878CC	13,180	1,100	1,800	2,800	5,500	16,500		
1878S	1,739,000	640	650	660	665	675	13,750	
1879 (30)	207,600	640	650	660	665	600	7,950	26,000
1879CC	10,708	1,300	2,100	3,500	6,000	20,000		
1879O	2,325	4,000	5,000	15,000	20,000	50,000	75,000	
1879S	1,223,800	640	650	660	665	800		
1880 (36)	51,420	640	650	660	670	1,600	10,400	21,000
1880S	836,000	640	650	660	665	700	9,400	
1881 (61)	2,199	3,000	4,000	8,000	10,000	29,000		23,500
1881S	727,000	640	650	660	665	675	11,000	
1882 (59)	571	4,200	12,000	18,000	23,000	45,000	75,000	23,500
1882CC	39,140	700	850	1,060	1,400	4,250		
1882S	1,125,000	640	650	660	665	675	8,500	
1883, Proof only (92)								40,000
1883CC	59,962	700	800	1,000	1,200	2,600	13,000	
1883S	1,189,000	640	650	660	665	675	5,500	
1884, Proof only (71)								38,000
1884CC	81,139	675	710	880	975	1,600	13,000	
1884S	916,000	640	650	660	665	675	3,750	
1885 (77)	751	3,700	4,750	6,200	7,060	21,000	35,000	21,000
1885CC	9,450	1,175	1,680	3,000	3,260	6,100	30,000	
1885S	683,500	640	650	660	665	675	4,200	
1886 (106)	1,000	6,000	9,500	18,000	22,000	30,000	50,000	21,000
1887, Proof only (121)								38,000
1887S	283,000	640	650	660	665	675	8,900	
1888 (105)	226,161	640	650	660	665	675	2,975	16,500
1888S	859,600	640	650	660	665	675	2,750	
1889 (41)	44,070	640	650	660	665	675	6,860	16,500
1889CC	30,945	675	800	1,150	1,220	2,000	9,800	
1889S	774,700	640	650	660	665	675	4,000	
1890 (55)	75,940	640	650	660	665	675	4,200	16,500
1890CC	91,209	675	685	760	825	1,350	17,000	
1890S	802,750	640	650	660	665	675	5,000	

Chart continued on next page.

	Mintage	VF-20	EF-40	AU-50	AU-55	MS-60	MS-63	PF-63
1891	(52)....... 1,390	$1,800	$2,800	$4,900	$9,000	$24,000		$15,500
1891CC	5,000	2,000	4,500	5,500	6,500	12,000	$28,000	
1891S	1,288,125	640	650	660	665	675	2,100	
1892	(93)....... 4,430	700	900	1,420	1,540	3,500	12,000	15,500
1892CC	27,265	710	750	1,080	1,160	2,200	15,750	
1892S	930,150	640	650	660	665	675	2,500	
1893	(59)..... 344,280	640	650	660	665	675	1,500	15,500
1893CC	18,402	750	900	1,020	1,100	2,100	10,000	
1893S	996,175	640	650	660	665	675	2,400	
1894	(50) ... 1,368,940	640	650	660	665	675	900	15,500
1894S	1,048,550	640	650	660	665	675	1,500	
1895	(51) ... 1,114,605	640	650	660	665	675	800	15,500
1895S	1,143,500	640	650	660	665	675	1,500	
1896	(128)..... 792,535	640	650	660	665	675	1,000	15,500
1896S	1,403,925	640	650	660	665	675	1,500	
1897	(86) ... 1,383,175	640	650	660	665	675	800	15,500
1897S	1,470,250	640	650	660	665	675	800	
1898	(75)..... 170,395	640	650	660	665	675	3,000	15,500
1898S	2,575,175	640	650	660	665	675	800	
1899	(84) ... 1,669,300	640	650	660	665	675	800	15,500
1899S	2,010,300	640	650	660	665	675	1,150	
1900	(124) ... 1,874,460	640	650	660	665	675	800	15,500
1900S	2,459,500	640	650	660	665	675	1,200	
1901	(96)..... 111,430	640	650	660	665	675	800	15,500
1901S	1,596,000	640	650	660	665	675	2,400	
1902	(114)...... 31,140	640	650	660	665	675	6,500	15,500
1902S	1,753,625	640	650	660	665	675	2,400	
1903	(158)..... 287,270	640	650	660	665	675	800	15,500
1903S	954,000	640	650	660	665	675	1,120	
1904	(98) ... 6,256,699	640	650	660	665	675	800	15,500
1904S	5,134,175	640	650	660	665	675	800	
1905	(92)...... 58,919	640	650	660	665	675	8,000	15,500
1905S	1,813,000	640	650	660	665	675	2,380	
1906	(94)...... 69,596	640	650	660	665	675	4,000	15,500
1906D	620,250	640	650	660	665	675	1,200	
1906S	2,065,750	640	650	660	665	675	1,450	
1907	(78) ... 1,451,786	640	650	660	665	675	800	15,500
1907D	842,250	640	650	660	665	675	1,275	
1907S	2,165,800	640	650	660	665	675	1,450	

SAINT-GAUDENS (1907–1933)

The $20 gold piece designed by Augustus Saint-Gaudens is considered by many to be the most beautiful United States coin. The first coins issued were 11,250 high-relief pieces struck for general circulation. The relief is much higher than that of later issues and the date 1907 is in Roman numerals. A few of the Proof coins were made using the lettered-edge collar from the Ultra High Relief version. These can be distinguished by a pronounced bottom left serif on the N in UNUM, and other minor differences. Flat-relief double eagles were issued later in 1907 with Arabic numerals, and continued through 1933.

The field of the rare, Ultra High Relief experimental pieces is extremely concave and connects directly with the edge without any border, giving it a sharp knifelike appearance. Liberty's skirt shows two folds on the side of her right leg; the Capitol building in the background at left is very small; the sun, on the reverse side, has 14 rays, as opposed to the regular high-relief coins, which have only 13 rays extending from the sun. High-relief Proofs are trial or experimental pieces.

VF-20 VERY FINE—Minor wear on Liberty's legs and toes. Eagle's left wing and breast feathers worn.
EF-40 EXTREMELY FINE—Drapery lines on chest visible. Wear on left breast, knee, and below. Eagle's feathers on breast and right wing bold.
AU-50 ABOUT UNCIRCULATED—Trace of wear on nose, breast, and knee. Wear visible on eagle's wings.
AU-55 CHOICE ABOUT UNCIRCULATED—Evidence of friction on design high points. Most of mint luster remains.
MS-60 UNCIRCULATED—No trace of wear. Light marks or blemishes.
MS-63 SELECT UNCIRCULATED—Some distracting contact marks or blemishes in prime focal areas. Impaired luster possible.
MATTE PF-63—Matte surfaces with only a few blemishes in secondary focal places. No major flaws.

Ultra High Relief Pattern, MCMVII (1907)

	PF
1907, Ultra High Relief, Plain Edge *(unique)*	—
1907, Ultra High Relief, Lettered Edge	—

Without Motto IN GOD WE TRUST (1907–1908)

High Relief, MCMVII (1907)

	Mintage	VF-20	EF-40	AU-50	AU-55	MS-60	MS-63	PF
1907, High Relief, Roman Numerals (MCMVII), Wire Rim	12,367	$5,500	$6,500	$7,500	$8,000	$10,000	$18,000	—

Arabic Numerals, No Motto (1907–1908)

Mintmark is on obverse, above date.

No Motto

Motto IN GOD WE TRUST (1908–1933)

	Mintage	VF-20	EF-40	AU-50	AU-55	MS-60	MS-63	MATTE PF-63
1907	361,667	$650	$660	$670	$675	$685	$700	
1908	4,271,551	650	660	670	675	685	700	
1908D	663,750	650	660	670	685	700	720	
1908, With Motto . . . . (101)	156,359	650	660	670	675	685	1,000	$16,000
1908D, With Motto	349,500	650	660	670	680	750	900	
1908S, With Motto	22,000	1,000	1,300	1,800	2,400	4,500	12,000	

Chart continued on next page.

1909, 9 Over 8

	Mintage	VF-20	EF-40	AU-50	AU-55	MS-60	MS-63	MATTE PF-63
1909, 9 Over 8	*	$650	$660	$680	$685	$800	$4,500	
1909	(67) 161,282	650	660	670	675	685	2,200	$16,000
1909D	52,500	650	660	675	690	1,200	5,500	
1909S	2,774,925	650	660	670	675	690	700	
1910	(167) 482,000	650	660	670	675	685	700	16,000
1910D	429,000	650	660	670	675	685	700	
1910S	2,128,250	650	660	670	675	685	700	
1911	(100) 197,250	650	660	670	675	700	1,360	16,000
1911D	846,500	650	660	670	675	685	700	
1911S	775,750	650	660	670	675	685	700	
1912	(74) 149,750	650	660	670	675	700	1,000	16,000
1913	(58) 168,780	650	660	670	675	685	2,000	16,000
1913D	393,500	650	660	670	675	685	720	
1913S	34,000	650	660	675	685	900	2,600	
1914	(70) 95,250	650	660	670	675	700	1,400	16,000
1914D	453,000	650	660	670	675	685	700	
1914S	1,498,000	650	660	670	675	685	700	
1915	(50) 152,000	650	660	670	675	690	1,500	16,000
1915S	567,500	650	660	670	675	685	700	
1916S	796,000	650	660	670	675	685	720	
1920	228,250	650	660	670	675	685	720	
1920S	558,000	9,000	11,000	13,000	15,000	28,000	55,500	
1921	528,500	12,000	13,000	17,000	21,000	50,000	125,000	
1922	1,375,500	650	660	670	675	685	700	
1922S	2,658,000	675	700	725	750	1,200	2,500	
1923	566,000	650	660	670	680	685	700	
1923D	1,702,250	650	660	670	680	685	700	
1924	4,323,500	650	660	670	680	685	700	
1924D	3,049,500	900	1,000	1,100	1,200	1,600	5,500	
1924S	2,927,500	900	1,000	1,100	1,200	1,600	5,500	
1925	2,831,750	650	660	670	675	685	700	
1925D	2,938,500	1,000	1,200	1,500	1,800	2,500	6,250	
1925S	3,776,500	900	1,200	1,500	1,800	5,000	15,000	
1926	816,750	650	660	670	675	685	700	
1926D	481,000	2,000	3,500	4,000	4,500	8,000	20,000	
1926S	2,041,500	700	1,100	1,400	1,400	1,600	3,200	
1927	2,946,750	650	660	670	675	685	700	
1927D	180,000		250,000	300,000	350,000	500,000	650,000	
1927S	3,107,000	3,000	4,500	5,000	5,500	10,000	40,000	
1928	8,816,000	650	660	670	675	685	700	
1929	1,779,750	4,000	6,200	7,000	8,000	9,500	20,000	
1930S	74,000	9,000	15,000	16,000	17,000	21,000	50,000	
1931	2,938,250	5,000	9,000	9,200	9,500	15,000	30,000	
1931D	106,500	5,200	9,000	9,200	10,000	20,000	35,000	
1932	1,101,750	5,000	10,000	11,000	12,000	14,000	30,000	
1933	445,500	*None placed in circulation*						

* Included in number below.

Collecting United States commemorative coins is like gathering snapshots for an album of important events, places, and people in the nation's history. Because they represent so many different aspects of America—from wars and Olympic games to presidents, state parks, and historical landmarks, every collector can assemble a set with its own special significance.

All U.S. commemorative coins are issued as legal tender, though in most cases the precious metal of the coins surpasses their face values. The weight and fineness for commemoratives follow those of standard-issue gold, silver, and clad coins.

CLASSIC COMMEMORATIVE SILVER AND GOLD

(1892–1893) World's Columbian Exposition

	Mintage	AU-50	MS-60	MS-63	MS-65
1892, Columbian Exposition	950,000	$10	$16	$40	$380
1893, Same type	1,550,405	9	16	38	425

(1893) World's Columbian Exposition, Isabella Quarter

	Mintage	AU-50	MS-60	MS-63	MS-65
1893, Columbian Exposition, Chicago	24,214	$300	$385	$500	$2,000

(1900) Lafayette Dollar

	Mintage	AU-50	MS-60	MS-63	MS-65
1900, Lafayette Dollar	36,026	$310	$500	$1,200	$5,000

(1903) Louisiana Purchase Exposition

	Mintage	AU-50	MS-60	MS-63	MS-65
1903, Louisiana Purchase/Thomas Jefferson	17,500	$300	$350	$500	$2,000
1903, Louisiana Purchase/William McKinley	17,500	300	350	500	2,000

(1904–1905) Lewis and Clark Exposition

	Mintage	AU-50	MS-60	MS-63	MS-65
1904, Lewis and Clark Exposition	10,025	$450	$600	$1,250	$6,000
1905, Lewis and Clark Exposition	10,041	500	700	1,800	9,000

(1915) Panama-Pacific Exposition

	Mintage	AU-50	MS-60	MS-63	MS-65
1915S, Panama-Pacific Exposition half dollar	27,134	$200	$275	$450	$1,500
1915S, Panama-Pacific Exposition, $1	15,000	300	325	450	1,500
1915S, Panama-Pacific Exposition, $2.50	6,749	800	1,000	2,000	4,500
1915S, Panama-Pacific, $50 Round	483	25,000	30,000	40,000	90,000

(1915) Panama-Pacific Exposition

	Mintage	AU-50	MS-60	MS-63	MS-65
1915S, Panama-Pacific, $50 Octagonal	645	$20,000	$25,000	$35,000	$85,000

(1916–1917) McKinley Memorial

	Mintage	AU-50	MS-60	MS-63	MS-65
1916, McKinley Memorial	15,000	$300	$325	$450	$1,500
1917, McKinley Memorial	5,000	350	400	750	2,500

(1918) Illinois Centennial

	Mintage	AU-50	MS-60	MS-63	MS-65
1918, Illinois Centennial	100,058	$70	$80	$110	$275

(1920) Maine Centennial

	Mintage	AU-50	MS-60	MS-63	MS-65
1920, Maine Centennial	50,028	$55	$85	$110	$300

(1920–1921) Pilgrim Tercentenary

With 1921 in Field on Obverse

	Mintage	AU-50	MS-60	MS-63	MS-65
1920, Pilgrim Tercentenary	152,112	$40	$60	$70	$275
1921, Same, With Date Added in Field	20,053	80	90	100	310

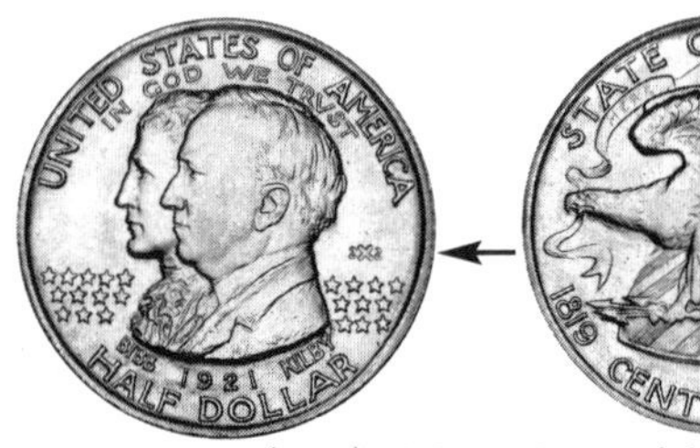

(1921) Alabama Centennial

Without 2x2 in Field

	Mintage	AU-50	MS-60	MS-63	MS-65
1921, Alabama Centennial, Plain	59,038	$95	$130	$265	$1,200
1921, Alabama Centennial, With "2X2" in Field of Obverse	6,006	150	175	320	1,250

(1921) Missouri Centennial

With 2★4 in Field

	Mintage	AU-50	MS-60	MS-63	MS-65
1921, Missouri Centennial, "2★4" in Field	5,000	$300	$400	$500	$2,600
1921, Missouri Centennial, Plain	5,428	200	350	450	2,300

(1922) Grant Memorial

	Mintage	AU-50	MS-60	MS-63	MS-65
1922, Grant Memorial, With Star half dollar*	4,256	$500	$800	$1,000	$4,000
1922, Same type, No Star in Obv Field half dollar	67,405	60	70	90	450
1922, Grant Memorial, With Star*	5,016	800	900	1,100	2,300
1922, Grant Memorial, No Star	5,000	800	900	1,100	2,300

* Fake stars usually have a flattened spot on the reverse.

(1923) Monroe Doctrine Centennial

	Mintage	AU-50	MS-60	MS-63	MS-65
1923S, Monroe Doctrine Centennial	274,077	$21	$35	$80	$1,600

(1924) Huguenot-Walloon Tercentenary

	Mintage	AU-50	MS-60	MS-63	MS-65
1924, Huguenot-Walloon Tercentenary	142,080	$65	$75	$110	$325

(1925) California Diamond Jubilee

	Mintage	AU-50	MS-60	MS-63	MS-65
1925S, California Diamond Jubilee	86,394	$90	$115	$150	$625

(1925) Fort Vancouver Centennial

	Mintage	AU-50	MS-60	MS-63	MS-65
1925, Fort Vancouver Centennial	14,994	$160	$200	$230	$760

(1925) Lexington-Concord Sesquicentennial

	Mintage	AU-50	MS-60	MS-63	MS-65
1925, Lexington-Concord Sesquicentennial	162,013	$40	$65	$80	$330

(1925) Stone Mountain Memorial

	Mintage	AU-50	MS-60	MS-63	MS-65
1925, Stone Mountain Memorial	1,314,709	$27	$40	$50	$150

(1926–1939) Oregon Trail Memorial

	Mintage	AU-50	MS-60	MS-65
1926, Oregon Trail Memorial	47,955	$65	$90	$170
1926S, Same type, S mint	83,055	65	90	170
1928, Oregon Trail Memorial (same as 1926)	6,028	90	110	190
1933D, Oregon Trail Memorial	5,008	180	200	300
1934D, Oregon Trail Memorial	7,006	80	100	200
1936, Oregon Trail Memorial	10,006	70	90	170
1936S, Same type, S mint	5,006	70	90	200
1937D, Oregon Trail Memorial	12,008	70	90	170
1938, Oregon Trail Memorial (same as 1926)	6,006			
1938D, Same type, D mint	6,005	*Set*	260	475
1938S, Same type, S mint	6,006			
1939, Oregon Trail Memorial (same as 1926)	3,004			
1939D, Same type, D mint	3,004	*Set*	850	1,200
1939S, Same type, S mint	3,005			
Oregon Trail Memorial, single type coin		65	90	170

(1926) Sesquicentennial of American Independence

	Mintage	AU-50	MS-60	MS-63	MS-65
1926, Sesquicentennial of American Independence	141,120	$40	$70	$100	$2,500
1926, American Independence, $2.50	46,019	235	300	420	3,200

(1927) Vermont Sesquicentennial

	Mintage	AU-50	MS-60	MS-63	MS-65
1927, Vermont Sesquicentennial (Battle of Bennington)	28,142	$110	$145	$165	$530

(1928) Hawaiian Sesquicentennial

	Mintage	AU-50	MS-60	MS-63	MS-65
1928, Hawaiian Sesquicentennial	9,958	$900	$1,300	$1,700	$4,200
1928, Hawaiian Sesquicentennial Sandblast Proof Presentation Piece	50			7,500	16,000

(1934–1938) Daniel Boone Bicentennial

1934 Added on Reverse

	Mintage	AU-50	MS-60	MS-63	MS-65
1934, Daniel Boone Bicentennial	10,007	$70	$80	$95	$150
1935, Same type	10,010				
1935D, Same type, D mint	5,005	*Set*	200	250	400
1935S, Same type, S mint	5,005				
1935, Same as 1934, but 1934 on Reverse	10,008				
1935D, Same type, D mint	2,003	*Set*	400	475	1,100
1935S, Same type, S mint	2,004				
1936, Daniel Boone (same as above)	12,012				
1936D, Same type, D mint	5,005	*Set*	200	250	400
1936S, Same type, S mint	5,006				
1937, Daniel Boone (same as above)	9,810				
1937D, Same type, D mint	2,506	*Set*	380	450	800
1937S, Same type, S mint	2,506				

	Mintage	AU-50	MS-60	MS-63	MS-65
1938, Daniel Boone (same as previous page)	2,100				
1938D, Same type, D mint	2,100	*Set*	$500	$700	$925
1938S, Same type, S mint	2,100				
Daniel Boone Bicentennial, single type coin		$70	80	95	150

(1934) Maryland Tercentenary

	Mintage	AU-50	MS-60	MS-63	MS-65
1934, Maryland Tercentenary	25,015	$80	$90	$110	$200

(1934–1938) Texas Independence Centennial

	Mintage	AU-50	MS-60	MS-63	MS-65
1934, Texas Independence Centennial	61,463	$60	$80	$90	$150
1935, Texas Centennial (same as 1934)	9,996				
1935D, Same type, D mint	10,007	*Set*	200	235	350
1935S, Same type, S mint	10,008				
1936, Texas Centennial (same as 1934)	8,911				
1936D, Same type, D mint	9,039	*Set*	200	235	350
1936S, Same type, S mint	9,055				
1937, Texas Centennial (same as 1934)	6,571				
1937D, Same type, D mint	6,605	*Set*	200	235	350
1937S, Same type, S mint	6,637				
1938, Texas Centennial (same as 1934)	3,780				
1938D, Same type, D mint	3,775	*Set*	350	395	750
1938S, Same type, S mint	3,814				
Texas Centennial, single type coin		60	80	90	150

(1935–1939) Arkansas Centennial

	Mintage	AU-50	MS-60	MS-63	MS-65
1935, Arkansas Centennial	13,012				
1935D, Same type, D mint	5,505	*Set*	$165	$220	$400
1935S, Same type, S mint	5,506				
1936, Arkansas Centennial (same as 1935; date 1936 on reverse)	9,660				
1936D, Same type, D mint	9,660	*Set*	165	220	425
1936S, Same type, S mint	9,660				
1937, Arkansas Centennial (same as 1935)	5,505				
1937D, Same type, D mint	5,505	*Set*	165	220	475
1937S, Same type, S mint	5,505				
1938, Arkansas Centennial (same as 1935)	3,156				
1938D, Same type, D mint	3,155	*Set*	225	250	850
1938S, Same type, S mint	3,155				
1939, Arkansas Centennial (same as 1935)	2,104				
1939D, Same type, D mint	2,104	*Set*	460	600	1,700
1939S, Same type, S mint	2,105				
Arkansas Centennial, single type coin		$40	60	70	130

(1935–1936) California-Pacific International Exposition

	Mintage	AU-50	MS-60	MS-63	MS-65
1935S, California-Pacific Exposition	70,132	$45	$60	$70	$90
1936D, California-Pacific Exposition	30,092	45	65	80	95

(1935) Connecticut Tercentenary

	Mintage	AU-50	MS-60	MS-63	MS-65
1935, Connecticut Tercentenary	25,018	$125	$160	$180	$325

(1935) Hudson, New York, Sesquicentennial

	Mintage	AU-50	MS-60	MS-63	MS-65
1935, Hudson, NY, Sesquicentennial	10,008	$325	$400	$500	$1,000

(1935) Old Spanish Trail

	Mintage	AU-50	MS-60	MS-63	MS-65
1935, Old Spanish Trail	10,008	$525	$650	$725	$1,000

(1936) Albany, New York, Charter

	Mintage	AU-50	MS-60	MS-63	MS-65
1936, Albany, New York, Charter	17,671	$160	$175	$190	$235

(1936) Arkansas Centennial – Robinson

	Mintage	AU-50	MS-60	MS-63	MS-65
1936, Arkansas Centennial (Robinson)	25,265	$65	$75	$85	$225

(1936) Battle of Gettysburg Anniversary

	Mintage	AU-50	MS-60	MS-63	MS-65
1936, Battle of Gettysburg Anniversary	26,928	$200	$225	$275	$410

(1936) Bridgeport, Connecticut, Centennial

	Mintage	AU-50	MS-60	MS-63	MS-65
1936, Bridgeport, CT, Centennial	25,015	$80	$100	$110	$150

(1936) Cincinnati Music Center Centennial

	Mintage	AU-50	MS-60	MS-63	MS-65
1936, Cincinnati Music Center Centennial	5,005				
1936D, Same type, D mint	5,005	*Set*	$450	$475	$1,400
1936S, Same type, S mint	5,006				
Cincinnati Music Center, single type coin		$140	150	165	375

(1936) Cleveland Centennial/Great Lakes Exposition

	Mintage	AU-50	MS-60	MS-63	MS-65
1936, Cleveland, Great Lakes Exposition	50,030	$60	$70	$80	$125

(1936) Columbia, South Carolina, Sesquicentennial

	Mintage	AU-50	MS-60	MS-63	MS-65
1936, Columbia, SC, Sesquicentennial	9,007				
1936D, Same type, D mint	8,009	*Set*	$425	$475	$575
1936S, Same type, S mint	8,007				
Columbia, SC, Sesqui, single type coin		$135	140	175	190

(1936) Delaware Tercentenary

	Mintage	AU-50	MS-60	MS-63	MS-65
1936, Delaware Tercentenary	20,993	$150	$175	$190	$245

(1936) Elgin, Illinois, Centennial

	Mintage	AU-50	MS-60	MS-63	MS-65
1936, Elgin, Illinois, Centennial	20,015	$110	$140	$165	$185

(1936) Long Island Tercentenary

	Mintage	AU-50	MS-60	MS-63	MS-65
1936, Long Island Tercentenary	81,826	$45	$50	$65	$225

(1936) Lynchburg, Virginia, Sesquicentennial

	Mintage	AU-50	MS-60	MS-63	MS-65
1936, Lynchburg, VA, Sesquicentennial	20,013	$110	$135	$145	$190

(1936) Norfolk, Virginia, Bicentennial

	Mintage	AU-50	MS-60	MS-63	MS-65
1936, Norfolk, VA, Bicentennial	16,936	$250	$285	$320	$375

(1936) Providence, Rhode Island, Tercentenary

	Mintage	AU-50	MS-60	MS-63	MS-65
1936, Rhode Island Tercentenary	20,013				
1936D, Same type, D mint	15,010	*Set*	$170	$200	$425
1936S, Same type, S mint	15,011				
Rhode Island Tercentenary, single type coin		$50	60	70	150

(1936) San Francisco – Oakland Bay Bridge Opening

	Mintage	AU-50	MS-60	MS-63	MS-65
1936S, San Francisco - Oakland Bay Bridge.	71,424	$80	$90	$100	$185

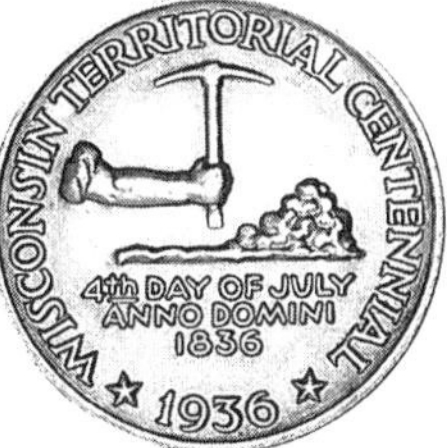

(1936) Wisconsin Territorial Centennial

	Mintage	AU-50	MS-60	MS-63	MS-65
1936, Wisconsin Territorial Centennial	25,015	$110	$130	$150	$200

(1936) York County, Maine, Tercentenary

	Mintage	AU-50	MS-60	MS-63	MS-65
1936, York County, Maine, Tercentenary.	25,015	$110	$125	$140	$175

(1937) Battle of Antietam Anniversary

See next page for chart.

	Mintage	AU-50	MS-60	MS-63	MS-65
1937, Battle of Antietam Anniversary	18,028	$320	$390	$450	$500

(1937) Roanoke Island, North Carolina, 350th Anniversary

	Mintage	AU-50	MS-60	MS-63	MS-65
1937, Roanoke Island, NC	29,030	$125	$150	$170	$185

(1938) New Rochelle, New York, 250th Anniversary

	Mintage	AU-50	MS-60	MS-63	MS-65
1938, New Rochelle, New York	15,266	$190	$250	$270	$300

(1946) Iowa Centennial

	Mintage	AU-50	MS-60	MS-63	MS-65
1946, Iowa Centennial	100,057	$55	$60	$75	$130

(1946–1951) Booker T. Washington Memorial

	Mintage		MS-60	MS-65
1946, Booker T. Washington Memorial **(a)**	1,000,546			
1946D, Same type, D mint	200,113	*Set*	$30	$85
1946S, Same type, S mint	500,279			
1947, Same type as 1946	100,017			
1947D, Same type, D mint	100,017	*Set*	40	135
1947S, Same type, S mint	100,017			
1948, Same type as 1946	8,005			
1948D, Same type, D mint	8,005	*Set*	80	110
1948S, Same type, S mint	8,005			
1949, Same type as 1946	6,004			
1949D, Same type, D mint	6,004	*Set*	120	170
1949S, Same type, S mint	6,004			
1950, Same type as 1946	6,004			
1950D, Same type, D mint	6,004	*Set*	65	110
1950S, Same type, S mint	512,091			
1951, Same type as 1946	510,082			
1951D, Same type, D mint	7,004	*Set*	50	100
1951S, Same type, S mint	7,004			
Booker T. Washington Memorial, single type coin			9	22

a. Minted; quantity melted unknown.

(1951–1954) Carver/Washington Commemorative

	Mintage		MS-60	MS-63	MS-65
1951, Carver/Washington	110,018				
1951D, Same type, D mint	10,004	*Set*	$40	$65	$275
1951S, Same type, S mint	10,004				
1952, Same type as 1951	2,006,292				
1952D, Same type, D mint	8,006	*Set*	40	65	210
1952S, Same type, S mint	8,006				
1953, Same type as 1951	8,003				
1953D, Same type, D mint	8,003	*Set*	40	65	275
1953S, Same type, S mint	108,020				

Chart continued on next page.

	Mintage	AU-50	MS-60	MS-63	MS-65
1954, Same type as 1951	12,006				
1954D, Same type, D mint	12,006	*Set*	$40	$65	$220
1954S, Same type, S mint	122,024				
Carver/Washington, single type coin		$10	11	13	25

MODERN COMMEMORATIVES

(1982) George Washington 250th Anniversary

	Mintage	MS-67	PF-67
1982D, George Washington 250th Anniversary	2,210,458	$3.50	
1982S, Same, Proof	(4,894,044)		$3.50

(1983–1984) Los Angeles Olympiad

	Mintage	MS-67	PF-67
1983P, Discus Thrower silver dollar	294,543	$9	
1983D, Same type, D mint	174,014	9	
1983S, Same type, S mint	(1,577,025) . . . 174,014	9	$10
1984P, Olympic Coliseum silver dollar	217,954	9	
1984D, Same type, D mint	116,675	10	
1984S, Same type, S mint	(1,801,210) . . . 116,675	10	10

(1983–1984) Los Angeles Olympiad

	Mintage	MS-67	PF-67
1984P, Olympic gold $10	(33,309)		$280
1984D, Olympic gold $10	(34,533)		280
1984S, Olympic gold $10	(48,551)		280
1984W, Olympic gold $10	(381,085) . . . 75,886	$280	280

(1986) Statue of Liberty

	Mintage	MS-67	PF-67
1986D, Statue of Liberty half dollar	928,008	$3	
1986S, Same type, S mint, Proof	(6,925,627)		$3
1986P, Statue of Liberty silver dollar	723,635	9	
1986S, Same type, S mint, Proof	(6,414,638)		9
1986W, Statue of Liberty gold $5	(404,013) 95,248	140	140

(1987) U.S. Constitution Bicentennial

	Mintage	MS-67	PF-67
1987P, U.S. Constitution Bicentennial silver dollar	451,629	$9	
1987S, Same type, S mint, Proof	(2,747,116)		$9
1987W, U.S. Constitution gold $5	(651,659) . . . 214,225	140	140

(1988) Seoul Olympiad

	Mintage	MS-67	PF-67
1988D, Olympiad silver dollar	191,368	$9	
1988S, Same type, S mint, Proof	(1,359,366)		$9
1988W, Olympiad gold $5	(281,465) 62,913	140	140

(1989) Congress Bicentennial

	Mintage	MS-67	PF-67
1989D, Congress Bicentennial half dollar	163,753	$5	
1989S, Congress Bicentennial half dollar	(767,897)		$5
1989D, Congress silver dollar	135,203	10	
1989S, Congress silver dollar	(762,198)		11
1989W, Congress Bicentennial gold $5	(164,690) 46,899	140	140

(1990) Eisenhower Centennial

	Mintage	MS-67	PF-67
1990W, Eisenhower Centennial silver dollar	241,669	$10	
1990P, Same type, P mint, Proof	(1,144,461)		$11

(1991) Korean War Memorial

	Mintage	MS-67	PF-67
1991D, Korean War Memorial silver dollar	213,049	$10	
1991P, Same type, P mint, Proof	(618,488)		$11

(1991) Mount Rushmore Golden Anniversary

	Mintage	MS-67	PF-67
1991D, Mount Rushmore Golden Anniversary half dollar	172,754	$11	
1991S, Same type, S mint, Proof	(753,257)		$10
1991P, Mount Rushmore silver dollar	133,139	20	
1991S, Same type, S mint, Proof	(738,419)		20
1991W, Mount Rushmore gold $5	(111,991) 31,959	200	140

(1991) United Service Organizations

	Mintage	MS-67	PF-67
1991D, U.S.O. silver dollar	124,958	$10	
1991S, Same type, S mint, Proof	(321,275)		$11

(1992) XXV Olympiad

	Mintage	MS-67	PF-67
1992P, Olympic clad half dollar	161,607	$5	
1992S, Same type, S mint, Proof	(519,645)		$5
1992D, Olympic silver dollar	188,039	15	
1992S, Same type, S mint, Proof	(504,505)		16
1992W, Olympic gold $5	(77,313) 27,732	200	150

(1992) Christopher Columbus Quincentenary

	Mintage	MS-67	PF-67
1992D, Columbus Quincentenary half dollar	106,949	$5	
1992S, Same type, S mint, Proof	(390,154)		$5
1992D, Columbus silver dollar	106,962	15	
1992P, Same type, P mint, Proof	(385,241)		20
1992W, Columbus gold $5	(79,730) 24,329	200	180

(1992) White House 200th Anniversary

	Mintage	MS-67	PF-67
1992D, White House 200th Anniversary silver dollar	123,803	$18	
1992W, Same type, W mint, Proof	(375,849)		$20

(1993) Bill of Rights

	Mintage	MS-67	PF-67
1993W, Bill of Rights silver half dollar	173,224	$10	
1993S, Same type, S mint, Proof	(559,758)		$9
1993D, Bill of Rights silver dollar	92,415	10	
1993S, Same type, S mint, Proof	(515,038)		11
1993W, Bill of Rights gold $5	(79,422) 22,897	200	180

(1993 [1994]) Thomas Jefferson

	Mintage	MS-67	PF-67
1993P, (1994) Thomas Jefferson silver dollar	266,927	$13	
1993S, (1994) Same type, S mint, Proof	(332,891)		$16

(1994) U.S. Capitol Bicentennial

	Mintage	MS-67	PF-67
1994D, U.S. Capitol Bicentennial silver dollar	68,332	$12	
1994S, Same type, S mint, Proof	(279,416)		$15

(1994) U.S. Prisoner of War Memorial

	Mintage	MS-67	PF-67
1994W, U.S. POW Memorial silver dollar	54,790	$50	
1994P, Same type, P mint, Proof	(220,100)		$30

(1994) Vietnam Veterans Memorial

	Mintage	MS-67	PF-67
1994W, Vietnam Veterans Memorial silver dollar	57,317	$50	
1994P, Same type, P mint, Proof	(226,262)		$40

(1994) Women in Military Service Memorial

	Mintage	MS-67	PF-67
1994W, Women Veterans Memorial silver dollar	53,054	$22	
1994P, Same type, P mint, Proof	(213,201)		$20

(1994) World Cup Tournament

	Mintage	MS-67	PF-67
1994D, World Cup Tournament clad half dollar	52,836	$5	
1994P, Same type, P mint, Proof	(122,412)		$5
1994D, World Cup Tournament silver dollar	81,698	14	
1994S, Same type, S mint, Proof	(576,978)		16
1994W, World Cup Tournament gold $5	(89,619) 22,464	200	175

(1995) Centennial Olympic Games

	Mintage	MS-67	PF-67
1995D, XXVI Olympiad, Basketball clad half dollar	171,001	$12	
1995S, Same type, S mint, Proof	(169,655)		$10
1995D, XXVI Olympiad, Baseball clad half dollar	164,605	12	
1995S, Same type, S mint, Proof	(118,087)		10
1996D, XXVI Olympiad, Swimming clad half dollar	49,533	80	
1996S, Same type, S mint, Proof	(114,315)		20
1996D, XXVI Olympiad, Soccer clad half dollar	52,836	60	
1996S, Same type, S mint, Proof	(112,412)		60
1995D, XXVI Olympiad, Gymnastics silver dollar	42,497	45	
1995P, Same type, P mint, Proof	(182,676)		30
1995D, XXVI Olympiad, Paralympics silver dollar	28,649	50	
1995P, Same type, P mint, Proof	(138,337)		32
1995D, XXVI Olympiad, Track and Field silver dollar	24,976	50	
1995P, Same type, P mint, Proof	(136,935)		25
1995D, XXVI Olympiad, Cycling silver dollar	19,662	80	
1995P, Same type, P mint, Proof	(118,795)		25
1996D, XXVI Olympiad, Tennis silver dollar	15,983	180	
1996P, Same type, P mint, Proof	(92,016)		50
1996D, XXVI Olympiad, Paralympics silver dollar	14,497	210	
1996P, Same type, P mint, Proof	(84,280)		40
1996D, XXVI Olympiad, Rowing silver dollar	16,258	220	
1996P, Same type, P mint, Proof	(151,890)		35
1996D, XXVI Olympiad, High Jump silver dollar	15,697	250	
1996P, Same type, P mint, Proof	(124,502)		30
1995W, XXVI Olympiad, Torch Runner gold $5	14,675	350	
1995W, Same type, W mint, Proof	(57,442)		200
1995W, XXVI Olympiad, Stadium gold $5	10,579	600	
1995W, Same type, W mint, Proof	(43,124)		250
1996W, XXVI Olympiad, Flag Bearer gold $5	9,174	500	
1996W, Same type, W mint, Proof	(32,886)		325
1996W, XXVI Olympiad, Cauldron gold $5	9,210	450	
1996W, Same type, W mint, Proof	(38,555)		300

UNITED STATES OF AMERICA E PLURIBUS UNUM IN GREAT DEEDS SOMETHING ABIDES. ON GREAT FIELDS SOMETHING STAYS. FORMS CHANGE AND PASS; BODIES DISAPPEAR; BUT SPIRITS LINGER TO CONSECRATE GROUND FOR THE VISIONPLACE OF SOULS. —JOSHUA CHAMBERLAIN ONE DOLLAR

LIBERTY IN GOD WE TRUST 1995

(1995) Civil War Battlefields

	Mintage	MS-67	PF-67
1995S, Civil War Battlefields clad half dollar	119,520	$25	
1995S, Same type, S mint, Proof	(330,002)		$22
1995P, Civil War Battlefields silver dollar	45,866	45	
1995S, Same type, S mint, Proof	(437,114)		45
1995W, Civil War Battlefields gold $5	12,735	400	
1995W, Same type, W mint, Proof	(55,246)		300

(1995) Special Olympics World Games

	Mintage	MS-67	PF-67
1995W, Special Olympics World Games silver dollar	89,301	$15	
1995P, Same type, P mint, Proof	(351,764)		$14

(1991–1995) 50th Anniversary of World War II

	Mintage	MS-67	PF-67
(1993) 1991–1995P, World War II clad half dollar. . . . . (317,396) . . .	197,032	$17	$15
(1993) 1991–1995D, World War II silver dollar	107,240	16	
(1993) Same type, W mint, Proof . . . . (342,041).			22
(1993) 1991–1995W, World War II gold $5. . . . . (67,026)	23,672	200	190

(1996) National Community Service

	Mintage	MS-67	PF-67
1996S, National Community Service silver dollar.	23,468	$140	
1996S, Same type, S mint, Proof. . . . . (100,787).			$50

(1996) Smithsonian Institution 150th Anniversary

	Mintage	MS-67	PF-67
1996D, Smithsonian Institution 150th Anniv silver dollar	30,593	$80	
1996P, Same type, P mint, Proof	(129,616)		$40
1996W, Smithsonian Institution gold $5	8,948	650	
1996W, Same type, W mint, Proof	(21,840)		325

(1997) Botanic Garden

	Mintage	MS-67	PF-67
1997P, Botanic Garden silver dollar	57,272	$25	
1997P, Same type, P mint, Proof	(264,528)		$25

(1997) Franklin D. Roosevelt

	Mintage	MS-67	PF-67
1997W, Franklin D. Roosevelt gold $5	11,805	$500	
1997W, Same type, W mint, Proof	(29,233)		$250

(1997) Jackie Robinson

	Mintage	MS-67	PF-67
1997S, Jackie Robinson silver dollar	30,180	$50	
1997S, Same type, S mint, Proof	(110,002)		$40
1997W, Jackie Robinson gold $5	5,174	2,750	
1997W, Same type, W mint, Proof	(24,072)		450

(1997) National Law Enforcement Officers Memorial

	Mintage	MS-67	PF-67
1997P, National Law Enforcement Memorial silver dollar	28,575	$100	
1997P, Same type, P mint, Proof	(110,428)		$80

(1998) Black Revolutionary War Patriots

	Mintage	MS-67	PF-67
1998S, Black Revolutionary War Patriots silver dollar	37,210	$90	
1998S, Same type, S mint, Proof	(75,070)		$60

(1998) Robert F. Kennedy

	Mintage	MS-67	PF-67
1998S, Robert F. Kennedy silver dollar	106,422	$17	
1998S, Same type, S mint, Proof	(99,020)		$23

(1999) Dolley Madison Commemorative

	Mintage	MS-67	PF-67
1999P, Dolley Madison silver dollar	89,104	$28	
1999P, Same type, P mint, Proof	(224,403)		$30

(1999) Yellowstone National Park

	Mintage	MS-67	PF-67
1999P, Yellowstone National Park silver dollar	62,000	$28	
1999P, Same type, S mint, Proof	(144,900)		$30

(1999) George Washington Death Bicentennial

	Mintage	MS-67	PF-67
1999W, George Washington gold $5	22,511	$225	
1999W, Same type, W mint, Proof	(41,693)		$225

(2000) Leif Ericson Millennium

	Mintage	MS-67	PF-67
2000P, Leif Ericson Millennium silver dollar	28,100	$50	
2000P, Same type, P mint, Proof	(142,900)		$40

(2000) Library of Congress Bicentennial

	Mintage	MS-67	PF-67
2000P, Library of Congress Bicentennial silver dollar	53,264	$22	
2000P, Same type, P mint, Proof	(198,503)		$22
2000W, Library of Congress bimetallic $10	7,261	1,800	
2000W, Same type, W mint, Proof	(27,445)		550

(2001) American Buffalo Commemorative

	Mintage	MS-67	PF-67
2001D, American Buffalo silver dollar	227,131	$150	
2001P, Same type, P mint, Proof	(272,869)		$175

(2001) Capitol Visitor Center

	Mintage	MS-67	PF-67
2001P, Capitol Visitor Center clad half dollar	99,157	$7	
2001P, Same type, P mint, Proof	(77,962)		$9
2001P, Capitol silver dollar	35,380	20	
2001P, Same type, P mint, Proof	(143,793)		25
2001P, Capitol gold $5	6,761	800	
2001P, Same type, P mint, Proof	(27,652)		250

(2002) Salt Lake City Olympic Games

	Mintage	MS-67	PF-67
2002P, Salt Lake Olympics silver dollar	35,287	$20	
2002P, Same type, P mint, Proof	(142,813)		$22
2002W, Salt Lake Olympics gold $5	5,727	250	
2002W, Same type, W mint, Proof	(8,882)		225

(2002) West Point Bicentennial

	Mintage	MS-67	PF-67
2002W, West Point silver dollar	101,236	$12	
2002W, Same type, W mint, Proof	(282,743)		$12

(2003) First Flight Centennial

(2003) First Flight Centennial

	Mintage	MS-67	PF-67
2003P, First Flight Centennial clad half dollar	57,726	$8	
2003P, Same type, P mint, Proof	(111,569)		$9
2003P, First Flight Centennial silver dollar	53,761	20	
2003P, Same type, P mint, Proof	(193,086)		18
2003W, First Flight Centennial gold $10	10,129	300	
2003W, Same type, W mint, Proof	(21,846)		300

(2004) Lewis and Clark Bicentennial

	Mintage	MS-67	PF-67
2004P, Lewis and Clark Bicentennial silver dollar	90,323	$20	
2004P, Same type, P mint, Proof	(288,492)		$18

(2004) Thomas Alva Edison

	Mintage	MS-67	PF-67
2004P, Thomas Alva Edison silver dollar	68,031	$20	
2004P, Same type, P mint, Proof	(213,409)		$22

(2005) Chief Justice John Marshall

	Mintage	MS-67	PF-67
2005P, Chief Justice John Marshall silver dollar	48,953	$20	
2005P, Same type, P mint, Proof	(141,993)		$22

(2005) Marine Corps 230th Anniversary

	Mintage	MS-67	PF-67
2005P, Marine Corps 230th Anniversary silver dollar	49,671	$25	
2005P, Same type, P mint, Proof	(548,810)		$27

(2006) Benjamin Franklin

	Mintage	MS-67	PF-67
2006P, Benjamin Franklin "Scientist" silver dollar	58,000	$30	
2006P, Same type, P mint, Proof	(142,000)		$30
2006P, Benjamin Franklin "Founding Father" silver dollar	58,000	30	
2006P, Same type, P mint, Proof	(142,000)		30

(2006) San Francisco Old Mint

	Mintage	MS-67	PF-67
2006S, San Francisco, Old Mint silver dollar	*67,100*	$20	
2006S, Same type, S mint, Proof	*(160,870)*		$22
2006S, San Francisco Old Mint gold $5	*17,500*	175	
2006S, Same type, S mint, Proof	*(44,174)*		175

(2007) Jamestown 400th Anniversary

	Mintage	MS-67	PF-67
2007P, Jamestown 400th Anniversary silver dollar		$20	
2007P, Same type, P mint, Proof			$22

GOVERNMENT COMMEMORATIVE SETS

Values are for commemorative coins and sets in all of their original packaging.

(1983–1984) Los Angeles Olympiad

	Price
1983 and 1984 Proof dollars	$18
1983 and 1984 6-coin set. One each of 1983 and 1984 dollars, both Proof and Uncirculated gold $10 **(a)**	600
1983 3-piece collector set. 1983 P, D, and S Uncirculated dollars	27
1984 3-piece collector set. 1984 P, D, and S Uncirculated dollars	30
1983 and 1984 gold and silver Uncirculated set. One each of 1983 and 1984 Uncirculated dollar and one 1984 Uncirculated gold $10	300
1983 and 1984 gold and silver Proof set. One each of 1983 and 1984 Proof dollars and one 1984 Proof gold $10	300

(1986) Statue of Liberty

	Price
2-coin set. Proof silver dollar and clad half dollar	$12
3-coin set. Proof silver dollar, clad half dollar, and gold $5	150
2-coin set. Uncirculated silver dollar and clad half dollar	12
2-coin set. Uncirculated and Proof gold $5	150
3-coin set. Uncirculated silver dollar, clad half dollar, and gold $5	150
6-coin set. One each of Proof and Uncirculated half dollar, silver dollar, and gold $5 **(a)**	300

(1987) Constitution

	Price
2-coin set. Uncirculated silver dollar and gold $5	$150
2-coin set. Proof silver dollar and gold $5	150
4-coin set. One each of Proof and Uncirculated silver dollar and gold $5 **(a)**	300

(1988) Seoul Olympiad

	Price
2-coin set. Uncirculated silver dollar and gold $5	$150
2-coin set. Proof silver dollar and gold $5	150
4-coin set. One each of Proof and Uncirculated silver dollar and gold $5 **(a)**	300

(1989) Congress

	Price
2-coin set. Proof clad half dollar and silver dollar	$15
3-coin set. Proof clad half dollar, silver dollar, and gold $5	155
2-coin set. Uncirculated clad half dollar and silver dollar	15
3-coin set. Uncirculated clad half dollar, silver dollar, and gold $5	155
6-coin set. One each of Proof and Uncirculated clad half dollar, silver dollar, and gold $5 **(a)**	310.

(1991) Mount Rushmore

	Price
2-coin set. Uncirculated clad half dollar and silver dollar	$30
2-coin set. Proof clad half dollar and silver dollar	30
3-coin set. Uncirculated clad half dollar, silver dollar, and gold $5	230
3 coin set. Proof half dollar, silver dollar, and gold $5	170
6-coin set. One each of Proof and Uncirculated clad half dollar, silver dollar, and gold $5 **(a)**	400

a. Packaged in cherrywood box.

(1992) XXV Olympiad

	Price
2-coin set. Uncirculated clad half dollar and silver dollar	$20
2-coin set. Proof clad half dollar and silver dollar	20
3-coin set. Uncirculated clad half dollar, silver dollar, and gold $5	220
3-coin set. Proof clad half dollar, silver dollar, and gold $5	170
6-coin set. One each of Proof and Uncirculated clad half dollar, silver dollar, and gold $5 **(a)**	400

(1992) Christopher Columbus

	Price
2-coin set. Uncirculated clad half dollar and silver dollar	$20
2-coin set. Proof clad half dollar and silver dollar	25
3-coin set. Uncirculated clad half dollar, silver dollar, and gold $5	220
3-coin set. Proof half dollar, silver dollar, and gold $5	200
6-coin set. One each of Proof and Uncirculated clad half dollar, silver dollar, and gold $5 **(a)**	420

(1993) Bill of Rights

	Price
2-coin set. Uncirculated silver half dollar and silver dollar	$20
2-coin set. Proof silver half dollar and silver dollar	20
3-coin set. Uncirculated silver half dollar, silver dollar, and gold $5	220
3-coin set. Proof half dollar, silver dollar, and gold $5	200
6-coin set. One each of Proof and Uncirculated silver half dollar, silver dollar, and gold $5 **(a)**	420
"Young Collector" set. Silver half dollar	12
"Educational" set. Silver half dollar and James Madison medal	10
Proof silver half dollar and twenty-five-cent stamp	15

(1993) Thomas Jefferson

	Price
3-piece set (issued in 1994). Silver dollar, Jefferson nickel, and $2 note	$50

(1993) World War II

	Price
2-coin set. Uncirculated clad half dollar and silver dollar	$30
2-coin set. Proof clad half dollar and silver dollar	35
3-coin set. Uncirculated clad half dollar, silver dollar, and gold $5	230
3-coin set. Proof clad half dollar, silver dollar, and gold $5	215
6-coin set. One each of Proof and Uncirculated clad half dollar, silver dollar, and gold $5 **(a)**	450
"Young Collector" set. Clad half dollar	15
"Victory" set. Silver dollar and French franc	16
Victory Medal set. Uncirculated clad half dollar and reproduction medal	17

(1994) U.S. Veterans

	Price
3-coin set. Uncirculated POW, Vietnam, and Women in Military Service silver dollars	$120
3-coin set. Proof POW, Vietnam, and Women in Military Service silver dollars	90

a. Packaged in cherrywood box.

(1994) World Cup Soccer

	Price
2-coin set. Uncirculated clad half dollar and silver dollar	$19
2-coin set. Proof clad half dollar and silver dollar	20
3-coin set. Uncirculated clad half dollar, silver dollar, and gold $5	220
3-coin set. Proof clad half dollar, silver dollar, and gold $5	200
6-coin set. One each of Proof and Uncirculated clad half dollar, silver dollar, and gold $5	420
"Young Collector" set. Uncirculated clad half dollar	8
"Special Edition" set. Proof clad half dollar and silver dollar	22

(1995) Civil War Battlefield Preservation

	Price
2-coin set. Uncirculated clad half dollar and silver dollar	$70
2-coin set. Proof clad half dollar and silver dollar	65
3-coin set. Uncirculated clad half dollar, silver dollar, and gold $5	470
3-coin set. Proof clad half dollar, silver dollar, and gold $5	365
6-coin set. One each of Proof and Uncirculated clad half dollar, silver dollar, and gold $5 **(a)**	835
"Young Collector" set. Uncirculated clad half dollar	25
2-coin "Union" Set. Clad half dollar and silver dollar	70
3-coin "Union" Set. Clad half dollar, silver dollar, and gold $5	375

(1995) Special Olympics

	Price
2-coin set. Proof Special Olympics silver dollar, 1995S Kennedy half dollar	$60

(1995–1996) Centennial Olympic Games

	Price
4-coin set #1. Uncirculated half dollar (Basketball), dollars (Gymnast, Paralympics), gold $5 (Torch Bearer)	$450
4-coin set #2. Proof half dollar (Basketball), dollars (Gymnast, Paralympics), gold $5 (Torch Bearer)	270
2-coin set #1. Proof silver dollars (Gymnast, Paralympics)	60
"Young Collector" set. Uncirculated Basketball, Swimming, or Soccer half dollar	—
1995–1996 16-coin Uncirculated set. One each of all Uncirculated coins **(a)**	1,400
1995–1996 16-coin Proof set. One each of all Proof coins **(a)**	1,400
1995–1996 8-coin Proof set. One each of all Proof coins **(a)**	
1995–1996 32-coin set. One each of all Uncirculated and Proof coins **(a)**	3,500

(1996) National Community Service

	Price
Proof silver dollar and Saint-Gaudens stamp	$40

(1996) Smithsonian Institution 150th Anniversary

	Price
2-coin set. Proof silver dollar and $5 gold	$365
4-coin set. One each of Proof and Uncirculated silver dollar and $5 gold **(a)**	1,000
"Young Collector" set. Proof silver dollar	40

(1997) Botanic Garden

	Price
Silver dollar, Jefferson nickel, and $1 note	$125

a. Packaged in cherrywood box.

(1997) Jackie Robinson

	Price
2-coin set. Proof silver dollar and gold $5	$500
4-coin set. One each of Proof and Uncirculated silver dollar and gold $5 **(a)**	3,300
3-piece "Legacy" set. Baseball card, pin, and gold $5	500

(1997) National Law Enforcement Officers Memorial

	Price
Insignia set. Silver dollar, lapel pin, and patch	$150

(1998) Black Revolutionary War Patriots

	Price
2-coin set. Uncirculated and Proof silver dollars	$150
"Young Collector" set. Uncirculated silver dollar	90
Black Revolutionary War Patriots set. Silver dollar and four stamps	90

(1998) Robert F. Kennedy

	Price
2-coin set. RFK silver dollar and JFK silver half dollar	$225
2-coin set. RFK silver dollar, Proof and Uncirculated	40

(1999) Dolley Madison Commemorative

	Price
2-coin set. Proof and Uncirculated silver dollars	$55

(1999) George Washington Death

	Price
2-coin set. One each of Proof and Uncirculated gold $5	$450

(1999) Yellowstone National Park

	Price
2-coin set. One each of Proof and Uncirculated silver dollars	$60

(2000) Leif Ericson Millennium

	Price
2-coin set. Proof silver dollar and Icelandic 1,000 kronur	$50

(2000) Millennium Coin and Currency Set

	Price
3-piece set. Uncirculated 2000 Sacagawea dollar; Uncirculated 2000 Silver Eagle; George Washington one-dollar note series 1999	$60

(2001) American Buffalo

	Price
2-coin set. One each of Proof and Uncirculated silver dollars	$325
"Coinage and Currency" set. Uncirculated silver dollar, two 2005 nickels, replica medal, replica $10 Bison note, and three stamps	125

(2001) Capitol Visitor Center

	Price
3-coin set. Proof clad half dollar, silver dollar, and gold $5	$280

(2002) Salt Lake Olympic Games

	Price
2-coin set. Proof silver dollar and gold $5	$250
4-coin set. One each of Proof and Uncirculated silver dollar and gold $5	520

(2004) Lewis and Clark

	Price
Pouch set. Proof silver dollar and beaded pouch	$100
"Coinage and Currency" set. Uncirculated silver dollar, two 2005 nickels, replica medal, replica $10 Bison note, three stamps	40
Western Journey nickel set. Proof silver dollar, two 2005 Proof nickels, silver-plated Peace Medal	22

(2004) Thomas Alva Edison

	Price
Edison set. Uncirculated silver dollar and light bulb	$30

(2005) Chief Justice John Marshall

	Price
Coin and Chronicles Set. Uncirculated silver dollar, booklet, BEP intaglio portrait	$30

(2005) Marine Corps 230th Anniversary

	Price
Marine Corps Uncirculated silver dollar and stamp set	$50
American Legacy Collection. Proof Marine Corps dollar, Proof John Marshall dollar, 10-piece Proof set	90

(2006) Benjamin Franklin

	Price
Coin and Chronicles Set. Uncirculated "Scientist" silver dollar, four stamps, *Poor Richard's Almanack* replica, intaglio print	$40

(2006) San Francisco Old Mint

	Price
American Legacy Collection. Proof 2006P Benjamin Franklin, Founding Father silver dollar; Proof 2006S San Francisco Old Mint silver dollar; Proof cent, nickel, dime, quarter, half dollar, and dollar	$60

PROOF COINS AND SETS

Proof coins can usually be distinguished by their sharpness of detail, high wire edge, and extremely brilliant, mirrorlike surface. Proofs are sold by the Mint at a premium.

Proof coins were not struck during 1943–1949 or 1965–1967. Sets from 1936 through 1972 include the cent, nickel, dime, quarter, and half dollar; from 1973 through 1981 the dollar was also included. *Values shown are for original unblemished sets.*

Figures in parentheses represent the total number of full sets minted.

Year	Mintage	Issue Price	Current Value
1936	(3,837)	$1.89	$4,250.00
1937	(5,542)	1.89	2,300.00
1938	(8,045)	1.89	1,100.00
1939	(8,795)	1.89	950.00
1940	(11,246)	1.89	750.00
1941	(15,287)	1.89	750.00
1942, Both nickels	(21,120)	1.89	750.00
1942, One nickel	*	1.89	650.00
1950	(51,386)	2.10	400.00
1951	(57,500)	2.10	375.00
1952	(81,980)	2.10	180.00
1953	(128,800)	2.10	150.00
1954	(233,300)	2.10	75.00
1955, Box pack	(378,200)	2.10	70.00
1955, Flat pack	*	2.10	85.00
1956	(669,384)	2.10	35.00
1957	(1,247,952)	2.10	12.00
1958	(875,652)	2.10	30.00
1959	(1,149,291)	2.10	13.00
1960, With Large Date cent	(1,691,602)	2.10	11.00
1960, With Small Date cent	*	2.10	18.00
1961	(3,028,244)	2.10	7.00
1962	(3,218,019)	2.10	7.00
1963	(3,075,645)	2.10	8.00
1964	(3,950,762)	2.10	7.00
1968S	(3,041,506)	5.00	4.00
1969S	(2,934,631)	5.00	4.00
1970S	(2,632,810)	5.00	5.00
1970S, With Small Date cent	*	5.00	55.00
1971S	(3,220,733)	5.00	3.00
1972S	(3,260,996)	5.00	2.50
1973S	(2,760,339)	7.00	5.00
1974S	(2,612,568)	7.00	6.00
1975S, With 1976 quarter, half, and dollar	(2,845,450)	7.00	6.00
1976S	(4,149,730)	7.00	6.00
1976S, 3-piece set	(3,998,621)	15.00	10.00
1977S	(3,251,152)	9.00	4.50
1978S	(3,127,781)	9.00	5.00
1979S, Filled S	(3,677,175)	9.00	4.50
1979S, Clear S	*	9.00	65.00
1980S	(3,554,806)	10.00	4.00
1981S	(4,063,083)	11.00	4.00
1982S	(3,857,479)	11.00	2.50
1983S	(3,138,765)	11.00	3.50
1983S, Prestige Set (Olympic dollar)	(140,361)	59.00	50.00
1984S	(2,748,430)	11.00	3.50
1984S, Prestige Set (Olympic dollar)	(316,680)	59.00	15.00
1985S	(3,362,821)	11.00	3.25
1986S	(2,411,180)	11.00	6.50
1986S, Prestige Set (Statue of Liberty half, dollar)	(599,317)	48.50	20.00
1987S	(3,792,233)	11.00	3.50
1987S, Prestige Set (Constitution dollar)	(435,495)	45.00	14.00
1988S	(3,031,287)	11.00	4.00

* Included in number above.

Year	Mintage	Issue Price	Current Value
1988S, Prestige Set (Olympic dollar)	(231,661)	$45.00	$20.00
1989S	(3,009,107)	11.00	4.00
1989S, Prestige Set (Congressional half, dollar)	*	45.00	25.00
1990S	(2,793,433)	11.00	5.00
1990S, With No S cent	(3,555)	11.00	4,000.00
1990S, With No S cent (Prestige Set)	*	45.00	4,400.00
1990S, Prestige Set (Eisenhower dollar)	(506,126)	45.00	15.00
1991S	(2,610,833)	11.00	7.00
1991S, Prestige Set (Mt. Rushmore half, dollar)	(256,954)	59.00	37.00
1992S	(2,675,618)	11.00	4.00
1992S, Prestige Set (Olympic half, dollar)	(183,293)	56.00	50.00
1992S, Silver	(1,009,586)	21.00	8.00
1992S, Silver Premier Set	(308,055)	37.00	8.50
1993S	(2,409,394)	12.50	7.00
1993S, Prestige Set (Madison half, dollar)	(224,045)	57.00	20.00
1993S, Silver	(570,213)	21.00	20.00
1993S, Silver Premier Set	(191,140)	37.50	20.00
1994S	(2,308,701)	12.50	7.00
1994S, Prestige Set (World Cup half, dollar)	(175,893)	57.00	25.00
1994S, Silver	(636,009)	21.00	23.00
1994S Silver Premier Set	(149,320)	37.50	23.00
1995S	(2,010,384)	12.50	25.00
1995S, Prestige Set (Civil War half, dollar)	(107,112)	57.00	80.00
1995S, Silver	(549,878)	21.00	50.00
1995S, Silver Premier Set	(130,107)	37.50	50.00
1996S	(1,695,244)	12.50	10.00
1996S, Prestige Set (Olympic half, dollar)	(55,000)	57.00	275.00
1996S, Silver	(623,655)	21.00	25.00
1996S, Silver Premier Set	(151,366)	37.50	25.00
1997S	(1,975,000)	12.50	20.00
1997S, Prestige Set (Botanic dollar)	(80,000)	48.00	100.00
1997S, Silver	(605,473)	21.00	40.00
1997S, Silver Premier Set	(136,205)	37.50	40.00
1998S	(2,086,507)	12.50	14.00
1998S, Silver	(638,134)	21.00	18.00
1998S, Silver Premier Set	(240,658)	37.50	22.00
1999S, 9-piece set	(2,543,401)	19.95	40.00
1999S, 5-piece quarter set	(1,169,958)	13.95	35.00
1999S, Silver 9-piece set	(804,565)	31.95	225.00
2000S, 10-piece set	(3,082,572)	19.95	12.00
2000S, 5-piece quarter set	(937,600)	13.95	6.00
2000S, Silver 10-piece set	(965,421)	31.95	16.50
2001S, 10-piece set	(2,294,909)	19.95	60.00
2001S, 5-piece quarter set	(799,231)	13.95	30.00
2001S, Silver 10-piece set	(889,697)	31.95	100.00
2002S, 10-piece set	(2,319,766)	19.95	20.00
2002S, 5-piece quarter set	(764,479)	13.95	13.00
2002S, Silver 10-piece set	(892,229)	31.95	35.00
2003S, 10-piece set	(2,172,684)	19.95	13.00
2003S, 5-piece quarter set	(1,235,832)	13.95	10.00
2003S, Silver 10-piece set	(1,125,755)	31.95	18.00
2004S, 11-piece set	(1,789,488)	22.95	30.00
2004S, 5-piece quarter set	(951,196)	15.95	16.00
2004S, Silver 11-piece set	(1,175,934)	37.95	20.00
2004S, Silver 5-piece quarter set	(593,852)	23.95	15.00
2005S, 11-piece set	*(2,275,000)*	22.95	13.00
2005S, 5-piece quarter set	*(987,960)*	15.95	9.00
2005S, Silver 11-piece set	*(1,069,679)*	37.95	25.00
2005S, Silver 5-piece quarter set	*(608,970)*	23.95	14.00
2006S, 10-piece set	*(1,934,965)*	22.95	17.00
2006S, 5-piece quarter set	*(882,000)*	15.95	10.00
2006S, Silver 11-piece set	*(988,140)*	37.95	15.00

* Included in number above.

Chart continued on next page.

Year	Mintage	Issue Price	Current Value
2006S, Silver 5-piece quarter set	*(531,000)*	$23.95	$14
2007S, 15-piece set			
2007S, 5-piece quarter set			
2007S, 4-piece Presidential set			
2007S, Silver 11-piece set			
2007S, Silver 5-piece quarter set			

UNCIRCULATED MINT SETS

Official Mint Sets are specially packaged by the government for sale to collectors. They contain uncirculated specimens of each year's coins for every denomination issued from each mint. Sets from 1947 through 1958 contain two examples of each regular-issue coin. No official sets were produced in 1950, 1982, or 1983. Privately assembled sets are valued according to individual coin prices. Only official sets are included in the following list. Unlike the Proof sets, these are normal coins intended for circulation and are not minted with any special consideration for quality.

Year	Mintage	Issue Price	Current Value
1947 P-D-S	*5,000*	$4.87	$700.00
1948 P-D-S	*6,000*	4.92	350.00
1949 P-D-S	*5,000*	5.45	475.00
1951 P-D-S	8,654	6.75	525.00
1952 P-D-S	11,499	6.14	500.00
1953 P-D-S	15,538	6.14	300.00
1954 P-D-S	25,599	6.19	150.00
1955 P-D-S	49,656	3.57	100.00
1956 P-D	45,475	3.34	90.00
1957 P-D	34,324	4.40	150.00
1958 P-D	50,314	4.43	90.00
1959 P-D	187,000	2.40	30.00
1960 P-D	260,485	2.40	16.00
1961 P-D	223,704	2.40	25.00
1962 P-D	385,285	2.40	12.00
1963 P-D	606,612	2.40	12.00
1964 P-D	1,008,108	2.40	12.00
1965*		4.00	5.00
1966*		4.00	5.00
1967*		4.00	11.00
1968 P-D-S	2,105,128	2.50	3.50
1969 P-D-S	1,817,392	2.50	4.00
1970 P-D-S	2,038,134	2.50	10.00
1971 P-D-S	2,193,396	3.50	4.00
1972 P-D-S	2,750,000	3.50	4.00
1973 P-D-S	1,767,691	6.00	11.00
1974 P-D-S	1,975,981	6.00	4.00
1975 P-D	1,921,488	6.00	5.50
1776–1976, (3-piece set)	4,908,319	9.00	7.50
1976 P-D	1,892,513	6.00	4.50
1977 P-D	2,006,869	$7.00	$4.50
1978 P-D	2,162,609	7.00	4.50
1979 P-D	2,526,000	8.00	4.00
1980 P-D-S	2,815,066	9.00	4.85
1981 P-D-S	2,908,145	11.00	7.50
1984 P-D	1,832,857	7.00	3.50
1985 P-D	1,710,571	7.00	4.00
1986 P-D	1,153,536	7.00	8.00
1987 P-D	2,890,758	7.00	4.00
1988 P-D	1,646,204	7.00	4.00
1989 P-D	1,987,915	7.00	4.00
1990 P-D	1,809,184	7.00	4.00
1991 P-D	1,352,101	7.00	5.00
1992 P-D	1,500,143	7.00	4.00
1993 P-D	1,297,431	8.00	4.50
1994 P-D	1,234,813	8.00	4.50
1995 P-D	1,038,787	8.00	10.00
1996 P-D, Plus 1996W dime	1,457,949	8.00	15.00
1997 P-D	950,473	8.00	13.00
1998 P-D	1,187,325	8.00	4.50
1999 P-D (18 pieces)	1,243,867	14.95	15.00
2000 P-D (20 pieces)	1,490,160	14.95	6.00
2001 P-D (20 pieces)	1,116,915	14.95	10.00
2002 P-D (20 pieces)	1,139,388	14.95	7.00
2003 P-D (20 pieces)	1,001,532	14.95	13.00
2004 P-D (22 pieces)	844,484	16.95	40.00
2005 P-D (22 pieces)	1,160,000	16.95	12.00
2006 P-D (20 pieces)		16.95	12.00
2007 P-D (28 pieces)		22.95	18.00

Note: Sets issued from 2005 onward have a special Satin Finish that is somewhat different from the finish on Uncirculated coins made for general circulation.
* Special Mint Set.

$1 SILVER EAGLES

Values below are based on spot silver value of $10 per ounce.

	Mintage	Unc.	PF
$1 1986	5,393,005	$14	
$1 1986S	(1,446,778)		$21
$1 1987	11,442,335	13	
$1 1987S	(904,732)		21
$1 1988	5,004,646	13	
$1 1988S	(557,370)		28
$1 1989	5,203,327	13	
$1 1989S	(617,694)		21
$1 1990	5,840,210	13	
$1 1990S	(695,510)		21
$1 1991	7,191,066	13	
$1 1991S	(511,925)		23
$1 1992	5,540,068	13	
$1 1992S	(498,654)		21
$1 1993	6,763,762	13	
$1 1993P	(405,913)		75
$1 1994	4,227,319	13	
$1 1994P	(372,168)		120
$1 1995	4,672,051	13	
$1 1995P	(438,511)		110
$1 1995W	(30,125)		3,000
$1 1996	3,603,386	40	
$1 1996P	(500,000)		35
$1 1997	4,295,004	$13	
$1 1997P	(435,368)		$50
$1 1998	4,847,549	13	
$1 1998P	(450,000)		22
$1 1999	7,408,640	13	
$1 1999P	(549,769)		25
$1 2000(W)	9,239,132	13	
$1 2000W	(600,000)		
$1 2001(W)	9,001,711	13	
$1 2001W	(746,398)		21
$1 2002(W)	10,539,026	13	
$1 2002W	(647,342)		21
$1 2003(W)	8,495,008	13	
$1 2003W	(747,831)		21
$1 2004(W)	8,882,754	13	
$1 2004W	(801,602)		21
$1 2005(W)	8,891,025	13	
$1 2005W	(701,606)		21
$1 2006(W)		13	
$1 2006W			50
$1 2006P, Reverse Proof			100
$1 2007(W)		13	
$1 2007W			21

AMERICAN EAGLE GOLD COINS

Bullion values are based on spot gold at $550 per ounce.

See next page for chart.

$5 Tenth-Ounce Gold

	Mintage	Unc.	PF
$5 MCMLXXXVI (1986)	912,609	$65	
$5 MCMLXXXVII (1987)	580,266	65	
$5 MCMLXXXVIII (1988)	159,500	120	
$5 MCMLXXXVIII (1988)P	(143,881)		$70
$5 MCMLXXXIX (1989)	264,790	65	
$5 MCMLXXXIX (1989)P	(84,647)		70
$5 MCMXC (1990)	210,210	65	
$5 MCMXC (1990)P	(99,349)		70
$5 MCMXCI (1991)	165,200	65	
$5 MCMXCI (1991)P	(70,334)		70
$5 1992	209,300	65	
$5 1992P	(64,874)		70
$5 1993	210,709	65	
$5 1993P	(58,649)		70
$5 1994	206,380	65	
$5 1994W	(62,849)		70
$5 1995	223,025	65	
$5 1995W	(62,673)		70
$5 1996	401,964	65	
$5 1996W	(56,700)		70
$5 1997	528,266	65	
$5 1997W	(34,984)		$100
$5 1998	1,344,520	$65	
$5 1998W	(20,000)		100
$5 1999	2,750,338	65	
$5 1999W	(48,426)		100
$5 2000	569,153	65	
$5 2000W	(49,970)		70
$5 2001	269,147	65	
$5 2001W	(37,547)		100
$5 2002	230,027	65	
$5 2002W	(40,864)		70
$5 2003	245,029	65	
$5 2003W	(46,000)		70
$5 2004	250,016	65	
$5 2004W	(15,636)		70
$5 2005	300,043	65	
$5 2005W	(17,546)		70
$5 2006(W)		65	
$5 2006W			70
$5 2007(W)		65	
$5 2007W			70

$10 Quarter-Ounce Gold

	Mintage	Unc.	PF
$10 MCMLXXXVI (1986)	726,031	$160	
$10 MCMLXXXVII (1987)	269,255	160	
$10 MCMLXXXVIII (1988)	49,000	160	
$10 MCMLXXXVIII (1988)P	(98,028)		$170
$10 MCMLXXXIX (1989)	81,789	160	
$10 MCMLXXXIX (1989)P	(54,170)		170
$10 MCMXC (1990)	41,000	160	
$10 MCMXC (1990)P	(62,674)		170
$10 MCMXCI (1991)	36,100	270	
$10 MCMXCI (1991)P	(50,839)		170
$10 1992	59,546	160	
$10 1992P	(46,269)		170
$10 1993	71,864	160	
$10 1993P	(46,464)		170
$10 1994	72,650	160	
$10 1994W	(48,172)		170
$10 1995	83,752	160	
$10 1995W	(47,484)		170
$10 1996	60,318	160	
$10 1996W	(37,900)		170
$10 1997	108,805	$160	
$10 1997W	(29,808)		$250
$10 1998	309,829	160	
$10 1998W	(29,733)		250
$10 1999	564,232	160	
$10 1999W	(34,416)		170
$10 2000	128,964	160	
$10 2000W	(36,033)		170
$10 2001	71,280	160	
$10 2001W	(25,630)		250
$10 2002	62,027	160	
$10 2002W	(29,242)		170
$10 2003	74,029	160	
$10 2003W	(31,000)		170
$10 2004	72,014	160	
$10 2004W	(9,344)		170
$10 2005	72,015	160	
$10 2005W	(7,992)		170
$10 2006(W)		160	
$10 2006W			170
$10 2007(W)		160	
$10 2007W			170

$25 Half-Ounce Gold

	Mintage	Unc.	PF
$25 MCMLXXXVI (1986)	599,566	$325	
$25 MCMLXXXVII (1987)	131,255	325	
$25 MCMLXXXVII (1987)P	(143,398)		$350
$25 MCMLXXXVIII (1988)	45,000	$350	

	Mintage	Unc.	PF
$25 MCMLXXXVIII (1988)P	(76,528)		$350
$25 MCMLXXXIX (1989)	44,829	$400	
$25 MCMLXXXIX (1989)P	(44,798)		350
$25 MCMXC (1990)	31,000	475	
$25 MCMXC (1990)P	(51,636)		350
$25 MCMXCI (1991)	24,100	750	
$25 MCMXCI (1991)P	(53,125)		350
$25 1992	54,404	325	
$25 1992P	(40,976)		350
$25 1993	73,324	325	
$25 1993P	(43,319)		350
$25 1994	62,400	325	
$25 1994W	(44,584)		350
$25 1995	53,474	325	
$25 1995W	(45,442)		350
$25 1996	39,287	325	
$25 1996W	(34,700)		350
$25 1997	79,605	$325	
$25 1997W	(26,801)		$450
$25 1998	169,029	325	
$25 1998W	(25,549)		350
$25 1999	263,013	325	
$25 1999W	(30,452)		350
$25 2000	79,287	325	
$25 2000W	(32,027)		350
$25 2001	48,047	325	
$25 2001W	(23,261)		450
$25 2002	70,027	325	
$25 2002W	(26,646)		350
$25 2003	79,029	325	
$25 2003W	(33,000)		350
$25 2004	98,040	325	
$25 2004W	(7,835)		350
$25 2005	80,023	325	
$25 2005W	(7,054)		350
$25 2006(W)		325	
$25 2006W			375
$25 2007(W)		325	
$25 2007W			350

$50 One-Ounce Gold

	Mintage	Unc.	PF
$50 MCMLXXXVI (1986)	1,362,650	$650	
$50 MCMLXXXVI (1986)W	(446,290)		$700
$50 MCMLXXXVII (1987)	1,045,500	650	
$50 MCMLXXXVII (1987)W	(147,498)		700
$50 MCMLXXXVIII (1988)	465,000	650	
$50 MCMLXXXVIII (1988W)	(87,133)		700
$50 MCMLXXXIX (1989)	415,790	650	
$50 MCMLXXXIX (1989W)	(54,570)		700
$50 MCMXC (1990)	373,210	650	
$50 MCMXC (1990)W	(62,401)		700
$50 MCMXCI (1991)	243,100	650	
$50 MCMXCI (1991)W	(50,411)		700
$50 1992	275,000	650	
$50 1992W	(44,826)		700
$50 1993	480,192	650	
$50 1993W	(34,389)		700
$50 1994	221,633	650	
$50 1994W	(46,674)		$700
$50 1995	200,636	$650	
$50 1995W	(46,484)		700
$50 1996	189,148	650	
$50 1996W	(36,000)		700
$50 1997	664,508	650	
$50 1997W	(27,554)		1,000
$50 1998	1,468,530	650	
$50 1998W	(26,060)		1,000
$50 1999	1,505,026	650	
$50 1999W	(31,446)		700
$50 2000	433,319	650	
$50 2000W	(33,006)		700
$50 2001	143,605	650	
$50 2001W	(24,580)		1,000
$50 2002	222,029	650	
$50 2002W	(27,499)		700
$50 2003	416,032	650	
$50 2003W	(33,000)		700
$50 2004	417,019	650	
$50 2004W	(8,720)		700
$50 2005	356,555	650	
$50 2005W	(9,784)		700
$50 2006(W)		650	
$50 2006W			700
$50 2006W, Reverse Proof			2,500
$50 2007(W)		650	
$50 2007W			700

Gold Bullion Sets

	PF
1987 Gold Set. $50, $25	$1,300
1988 Gold Set. $50, $25, $10, $5	1,300
1989 Gold Set. $50, $25, $10, $5	1,300
1990 Gold Set. $50, $25, $10, $5	1,300
1991 Gold Set. $50, $25, $10, $5	1,300
1992 Gold Set. $50, $25, $10, $5	1,300
1993 Gold Set. $50, $25, $10, $5	1,300
1993 Bicentennial Gold Set. $25, $10, $5, $1 silver eagle, and medal	675
1994 Gold Set. $50, $25, $10, $5	1,300
1995 Gold Set. $50, $25, $10, $5	1,300
1995 Anniversary Gold Set. $50, $25, $10, $5, and $1 silver eagle	4,300
1996 Gold Set. $50, $25, $10, $5	1,300
1997 Gold Set. $50, $25, $10, $5	$1,800
1997 Impressions of Liberty Set. $100 platinum, $50 gold, $1 silver	1,975
1998 Gold Set. $50, $25, $10, $5	1,300
1999 Gold Set. $50, $25, $10, $5	1,300
2000 Gold Set. $50, $25, $10, $5	1,300
2001 Gold Set. $50, $25, $10, $5	1,800
2002 Gold Set. $50, $25, $10, $5	1,300
2003 Gold Set. $50, $25, $10, $5	1,300
2004 Gold Set. $50, $25, $10, $5	1,300
2005 Gold Set. $50, $25, $10, $5	1,300
2006 Gold Set. $50, $25, $10, $5	1,300
2007 Gold Set. $50, $25, $10, $5	1,300

2006 20th Anniversary Sets

2006W $50 Gold Set. Uncirculated, Proof, Reverse Proof	
2006 Silver Dollars, Uncirculated, Proof, Reverse Proof	
2006W 1-oz. Gold- and Silver-Dollar Set. Uncirculated	

FIRST SPOUSE $10 GOLD BULLION COINS

Half-Ounce 24-Karat Gold

Martha Washington $10 gold bullion coin.

Abigail Adams $10 gold bullion coin.

Symbolic representation of Liberty, used in place of portrait of Martha Jefferson, who died before Thomas Jefferson was elected.

Dolley Madison $10 gold bullion coin.

U.S. Mint artist renderings; not actual coins.

$10 2007, Martha Washington	
$10 2007, Abigail Adams	
$10 2007, Martha Jefferson / Liberty Representation	
$10 2007, Dolley Madison	

$50 AMERICAN BUFFALO .9999 FINE GOLD BULLION

	Unc.	PF		Unc.	PF
$50 2006W	. . . .		$50 2007W	. . . .	
$50 2006W	. . . .		$50 2007W	. . . .	

AMERICAN EAGLE PLATINUM COINS

The one-ounce American Eagle platinum coin is designated $100 and contains one ounce of pure platinum. Fractional denominations containing 1/2 ounce, 1/4 ounce, or 1/10 ounce are called $50, $25, and $10, respectively.

Obverse for Bullion and Proof, All Years

Reverse for Bullion, All Years; for Proof in 1997

Vistas of Liberty Reverse Designs

1998, Eagle Over New England

1999, Eagle Above Southeastern Wetlands

2000, Eagle Above America's Heartland

2001, Eagle Above America's Southwest

2002, Eagle Fishing in America's Northwest

See next page for chart.

$10 Tenth-Ounce Platinum

	Mintage	Unc.	PF
$10 1997	70,250	$120	
$10 1997W	(37,025)		$130
$10 1998	39,525	120	
$10 1998W	(19,832)		130
$10 1999	55,955	120	
$10 1999W	(19,123)		130
$10 2000	34,027	120	
$10 2000W	(15,651)		130
$10 2001	52,017	120	
$10 2001W	(25,000)		130
$10 2002	23,005	120	
$10 2002W	(12,365)		130
$10 2003	22,007	$120	
$10 2003W	(9,249)		$160
$10 2004	15,010	120	
$10 2004W	(3,171)		500
$10 2005	14,013	120	
$10 2005W	(2,583)		160
$10 2006(W)		120	
$10 2006W, Burnished		200	
$10 2006W			130
$10 2007(W)		120	
$10 2007W			130

$25 Quarter-Ounce Platinum

	Mintage	Unc.	PF
$25 1997	27,100	$300	
$25 1997W	(18,661)		$310
$25 1998	38,887	300	
$25 1998W	(14,860)		310
$25 1999	39,734	300	
$25 1999W	(13,514)		310
$25 2000	20,054	300	
$25 2000W	(11,995)		310
$25 2001	21,815	300	
$25 2001W	(8,858)		310
$25 2002	27,405	300	
$25 2002W	(9,282)		310
$25 2003	25,207	$300	
$25 2003W	(6,829)		$350
$25 2004	18,010	300	
$25 2004W	(2,583)		1,200
$25 2005	12,013	300	
$25 2005W	(932)		400
$25 2006(W)		300	
$25 2006W, Burnished		550	
$25 2006W			310
$25 2007(W)		300	
$25 2007W			310

$50 Half-Ounce Platinum

	Mintage	Unc.	PF
$50 1997	20,500	$600	
$50 1997W	(15,463)		$610
$50 1998	32,415	600	
$50 1998W	(13,821)		610
$50 1999	32,309	600	
$50 1999W	(11,098)		610
$50 2000	18,892	600	
$50 2000W	(11,049)		610
$50 2001	12,815	600	
$50 2001W	(8,268)		610
$50 2002	24,005	600	
$50 2002W	(8,772)		610
$50 2003	17,409	$600	
$50 2003W	(6,963)		$650
$50 2004	13,236	600	
$50 2004W	(1,073)		1,800
$50 2005	9,013	600	
$50 2005W	(846)		610
$50 2006(W)		600	
$50 2006W, Burnished		1,200	
$50 2006W			610
$50 2007(W)		600	
$50 2007W			610

$100 One-Ounce Platinum

	Mintage	Unc.	PF
$100 1997	56,000	$1,200	
$100 1997W	(18,000)		$1,225
$100 1998	133,002	1,200	
$100 1998W	(14,203)		1,225
$100 1999	56,707	1,200	
$100 1999W	(12,351)		1,225
$100 2000	10,003	1,200	
$100 2000W	(12,453)		1,225
$100 2001	14,070	1,200	
$100 2001W	(8,990)		1,225
$100 2002	11,502	1,200	
$100 2002W	(9,834)		1,225
$100 2003	8,007	$1,200	
$100 2003W	(8,106)		$1,225
$100 2004	7,009	1,200	
$100 2004W	(2,017)		2,500
$100 2005	6,310	1,200	
$100 2005W	(1,663)		1,500
$100 2006(W)		1,200	
$100 2006W, Burnished		2,200	
$100 2006W			1,225
$100 2007(W)		1,200	
$100 2007W			1,225

Platinum Bullion Sets

	PF
1997 Platinum Set. $100, $50, $25, $10	$2,200
1998 Platinum Set. $100, $50, $25, $10	2,200
1999 Platinum Set. $100, $50, $25, $10	2,200
2000 Platinum Set. $100, $50, $25, $10	2,200
2001 Platinum Set. $100, $50, $25, $10	2,200
2002 Platinum Set. $100, $50, $25, $10	2,200
2003 Platinum Set. $100, $50, $25, $10	$2,200
2004W Platinum Set. $100, $50, $25, $10	6,000
2005W Platinum Set. $100, $50, $25, $10	2,600
2006W Platinum Set. $100, $50, $25, $10	2,200
2007W Platinum Set. $100, $50, $25, $10	2,200

Private coins were circulated in most instances because of a shortage of regular coinage. Some numismatists use the general term *private gold* to refer to coins struck outside of the United States Mint. In the sense that no state or territory had authority to coin money, *private gold* simply refers to those interesting necessity pieces of various shapes, denominations, and degrees of intrinsic worth which were circulated in isolated areas of our country by individuals, assayers, bankers, etc. Some will use the words "Territorial" and "State" to cover certain issues because they were coined and circulated in a territory or state. While the state of California properly sanctioned the ingots stamped by F.D. Kohler as state assayer, in no instance were any of the gold pieces struck by authority of any of the territorial governments.

The stamped ingots put out by Augustus Humbert, the United States assayer of gold, were not recognized at the United States Mint as an official issue of coins, but simply as ingots, though Humbert placed the value and fineness on the pieces as an official agent of the federal government.

TEMPLETON REID
Georgia Gold 1830

The first private gold coinage under the Constitution was struck by Templeton Reid, a jeweler and gunsmith, in Milledgeville, Georgia in July 1830. To be closer to the mines, he moved to Gainesville, where most of his coins were made. Although weights were accurate, Reid's assays were not, and his coins were slightly short of claimed value. Accordingly, he was severely attacked in the newspapers and soon lost the public's confidence.

	VG	VF
1830, $2.50	$25,000	$40,000
1830, $5	60,000	100,000
1830, TEN DOLLARS	110,000	180,000
(No Date) TEN DOLLARS	100,000	150,000

California Gold 1849

1849, TEN DOLLAR CALIFORNIA GOLD *(unique, in Smithsonian)*. . . . .

THE BECHTLERS RUTHERFORD COUNTY, NC, 1831–1852

Two skilled German metallurgists, Christopher Bechtler and his son August, and later Christopher Bechtler, Junior, a nephew of Christopher the elder, operated a private mint at Rutherfordton, North Carolina. Rutherford County, in which Rutherfordton is located, was the principal source of the nation's gold supply from 1790 to 1848.

Christopher Bechtler

	VF	EF	AU	Unc.
ONE DOLLAR CAROLINA, 28.G, N Reversed	$1,000	$1,800	$2,400	$4,750
ONE GOLD DOLLAR N. CAROLINA, 28.G, No Star.	2,100	3,000	4,500	8,500
ONE GOLD DOLLAR N. CAROLINA, 30.G.	1,300	2,000	3,000	7,000
2.50 CAROLINA, 67.G., 21 CARATS.	2,900	5,000	6,000	11,000
2.50 CAROLINA, 70.G, 20 CARATS	3,000	5,500	6,500	13,000
2.50 GEORGIA, 64.G, 22 CARATS	3,000	6,000	6,700	13,000
2.50 NORTH CAROLINA, 75.G., 20 CARATS. RUTHERFORD in a Circle. Border of Large Beads	8,000	13,000	18,000	35,000
2.50 NORTH CAROLINA, Without 75.G.	8,500	13,500	19,000	37,000

Without 150.G.

	VF	EF	AU	Unc.
5 DOLLARS CAROLINA, RUTHERFORD, 140.G., 20 CARATS. AUGUST 1, 1834				
Plain Edge	$3,500	$4,750	$6,500	$11,000
Reeded Edge	7,000	13,000	18,000	26,000
5 DOLLARS BECHTLER, Without Star and C.	—			
5 DOLLARS CAROLINA GOLD, 134.G., 21 CARATS, With Star	3,000	4,000	6,000	10,000
5 DOLLARS GEORGIA GOLD, RUTHERFORD, 128.G., 22 CARATS	3,500	5,000	8,000	14,000
5 DOLLARS GEORGIA GOLD, RUTHERF., 128.G., 22 CARATS	3,500	5,000	8,000	14,000
5 DOLLARS CAROLINA GOLD, RUTHERF., 140.G., 20 CARATS, AUGUST 1, 1834	3,850	4,750	6,500	14,000
Similar, but "20" Distant From CARATS	4,000	6,000	8,500	14,000
5 DOLLARS NORTH CAROLINA GOLD, 150.G., 20 CARATS	9,000	12,500	20,000	35,000
Similar, Without 150.G		—	—	

August Bechtler

	VF	EF	AU	Unc.
1 DOL:, CAROLINA GOLD, 27.G., 21.C.	$700	$1,100	$1,500	$2,500
5 DOLLARS, CAROLINA GOLD, 134.G:, 21 CARATS	2,750	4,100	6,000	15,500

	VF	EF	AU	Unc.
5 DOLLARS, CAROLINA GOLD, 141.G., 20 CARATS	$5,000	$7,000	$11,000	$16,000
5 DOLLARS, CAROLINA GOLD, 128.G., 22 CARATS	5,000	7,000	11,000	18,750

NORRIS, GREGG & NORRIS SAN FRANCISCO 1849

These pieces are considered the first of the California private gold coins. A newspaper account dated May 31, 1849, described a five-dollar gold coin struck at Benicia City, though with the imprint San Francisco, and the private stamp of Norris, Gregg & Norris.

	F	VF	EF	AU	Unc.
1849, Half Eagle, Plain Edge.	$2,300	$3,300	$5,500	$8,000	$15,000
1849, Half Eagle, Reeded Edge.	2,300	3,300	5,500	8,000	15,000
1850, HALF EAGLE, With STOCKTON Beneath Date *(unique)*					

MOFFAT & CO. SAN FRANCISCO 1849–1853

The firm of Moffat & Company was perhaps the most important of the California private coiners. The assay office they conducted was semi-official in character, and successors to this firm later sold its facilities to the Treasury Department, which used them to create the San Francisco Mint.

In June or July, 1849, Moffat & Co. began to issue small rectangular pieces of gold in values from $9.43 to $264. The $9.43, $14.25, and $16.00 varieties are the only types known today.

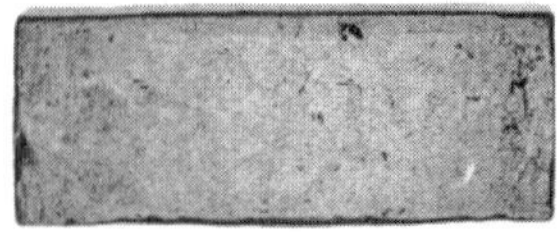

	EF
$9.43 Ingot *(unique)*	—
$14.25 Ingot *(unique)*	—
$16.00 Ingot	$35,000

The dies for the $10 piece were cut by Albert Kuner. The words MOFFAT & CO. appear on Liberty's coronet instead of the word LIBERTY as in regular United States issues.

	F	VF	EF	AU	Unc.
1849, FIVE DOL. *(all varieties)*	$800	$1,200	$1,800	$3,000	$6,750
1850, FIVE DOL. *(all varieties)*	800	1,200	1,800	3,400	7,000
1849, TEN DOL.	1,600	2,500	5,000	9,000	18,000
1849, TEN D.	1,700	2,500	5,500	10,000	20,000

UNITED STATES ASSAY OFFICE
Augustus Humbert
United States Assayer of Gold, 1851

When Augustus Humbert was appointed United States Assayer, he placed his name and the government imprint on the ingots of gold issued by Moffat & Co. The assay office, a provisional government mint, was a temporary expedient to accommodate the Californians until the establishment of a permanent branch mint. The $50 gold piece was accepted as legal tender on a par with standard U.S. gold coins.

Lettered Edge Varieties

	F	VF	EF	AU	Unc.
1851, 50 D C 880 THOUS., No 50 on Reverse. Sunk in Edge: AUGUSTUS HUMBERT UNITED STATES ASSAYER OF GOLD CALIFORNIA 1851	$8,000	$12,000	$17,000	$23,000	$50,000

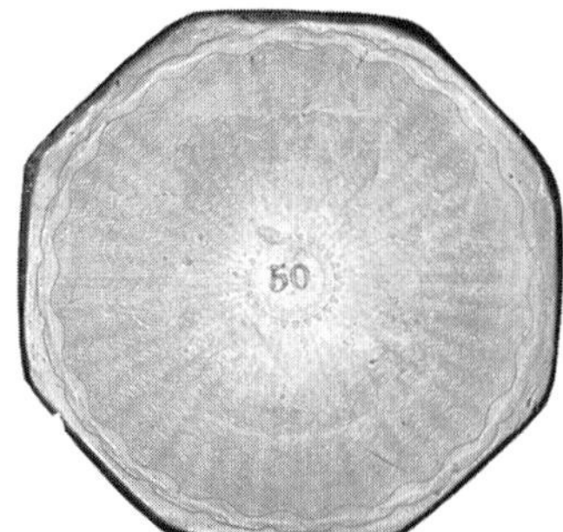

50 on Reverse

	F	VF	EF	AU	Unc.
1851, 50 D C, 880 THOUS., Similar to Last Variety, but 50 on Reverse	$9,000	$17,000	$24,000	$38,000	$70,000
1851, 50 D C, 887 THOUS., With 50 on Reverse	8,500	15,000	20,000	30,000	60,000

Reeded Edge Varieties

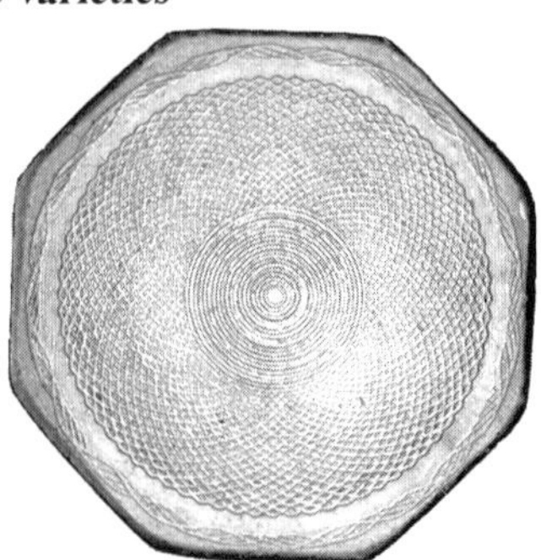

	F	VF	EF	AU	Unc.
1851, FIFTY DOLLS, 880 THOUS., "Target" Reverse	$6,000	$8,000	$12,000	$18,000	$30,000
1851, FIFTY DOLLS, 887 THOUS., "Target" Reverse	6,000	8,000	12,000	18,000	30,000
1852, FIFTY DOLLS, 887 THOUS.	6,000	8,000	12,000	18,000	32,000

Moffat & Co. proceeded in January, 1852 to issue a new ten-dollar piece bearing the stamp MOFFAT & CO.

	F	VF	EF	AU	Unc.
1852, TEN D. MOFFAT & CO.	$1,700	$2,800	$6,000	$15,000	$32,000

	F	VF	EF	AU	Unc.
1852, TEN DOLS., 1852, 2 Over 1	$1,500	$2,500	$4,000	$6,500	$13,000
1852, TEN DOLS.	1,200	1,850	2,600	4,500	11,000

	F	VF	EF	AU	Unc.
1852, TWENTY DOLS., 1852, 2 Over 1	$2,750	$4,500	$9,500	$17,000	$40,000

United States Assay Office of Gold – 1852

The firm of Moffat & Co. was reorganized as Curtis, Perry & Ward, which assumed the government contract to conduct the United States Assay Office of Gold.

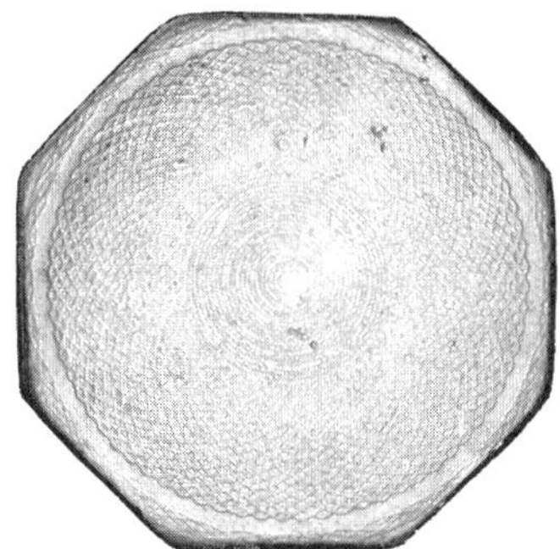

	F	VF	EF	AU	Unc.
1852, FIFTY DOLLS., 887 THOUS.	$6,000	$8,000	$13,000	$17,000	$32,000
1852, FIFTY DOLLS., 900 THOUS.	6,000	8,000	13,500	19,000	34,000

	F	VF	EF	AU	Unc.
1852, TEN DOLS., 884 THOUS.	$900	$1,500	$2,200	$3,750	$9,000
1853, TEN D., 884 THOUS.	3,200	6,500	12,000	16,500	35,000
1853, TEN D., 900 THOUS.	2,000	3,000	5,000	9,000	13,000
1853, TWENTY D., 884 THOUS.	3,750	6,250	9,500	15,000	23,000
1853, TWENTY D., 900 THOUS.	1,100	1,500	2,200	3,000	6,250

United States Assay Office of Gold – Moffat

The last Moffat issue was an 1853 $20 piece that is very similar to the U.S. double eagle of that period. It was struck after the retirement of John L. Moffat from Moffat & Company.

	F	VF	EF	AU	Unc.
1853, TWENTY D.	$1,900	$2,500	$3,750	$6,500	$15,000

CINCINNATI MINING & TRADING CO. (1849)

The origin and location of this company are unknown. It might have been organized in Ohio, and conducted business in California.

	EF	Unc.
1849, FIVE DOLLARS	—	—
1849, TEN DOLLARS	$300,000	—

MASSACHUSETTS AND CALIFORNIA COMPANY

This company was believed to have been organized in Northampton, Massachusetts, in May 1849.

	F	VF	EF
1849, FIVE D.	$50,000	$80,000	$130,000

MINERS' BANK SAN FRANCISCO 1849

The institution of Wright & Co., exchange brokers located in Portsmouth Square, San Francisco, was known as the Miners' Bank.

A $10 piece was issued in the autumn of 1849, but the coins were not readily accepted because they were worth less than face value.

	VF	EF	AU	Unc.
(1849) TEN D.	$8,000	$15,000	$22,000	$40,000

J.S. ORMSBY SACRAMENTO 1849

The initials J.S.O., which appear on certain issues of California privately coined gold pieces, represent the firm of J.S. Ormsby & Co. The firm struck both $5 and $10 denominations, all undated.

	VF
(1849) 5 DOLLS *(unique)*	—
(1849) 10 DOLLS *(4 known)*	$140,000

PACIFIC COMPANY, SAN FRANCISCO 1849

The origin of the Pacific Company is uncertain. All data regarding the firm are based on conjecture.

Edgar H. Adams wrote that he believed that the coins bearing the stamp of the Pacific Company were produced by the coining firm of Broderick and Kohler. The coins were probably hand struck with the aid of a sledgehammer.

	EF
1849, 1 DOLLAR *(2 known)*	—
1849, 5 DOLLARS	$150,000
1849, 10 DOLLARS	175,000

F.D. KOHLER
CALIFORNIA STATE ASSAYER 1850

The State Assay Office was authorized on April 12, 1850. That year, Governor Burnett appointed F.D. Kohler, who thereupon sold his assaying business to Baldwin & Co. Kohler served at both the San Francisco and Sacramento offices. The State Assay Offices were discontinued when the U.S. Assay Office was established, on February 1, 1851.

	EF
$36.55 Sacramento	—
$37.31 San Francisco	—
$40.07 San Francisco	—
$45.34 San Francisco	—
$50.00 San Francisco	—
$54.09 San Francisco	—

DUBOSQ & COMPANY SAN FRANCISCO 1850

Theodore Dubosq, a Philadelphia jeweler, took melting and coining machinery to San Francisco in 1849.

	VF
1850, FIVE D.	$65,000
1850, TEN D.	65,000

BALDWIN & CO. SAN FRANCISCO 1850

George C. Baldwin and Thomas S. Holman were in the jewelry business in San Francisco and were known as Baldwin & Co. They were the successors to F.D. Kohler & Co., taking over its machinery and other equipment in May 1850.

	F	VF	EF	AU	Unc.
1850, FIVE DOL.	$3,000	$5,500	$11,000	$14,000	$19,000
1850, TEN DOLLARS, Horseman type	16,000	27,500	45,000	62,500	90,000

	F	VF	EF	AU	Unc.
1851, TEN D.	$4,500	$11,000	$17,500	$27,000	$60,000

	VF	EF	AU	Unc.
1851, TWENTY D.	$75,000	$135,000	—	—

SHULTZ & COMPANY SAN FRANCISCO 1851

The firm, located in back of Baldwin's establishment, operated a brass foundry beginning in 1851. Judge G.W. Shultz and William T. Garratt were partners in the enterprise.

	F	VF
1851, FIVE D.	$14,000	$30,000

DUNBAR & COMPANY SAN FRANCISCO 1851

Edward E. Dunbar operated the California Bank in San Francisco. Dunbar later returned to New York and organized the famous Continental Bank Note Co.

	EF
1851, FIVE D.	$125,000

WASS, MOLITOR & CO.
SAN FRANCISCO 1852–1855

The gold-smelting and assaying plant of Wass, Molitor & Co. was operated by two Hungarian patriots, Count S.C. Wass and A.P. Molitor. They maintained an excellent laboratory and complete apparatus for analysis and coinage of gold.

	F	VF	EF	AU	Unc.
1852, FIVE DOLLARS	$2,000	$4,000	$8,000	$13,000	$27,500

Large Head

Small Head

	F	VF	EF	AU	Unc.
1852, TEN D., Large Head	$1,300	$2,000	$3,800	$7,000	$12,000
1852, TEN D., Small Head	3,000	4,000	9,000	15,000	36,000
1855, TEN D.	6,000	9,000	12,000	16,000	27,500

Large Head

Small Head

	F	VF	EF	AU	Unc.
1855, TWENTY DOL., Large Head	—	—	$170,000	—	—
1855, TWENTY DOL., Small Head	$6,000	$15,000	19,000	$38,000	$70,000

	F	VF	EF	AU	Unc.
1855, 50 DOLLARS	$12,000	$16,000	$21,000	$43,500	$90,000

KELLOGG & CO. SAN FRANCISCO 1854–1855

When the U.S. Assay Office ceased operations, a period ensued during which no private firm was striking gold. The new San Francisco branch mint did not produce coins for some months after Curtis & Perry took the government contract. The lack of coin was again keenly felt by businessmen, who petitioned Kellogg & Richter to "supply the vacuum" by issuing private coin. Their plea was soon answered, for on February 9, 1854, Kellogg & Co. placed their first $20 piece in circulation.

	F	VF	EF	AU	Unc.	PF
1854, TWENTY D.	$1,300	$1,800	$2,500	$4,200	$10,000	
1855, TWENTY D.	1,300	1,800	3,000	4,500	12,000	
1855, FIFTY DOLLS.						$175,000

OREGON EXCHANGE COMPANY
OREGON CITY 1849
The Beaver Coins of Oregon

On February 16, 1849, the legislature passed an act providing for a mint and specified $5 and $10 gold coins without alloy. Oregon City, the largest city in the territory with a population of about 1,000, was designated as the location for the mint. At the time this act was passed, Oregon had been brought into the United States as a territory by act of Congress. When the new governor arrived on March 2, he declared the coinage act unconstitutional.

	F	VF	EF	AU	Unc.
1849, 5 D.	$13,000	$20,000	$27,500	$60,000	—
1849, TEN.D.	30,000	60,000	100,000	150,000	—

MORMON GOLD PIECES
SALT LAKE CITY, UTAH, 1849–1860

Brigham Young was the instigator of the coinage system and personally supervised the mint, which was housed in a little adobe building in Salt Lake City. The mint was inaugurated in 1849 as a public convenience.

	F	VF	EF	AU	Unc.
1849, TWO.AND.HALF.DO.	$4,500	$8,000	$13,000	$22,000	$35,000
1849, FIVE.DOLLARS	3,650	7,000	12,000	15,000	27,000

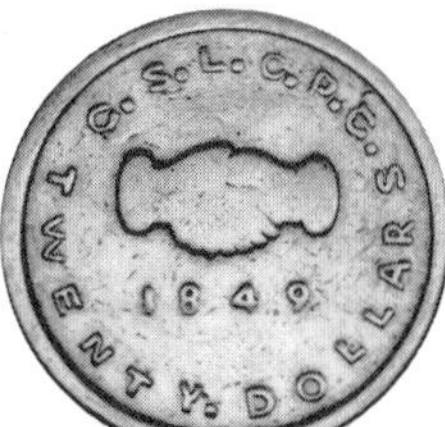

	F	VF	EF
1849, TEN.DOLLARS	$80,000	$120,000	$150,000
1849, TWENTY.DOLLARS	30,000	65,000	85,000

	F	VF	EF	AU	Unc.
1850, FIVE DOLLARS	$4,200	$7,500	$12,000	$18,000	$37,500
1860, 5.D.	8,000	15,000	20,000	27,000	40,000

COLORADO GOLD PIECES
Clark, Gruber & Co.
Denver 1860–1861

Clark, Gruber & Co. was a well-known private minting firm in Denver, Colorado, in the early 1860s.

	F	VF	EF	AU	Unc.
1860, 2 1/2 D.	$850	$1,250	$2,000	$3,200	$7,000
1860, FIVE D.	950	1,500	2,100	3,750	7,500

	F	VF	EF	AU	Unc.
1860, TEN D.	$4,000	$6,000	$9,000	$15,000	$24,000
1860, TWENTY D.	25,000	40,000	70,000	120,000	250,000

	F	VF	EF	AU	Unc.
1861, 2 1/2 D.	$900	$1,400	$2,100	$3,500	$8,500
1861, FIVE D.	1,200	1,700	2,600	4,700	17,000
1861, TEN D.	1,200	1,800	2,750	4,800	15,000

	F	VF	EF	AU
1861, TWENTY D.	$5,750	$13,000	$25,000	$45,000

John Parsons & Company
Tarryall Mines – Colorado, 1861

Very little is known regarding the mint of John Parsons and Co., although it is reasonably certain that it operated in the South Park section of Park County, Colorado, near the original town of Tarryall, in the summer of 1861.

	VF
(1861) Undated 2 1/2 D.	$100,000
(1861) Undated FIVE D	150,000

J.J. Conway & Co.
Georgia Gulch, Colorado, 1861

Records show that the Conway mint operated for a short while in 1861. As in all gold mining areas, the value of gold dust caused disagreement among the merchants and the miners. The firm of J.J. Conway & Co. solved this difficulty by bringing out its gold pieces in August 1861.

	VF
(1861) Undated 2 1/2 DOLL'S	$65,000
(1861) Undated FIVE DOLLARS	100,000
(1861) Undated TEN DOLLARS	—

CALIFORNIA SMALL-DENOMINATION GOLD

There was a scarcity of small coins during the California Gold Rush and, starting in 1852, quarter, half, and dollar pieces were privately minted from native gold to alleviate the shortage. The need and acceptability of these pieces declined after 1856 and they then became popular as souvenirs. Authentic pieces all have CENTS, DOLLAR, or an abbreviation thereof on the reverse. The tokens are much less valuable. Modern restrikes and replicas have no numismatic value.

The values in the following charts are only for coins made before 1883 with the denomination on the reverse expressed as CENTS, DOL., DOLL., or DOLLAR.

Quarter Dollar – Octagonal

	EF-40	AU-50	MS-60
Liberty Head	$70	$90	$130
Indian Head	80	100	140
Washington Head	350	475	600

Quarter Dollar – Round

	EF-40	AU-50	MS-60
Liberty Head	$70	$90	$130
Indian Head	90	120	175
Washington Head	400	700	850

Half Dollar – Octagonal

	EF-40	AU-50	MS-60
Liberty Head	$80	$120	$145
Liberty Head / Eagle	550	650	1,200
Indian Head	150	175	300

Half Dollar – Round

	EF-40	AU-50	MS-60
Liberty Head	$85	$160	$225
Indian Head	120	140	200

Dollar – Octagonal

	EF-40	AU-50	MS-60
Liberty Head	$240	$335	$475
Liberty Head / Eagle	950	1,500	2,300
Indian Head	300	425	725

Dollar – Round

	EF-40	AU-50	MS-60
Liberty Head	$775	$1,000	$1,600
Indian Head	850	1,100	1,900

HARD TIMES TOKENS (1832–1844)

During the financial crises of 1832 to 1844 many government coins were hoarded, and privately made tokens were used out of necessity. The so-called Hard Times tokens of this period were slightly smaller and lighter than normal large cents. They were made of copper or brass and are of two general groups: political tokens whose theme centered on President Jackson's fight against the United States Bank, and tradesmen's cards, issued by merchants. Many different designs and varieties exist.

	VF	EF
Hard Times Tokens, 1832–1844, most common pieces	$7	$18

CIVIL WAR TOKENS (1860s)

Civil War tokens are generally divided into two groups: tradesmen's tokens, and anonymously issued pieces with political or patriotic themes. They came into existence only because of the scarcity of government coins and disappeared as soon as the bronze coins of 1864 met the public demand for small copper change.

These tokens vary greatly in composition and design. A number were more or less faithful imitations of the copper-nickel cent. A few of this type have the word "not" in very small letters above the words ONE CENT.

	F	VF	EF	Unc.
Copper or Brass Tokens	$7	$8	$13	$25
Nickel or German Silver Tokens	15	22	32	65
White Metal Tokens	17	25	40	70
Copper-Nickel Tokens	30	40	50	100
Silver Tokens	75	100	150	250

Common-date silver coins are valued according to the price of silver bullion. In recent years the price of silver bullion has been subject to extreme fluctuation. Therefore, when you read this it is highly probable that the current bullion price may differ from the prevailing market price used in tabulating valuations of many 19th- and 20th-century silver coins (priced in italics) listed in this edition. The following chart will help to determine the approximate bullion value of these coins at various price levels. Or, the approximate value may be calculated by multiplying the current spot price of silver times the content for each coin as indicated below. Dealers generally purchase common silver coins at 15% below bullion value, and sell them at 15% above bullion value.

Bullion Values of Silver Coins

Silver Price Per Ounce	Wartime Nickel .05626 oz.	Dime .07234 oz.	Quarter .18084 oz.	Half Dollar .36169 oz.	Silver Clad Half Dollar .14792 oz.	Silver Dollar .77344 oz.
$9.00	$0.51	$0.65	$1.63	$3.26	$1.33	$6.96
9.50	0.53	0.69	1.72	3.44	1.41	7.35
10.00	0.56	0.72	1.81	3.62	1.48	7.73
10.50	0.59	0.76	1.90	3.80	1.55	8.12
11.00	0.62	0.80	1.99	3.98	1.63	8.51
11.50	0.65	0.83	2.08	4.16	1.70	8.89
12.00	0.68	0.87	2.17	4.34	1.78	9.28
12.50	0.70	0.90	2.26	4.52	1.85	9.67
13.00	0.73	0.94	2.35	4.70	1.92	10.05
13.50	0.76	0.98	2.44	4.88	2.00	10.44
14.00	0.79	1.01	2.53	5.06	2.07	10.83
14.50	0.82	1.05	2.62	5.24	2.14	11.21
15.00	0.84	1.09	2.71	5.43	2.22	11.60

The value of common-date gold coins listed in this book may be affected by the rise or fall in the price of gold bullion. Nearly all U.S. gold coins have an additional premium value beyond their bullion content, and thus are not subject to the minor variations described for silver coins. The premium amount is not necessarily tied to the bullion price of gold, but is usually determined by supply and demand levels for actual gold coins occurring in the numismatic marketplace. Because these factors can vary significantly, there is no reliable formula for calculating "percentage above bullion" prices that would remain accurate over time. For this reason the chart below lists bullion values based on gold content only. Consult your nearest coin dealer to ascertain current premium prices.

Bullion Values of Gold Coins

Gold Price Per Ounce	$5.00 Liberty Head 1839–1908 Indian Head 1908–1929 .24187 oz.	$10.00 Liberty Head 1838–1907 Indian Head 1907–1933 .48375 oz.	$20.00 1849–1933 .96750 oz.
$500.00	$120.94	$241.88	$483.75
525.00	126.98	253.97	507.94
550.00	133.03	266.06	532.13
575.00	139.08	278.16	556.31
600.00	145.12	290.25	580.50
625.00	151.17	302.34	604.69
650.00	157.22	314.44	628.88
675.00	163.26	326.53	653.06
700.00	169.31	338.63	677.25
725.00	175.36	350.72	701.44
750.00	181.40	362.81	725.63
800.00	193.50	387.00	774.00

Note: The U.S. bullion coins first issued in 1986 are unlike the older regular issues. They contain the following amounts of pure metal: silver $1, 1 oz.; gold $50, 1 oz.; gold $25, 1/2 oz.; gold $10, 1/4 oz.; gold $5, 1/10 oz.

INDEX